She Who Dares

Copyright © 2018: Authors & Co
ISBN-13: 978-1724524140

Table of Contents

Foreword – Abigail Horne 5
    About Abigail Horne 21
Sarah Stone 24
    About Sarah Stone 39
Alison Goodwin 41
    About Alison Goodwin 60
Caroline Strawson 63
    About Caroline Strawson 80
Chelle Shohet 82
    About Chelle Shohet 99
Diana Catherine 102
    About Diana Catherine 114
Demi Price 116
    About Demi Price 127
Donna Davies 129
    ABOUT DONNA DAVIES 142
Jennifer Barnfield 145
    About Jennifer Barnfield 166
Jennifer Stevens 169
    About Jennifer Stevens 179
Jo Gilbert 181
    About Jo Gilbert 194
Jo Swann 196
    About Jo Swann 211
Kimberley Banner 214

About Kimberley Banner 230
Laura Moss *232*
   About Laura Moss 246
Laura Rhian Warren *248*
   Laura Rhian Warren 266
Leigh Howes *269*
   About Leigh Howes 287
Linda Mawle *289*
   About Linda Mawle 301
Lindsey Fairhurst *303*
   About Lindsey Fairhurst 320
Lisa Dolman *322*
   About Lisa Dolman 334
Lorna Park *336*
   Lorna Park 352
Natalie Tilsley *355*
   About Natalie Tilsley 372
Nichola Sproson *374*
   About Nichola Sproson 390
Sarah Hardie *392*
   About Sarah Hardie 397
Susan Hughes *399*
   About Susan Hughes 414
Tina Pavlou *416*
   About Tina Pavlou 418

SHE WHO DARES

Foreword – Abigail Horne

Despite all of the bullshit you are going to tell yourself whilst reading this book, the world *does* need your awesomeness and ideas.

You have two internal voices – one that tells you to go for it, and the other that laughs in your face. Let me be the third voice that skips arounds your inner disagreement to give you some straight, honest talking about what you need and what you are more than capable of doing to make your business a success.

Believe it or not, right now you do have greatness within you. We all do. Admittedly, you may not be tapping into it, but it's there. Your birth right is to achieve everything that your heart desires, and chapter by chapter I want to make sure that you not only have that right, but the knowledge, skills, and support to make it happen.

When I look back over my career (which we will go through in more detail shortly), I genuinely feel inspired by my own actions. I have experienced a rollercoaster of overwhelming highs and soul-destroying lows, but what matters in those moments of doubt, pain and self-destruction is that I climbed back up off my knees and carried on.

In those moments of opportunity, I said yes. In those situations of fear, I took control and went for it anyway.

The question that I ask myself most frequently looking back is this, "What if I had listened to that voice that laughed in my face?"

Those very words make me shudder. I didn't know my own power back then and it would have been so easy to walk away, tell myself I can't, and not go on to change the lives of thousands of women around the world. Scary, huh?

So, let's fast forward. YOU HAVE MADE IT. How do you feel now? What does life look like and what does it feel like? In these moments you hush those voices and that is the place I want you to hold onto: the place where you are in complete and utter control.

You are here for a reason, reading this book because you trust that it will deliver what you need. So, my commitment to you is that we will all be totally transparent on what we have done that has worked, and again, honest in what hasn't worked in order to eliminate the possibility of making the same mistakes.

Although I have equal experience of business models that are "offline", I am a firm believer in leaning towards what lights you up inside and for me that is the online world. Someone once told me that you can make your first £100,000 online without any need for advertising and by just talking to the people in your current network.

When this proved to be true, the online space just became more and more addictive.

In my fifth year of self-employment I will reach that magic mark of making £1,000,000 from the online world and that is exactly what I want to help you tap into.

I made my first six figures with just 200 friends on Facebook, before the days of Instagram and without a clue about how to use Twitter or LinkedIn. I'm still no expert in any of these awesome platforms and I don't pretend to be.

What I am is able to share with you how I have best used them to my advantage as a total novice.

I admit that some of my success was too quick and we are going to talk about this as well. There's no point giving you all of the glitz and none of the 'glitch' because I'm positive that you will be able to learn as much from my failures as you do from my wins.

What I really want you to know about me whilst reading this chapter is just how normal I am. I'm 31, a wife to Aarran, a mum to six year old Teddy and have absolutely no super powers. I also have no domestic skills whatsoever but that's a whole other story.

I don't have a degree in business, but I do have several qualifications on paper that 'qualify' me to give you this advice (and, of course, my own experience), which I feel is worth the same, if not more.

I have been unconfident, depressed, lost, unsure and in total doubt during this journey, so I suppose I'm telling you if you are feeling anything similar that you can still do this.

The other side holds so much personal joy and fulfilment that you will be so proud that we came through this journey together.

So, why have I aimed this book at women and collaborated with lots of other awesome females in business? Well, because I am a woman, meaning I go through all the same challenges and emotions that you probably do.

Men have this incredible way of not overthinking, of not caring less of what others think, and facing fears a little more head on. We ladies are a little more complicated. Maybe it's our hormones, I'm not sure, but we certainly give ourselves a harder time than most men do in my experience.

I am not sure how you would define a feminist but just to save any confusion, I care equally about the success of men and women. The reason I choose to spend my life supporting women is because some amazing women have supported me, and because of their understanding, friendship, and advice, I know I am able to have that same impact on others.

When working with women you develop an understanding and closeness, and just to be totally frank, if I had these same working relationships with men, I'm not entirely convinced my husband would feel as happy in our marriage!

I also believe women struggle to reach out for help; that in asking for support or advice they are somehow admitting that they aren't capable, which just isn't true. We allow ourselves to burn out by working at 1000 miles per hour whist burning the candle at every available end just to show the world and ourselves that we can do it.

Yes, we are THAT crazy. We juggle business with babies whilst trying to maintain our figures (badly in my case) and maintain our homes (again, badly for me). We sacrifice television, girls' nights out and relaxing Sundays to work on our dreams and so each and every one of us deserves to succeed.

We laugh in the face of a 'nine till five' as that was our part time life, and now we are living our 100 hour a week passions. Better to live what we love though, right? Don't worry, by the end of this book you are going to achieve not just knowledge but the tips on balance from a whole variety of business women.

Also, some better systems to put in place to reduce those working weeks, although I know you will still struggle to put your phone away.

Female Entrepreneurship is most definitely on the rise. Gone are the days when we were accepting the corporate response that we cannot work flexibly around our families.

If I get on my super high horse, we still live in a world where there are conversations about gender pay gaps and let's face it, screw being paid less than men. As a girl boss we make our own way in this world and pay ourselves what we can instead with no limit on what is possible.

The day I smashed through my own financial glass ceiling of earning more in a month than I used to earn in a whole year of my employed career, I knew that I was capable of anything. YOU are capable of anything.

Before I go on to introduce you to some of the amazing women smashing through their own glass ceilings that I have the pleasure of working with, I want to take you back and give you an insight into my own past so that you have a clearer understanding of how we all ended up together right here in this book.

Let me share an extract from a bestselling book that I was featured in called "She Made It Happen". If you have already read this, feel free to skip through the italic section but not past the rest of my chapter. The best is definitely yet to come.

"Have you ever felt like you just don't belong? Like there is a box other women manage to fit into but as hard as you have tried you are just not made for that space?

That feeling was my every day normal, and I fought it for so long.

At school I was girl who aced absolutely everything with no effort but had no clue what I was working towards. I felt under so much pressure to find my path, pick my career and go on to do my A levels that I completely withdrew from education.

I remember looking at going into the army because a careers advisor had once told me that the army was there for people who don't necessarily know what they want to do, but I quickly gave up on that idea when I realised that I would be spending my life taking orders from someone else. I have NEVER been great with authority.

Doing my best to conform in some way, I went to college to study "Travel & Tourism". I have absolutely no idea why. I lasted for three whole weeks before I admitted to my family that as wasted as my brain probably was, education just wasn't for me. My family knew that anyway and supported me entirely, I'm grateful to have parents who have always encouraged me to live life on my own terms.

However, I remember being called a rebel by friends & teachers at that time. This young adult who could have had it all but instead decided to quit because whatever this journey was to university and beyond, it just wasn't for me. I literally watched my school friends continue through education whilst I sat on the sidelines feeling like a freak.

I worked from the age of 14, so from a young age I had a taste for earning my own money. It seemed a natural move for me when I left education to go straight into a large organisation to climb the career ladder instead, so that's exactly what I did.

At 17 years old, I started working for an energy company with a manager named Carol. What I didn't realise then was that this lady would become my first mentor. Carol was the first person who embraced my ambition, never asked about my qualifications, only spoke of what I could achieve with hard work, self-development and planning and to this day I am still so grateful for her.

It's funny the things that you never forget. Carol taught me about NLP and having an anchor for confidence. I can still touch a finger and feel immediately like I can own the room.

Carol told me that by the age of 30 she knew I would be at operational management level, but my goals over time became bigger and neither of us knew back then that by the age of 29 I would actually own my own energy company.

Back to the age of 18, I now had a second mentor to further nurture my skills, Jo Gilbert. I became the youngest manager in that nationwide energy company because I soaked up her advice like a sponge. I felt for the first time like I had the skills to become successful, and she gave me that belief.

Jo told me that I was a shining star and that I would be successful beyond words but what she didn't know is that we would become best friends for life. Jo has maintained to be one of the single most important women in my life for over a decade and it is because of her that I am me.

For many reasons I outgrew working for someone else. I was sick of my life, holidays, working hours and ideas having to go through other people and ultimately, I had just had enough. I had become a mum and all of a sudden time was more precious than ever.

I couldn't bare another moment away from my little boy, Ted, when I just didn't feel happy or fulfilled. When in turmoil I ask myself questions to really make sense of my thoughts, so I can make changes where necessary.

Here is what I asked myself one random Wednesday, "What is zapping your life of energy and joy, and what happiness will your future hold if you don't make a change today?"

I came to the conclusion that my job was killing my energy and every day I was becoming less passionate about my life. My time away from my son was dampening my joy and it had to change immediately. I was spending 40 hours a week in a soul-destroying office to pay my bills on a home I never got to enjoy.

Meanwhile, I was missing my son growing up because I was working to make someone else rich when we were just getting by.

Unless I made a change, nothing in my future would change. To me, it was that simple. I walked out of my job that Wednesday in April 2013 and that day was the start of the rest of my life.

Leaving a 10 year career was painful. I was scared and exposed but when your back is against a wall it's amazing what can happen! In that moment I literally became my own inspiration.

I decided that the reason I was still unable to fit in a box was because I was never meant to be in one. I am a powerful female entrepreneur, but that wasn't on the list of careers at school.

I am a creative female entrepreneur, but education didn't know how to support that. I am an unstoppable female entrepreneur and that is why a job would have never fulfilled me, no matter how high up the ladder I climbed.

I am a passionate female entrepreneur, and that is why I need to reach out to you and tell you that this confusion you may be feeling right now is okay! You are about to enter a chapter of your life where you will become your own inspiration, too.

At 27, I became self-employed. I started to live unapologetically the way I wanted and deserved to and it all felt so natural. Freedom really suits me. You just cannot clip these wings, and trust me haters have tried! I worked on average 90 hours a week into the middle of the night to ensure my time as a mum was as uninterrupted as possible.

My marriage suffered as my evenings weren't about watching TV together but about burying my head into my laptop or networking in person in other parts of the world. I want to mention at this point that although I was changing and going through so much personal growth, he never held me back. He didn't always understand but he supported me in every way he could and still does to this day.

In 2 very blurred years, I had turned my £23,400 job into an annual income of £230,000 and I in no way felt like I had reached my potential. Let's hold it there for now and talk about HOW that was achieved, because the reality is there are a lot of inward scars that have come with that outward success.

I made sacrifices, not all of which I'm proud of but it's the truth. Some friendships suffered, as did time with my loved ones. Some relationships needed to be severed, though, because every time someone angrily told me that I had changed, I congratulated myself because of course I had. That was the whole point! With self-development came knowledge, with knowledge came confidence, and with confidence came success.

Thank goodness for books, mentors, and online courses, hey! I completely embraced myself, flaws and all. I knew I wasn't perfect but perfection is boring. My success came from passion, a hurricane of energy, and my eyes on the prize. Nothing else.

That became a problem, though. What did I originally set out to achieve? Was I coming from significance or contribution? I didn't know anymore, if I'm honest.

Here come's where I quizzed myself again, "If this was your last week on this beautiful earth, what would be more important to you: the balance in your life, or the balance in your bank account?

Sh*t! In that moment, I realised that I had created wealth but that wasn't my goal! Unhealthy and wealthy, flipping great! I want to point out that it was no one's fault but my own for not having any sort self-care routine. My body was in a battle with my mind and was starting to fail.

I have a back condition that causes me severe pain and it was getting worse and worse. I was gaining weight quickly with living out of hotel rooms and it all came to an abrupt halt when I suffered a miscarriage and I completely blamed myself. My body won the battle over my mind and I started my downward spiral into crash and burn.

Before the start of this destructive period in my life, I had put all the wheels in motion for the launch of my own energy company. There was an element of having to go with the momentum I had already created but if it weren't for that I wouldn't have even got dressed in that year. I just wanted to hide from social media, from the world and from myself.

I wanted to put unstoppable Abi in a draw and shut her away whilst I disappeared into a shadow. It was a dark, dark time and it lasted a lot longer than I would ever allow myself to suffer now. Always remaining 100% committed even when I'm falling apart, I got through the launch which was surprisingly really successful, but I couldn't shake my unhappiness.

I had my dream home, successful companies, a family that adores me and I was MISERABLE. You can say this was selfish of me, but I swear it was the opposite. I had achieved everything that others dream of but that didn't make me feel good. I didn't want to be someone's inspiration, I wanted others do this for themselves otherwise what was the point?

I didn't want to be in what felt like a small percentage of those that made it in to successful self-employment, I wanted to pave the way for women everywhere to follow in my footsteps, yet something wasn't quite right, and I just can't settle for not quite right. It goes without saying that this period of self-sabotage started to have catastrophic effects on my businesses, income, and life.

Why am I telling you this? You are reading this to find out how success happened, not that I was feeling like a failure, but this 'failure' was the foundation for becoming the best and most authentic version of myself that I have ever been.

It also shows you that greatness is inside of you no matter where you are in life or what you are going through, and that you simply have to find gratitude for that greatness even in the darkest of times to become unstoppable.

The beauty of taking yourself deep into gratitude is that you start to remember who you are, what you have achieved and what you are made of. In turn, you are then able to forgive yourself, your mistakes, and prepare yourself for a comeback much greater than your setback.

In my usual talking to myself manner, I asked myself a further question, "When it comes to your legacy, how will the lives of others be positively impacted because you have lived?"

In that moment I physically needed to map out on whiteboards and sticky notes what I was born to do. I began to realise my purpose, something that I was so passionate about that I had no choice but step back up again. I needed to help women like me. The young woman who hasn't found her direction, the career woman who is capable of being the boss and the woman with ideas with no idea how to make them profitable.

Finally, that 6/7 figure female entrepreneur who hasn't yet realised that burnout will hit if the balance in her life doesn't become as important as the balance in her bank account. And it will hit HARD.

In realising my purpose and finally feeling aligned with my legacy, it was time for some inward reflection. Can I do this alone? Do I even want to do this alone? The answer to both was no. I could either outsource half of my vision and pay for the ongoing privilege or reach out to someone with the skills that makes up the other half of me and collaborate.

The difference being if someone else is collaborating with me, the chances are they would be coming from the same place of love and contribution, and that is what was needed. The weirdest thing happened, though, on deciding that I needed a work wife. The lady that I reached out to was working on the exact same idea.

Some may call it spooky, we call it the universe having our backs! What were the chances? It's not like we were best friends or lived locally, we had simply crossed paths work wise a couple of times and had great results together. Timing was everything and when we met to discuss our future we knew our relationship would be one that would last a lifetime.

Female Success Network was born. I was re-born and women around the world started to become a part of the movement. With co-founder Sarah Stone, we put our skills, knowledge, heart and soul into changing the lives of women just like us. Female Success Network isn't just about success in business, it supports whatever success means to a woman, so she knows that she is always supported and never alone.

Being a solopreneur can be soul destroying. You imagine this bliss of working for yourself but the illusion shatters quickly when you realise you are spending your days by yourself with no one to bounce ideas off or be accountable to.

We have created the change that we wanted to see, and it is so authentic and from such a heartfelt place within us that there could never be anything else quite like it. I have embraced being uniquely myself again whilst helping other women do the same and the process has been beautiful.

So, how did I make it happen? By being brave, bold, falling apart and then piecing myself back together. By forgiving myself, delving deep into gratitude and finding my purpose in my failings.

By stepping back up, admitting that I needed some help and then getting the hell on with it in spite of my fears, my flaws and for every other woman who is fighting to find herself whilst struggling to fit in a box.

That's how and more importantly WHY I made it happen.

So, take this moment in time to decide on whether you are fulfilling your purpose that will last beyond your years or are you just getting by. Wake up and decide to be the heroine of your life and stop playing the victim. There is only one woman's story that should be inspiring you right now and that is YOURS! Go, be brave and live the life that you deserve. Today."

On writing this extract, Female Success Network was just a few months old. I shared all the vision in the world with Sarah Stone, but we had not yet seen the results of our hard work and dedication to our clients. Today, we can share an update. In fact, we can share a whole book.

Sarah and I could not be prouder of what we have created or who we have had the absolute pleasure of working with. Whatever your age, your business, or your experience, you will be able to relate to someone that we have featured.

Although my personal passion is how to make money and create success online, you will see that lots of the small to medium enterprises that we work with very much have offline businesses as well.

I want you to learn from their thoughts, experiences, their highs and their lows, because every single woman in this book has more to offer than you could ever imagine.

Looking to the future, I want to share with you my excitement for Year 2 of Female Success Network and what the future holds for me personally.

Reflecting over all the work we have completed with the ladies in this book, we have been able to catalogue and systemise what has worked, what has made an impact, what has enabled the best results, and what has eliminated unnecessary mistakes. We have had all this confirmed by the amount of our clients who are actually staying with us for a whole second year.

What has been obvious to us though is that our impact has not yet been big enough. One of the reasons why being that working with business strategists 1:1 may not be within every start-up's budget. On taking our results, client wins, and impact into consideration, we have passionately developed "Success School" for the aspiring business women in need of expert guidance but not yet in a position to access our 1:1 support.

Success School is a program designed to educate and certify individuals in the essential areas of starting and scaling a successful business. You can find out more details by heading over to www.femalesuccessnetwork.com/successschool today.

On a personal note, I have been an astonishingly busy bee in a whole other area enhancing the visibility and credibility of female entrepreneurs around the world! As mentioned previously, a year ago I was featured in "She Made It Happen" which became an international bestseller.

Off the back of the release I was featured in media locally, nationally, and globally including in Forbes as a female entrepreneur to watch out for. I then went on to win the super achievers "Entrepreneur of the Year" award, 2018. JUST WOW. All from being in a book!

It made me take stock of how books really do help entrepreneurs get more exposure and be taken more seriously in the world of business. I went from barely being visible to an over-night sensation in the blink of an eye.

It made me super curious and passionate about the process and so, wanting to introduce this to my own clients, I worked with a book coach whilst separately gaining diplomas in both publishing and self-publishing to best serve my clients.

I trained and perfected my processes then launched Authors & Co to the world with a boom! I am working with clients all over the globe and to date have a 100% success rate in helping my authors achieve Number 1 Bestsellers within my Brand Yourself Bestseller ™ Program. I can honestly say I am in my element. The results and media I am seeing my authors achieve is insane!

Again, with the understanding that 1:1 work isn't always attainable, I have created an academy for aspiring authors to learn from my processes to successfully launch their very own book. You can find more information by heading over to www.authorsandco.com/authorsacademy.

Before handing you over to my incredible business partner and the wonderful women changing the business world one day at a time, I just want to say "thank you" for showing up for yourself and for others just by purchasing this book.

Your time is now.

Wishing you every success, and every bit of courage to fulfil your potential.

Abigail

About Abigail Horne

With 15 years experiencing in business and entrepreneurship, Abigail has worked with tens of thousands of individuals to help them fulfil their potential within corporate organisations and within self-employed businesses.

Although Abigail believes that the greatest form of learning comes with experience, she is not without an array of qualifications that have helped her become the confident and competent business women that she is today.

Abigails qualifications include, but are not limited to:

ILM certification in Coaching and Mentoring

Diploma in Business Planning & Implementation

Diploma in Publishing

Diploma in Self-Publishing

Diploma in English Literature and Creative Writing

Diploma in Numerology

Currently Undergoing –

Master Practitioner Qualification in strengths-based training to optimise business performance and reduce risk.

Abigail has been awarded the super achievers "Entrepreneur of the Year" award of 2018.

No stranger to the media Abigail has featured in Forbes, The Huffington Post, Fox, CBS and NBC as well as countless other media publications both on and offline.

Abigail is a passionate & honest entrepreneur driven by helping others succeed with greater knowledge, credibility and visibility.

Abigail's focus falls on the personal and professional development of women as a woman herself who has experienced and overcome many challenges. Abigail is a collaborator and orchestrates the talents of many women in one epic space that is "Female Success Network", co-founded with Sarah Stone.

Abigail understands that success is very personal and one size does not fit all. Her focus is not just on a woman's performance in business but on how areas such as health and relationships have a huge impact on the overall pursuit of success.

Email – hello@femalesuccessnetwork.com

hello@authorsandco.com

Visit – www.femalesuccessnetwork.com

www.authorsandco.com

FACEBOOK -
www.facebook.com/femalesuccessnetwork

www.facebook.com/authorsandco

INSTAGRAM –

www.instagram.com/female_success_network

www.instagram.com/authorsandco

LINKEDIN –

www.linkedin.com/abigail-elisabeth-horne

Sarah Stone

YOUR BELIEF IS YOUR REALITY.

I'm the girl who left school with very few qualifications and very little to aspire to.

If someone had told me that I would go on to create 4 businesses, travel the world for work, win an award for my business achievements and be the Co-Founder of a global platform which empowers, inspires and helps women achieve their version of success - I would have thought you were high on drugs and recommended you seek help!
Seriously.

Although I had a fire in my belly, the overwhelming passion to work hard and an inner resilience to my circumstances, home life and failed relationships, it was often misguided due to the social tags we tend to give ourselves.

Life didn't start too easily for my Mum and I. When I was just 6 months old, a lump the size of a grapefruit appeared on my abdomen right in front of my Mum's eyes whilst she was changing my nappy.

Childhood quickly disappeared as that lump was a cancerous Wilms Tumor, which then burst in my tiny body. I spent the next 4 years undergoing chemotherapy and radiotherapy in Pendlebury Children's Hospital, Manchester. During that time when my mum was living and caring for me full time in hospital, my dad decided to leave and never return. Nice touch, hey? Thanks Dad.

But, that wasn't the end of my story. I beat the odds. I beat childhood cancer.

School wasn't an easy ride either. The best part was making friends and sport. When it came to exams, my mind just went blank and in sheer panic I just created pretty sequences in the "a, b, c, d" columns. Needless to say, that it didn't get me the outcome I'd hoped for.

Things started to turn around when I had the opportunity to do work experience in a beautiful boutique hotel, Bartle Hall Hotel. I didn't realise at the time, but there I had my very own mentor, Victoria Pilbeam (such a cool name).

This very special lady saw something in me, which all my teachers had overlooked. Her approach was to visually guide me with physical hands-on learning. She clearly demonstrated everything and led by example to show me what I needed to aspire to. Being coached in a way which worked for me, I started to thrive. Excel, in fact!

Evidence of this came when regardless of my exam results, social tags, personal hardship and circumstances at home; the day after my last GCSE exam (when I was just 15 years old), I started full time employment and went on to blossom into a young professional women with dreams to be, do and achieve more in life.

I began to believe.

The more trust I earned, the more responsibility I was given and it felt amazing. My confidence grew and I realised that I was capable of anything I put my mind to.

Earning my own money, becoming financially independent and being in a position where I could contribute to my mum's bills, learn to drive and buy my own car was so rewarding. I could see that the hard work and long hours had paid off.

In a very serendipitous moment, my friend encouraged me to apply for a role with Warner Bros. It excited me, but I instantly thought I wasn't good enough, I didn't have the right qualifications and I was far too young. I decided to 'give it a go' and apply anyway, as I had absolutely nothing to lose.

Yep, you guessed it. I got the job! I was so proud and so were the team at Bartle Hall because they wanted to set me free so that I could spread my wings and go on to fly. I'll always be eternally grateful to them for giving me the best possible start as an adult, seeing my potential and allowing me to learn so many skills that I still use today.

Working in the entertainment industry was so special and really exciting. I went on to be promoted throughout the company and quickly became their youngest Administration Trainer and Promotions Executive.

As part of my role, I had the opportunity to attend and be part of some major film premieres. I've been lucky enough to meet the likes of George Clooney, Mark Wahlberg, John Travolta, Sylvester Stallone, the cast of Harry Potter, and 'Mr Grey' himself.

There have been some pretty epic 'after show' parties too, that could totally be a book in its own right! I don't say this to brag, name drop or impress you; I say it because they are all normal people doing a job and showing up to promote their role in a movie or enhance their personal brand.

It highlighted to me that, as a business owner, you have to do the same. Become your own brand ambassador because you will have to show up, be seen, be heard and stand out from the crowd to make your business aspirational.

If you have an overwhelming fire inside you for anything at all and it makes you happy, do it! Listen to your heart as your passion, commitment and enthusiasm will radiate from you and attract exactly what you put out there.

In 2000 I met my soulmate, Andy. We decided to move to Wales, buy a house and settle down to start a family. I left the glitz and glamour of the cinema industry to focus on a more sensible role with a good pension, flexible working and self-development opportunities.

Things took an unexpected turn in 2002 when at 21 weeks pregnant, I went into early labour. Far too soon for our baby girl, Charlotte, to enter the world.

It took quite a while to even try to recover from something as traumatic as this. However, the medical advice we received was to try again as my body was all set to become a mummy; I was all set to become a mummy too.

Sadly, I went on to miscarry again. This time at 22 weeks.
It hurt. Beyond words.

It was at this point that Andy and I decided that there was no way I could put myself through this again. Mentally, physically and emotionally, I was utterly broken.

I'm not sharing this to make anyone sad. I want to reassure you that whatever life throws at you, you can survive. There's always a way.

Going through trauma allows you to put things into perspective, to be eternally grateful for everything you do have and all the things you CAN do!

When you've hit rock bottom it's hard to even think that things will get better. It really doesn't help when people try to re-assure you with 'don't worry, you can try again' or 'it wasn't meant to be'. The hardest part of this period of loss was when people looked at me with pity in their eyes. I just wanted to hide from everyone.

It's a very natural feeling to feel isolated and alone because you truly believe that no-one could possibly understand the pain and upset but guess what? I quickly realised that I wasn't alone and that I had a choice to make. I needed to remind myself that joy and hope existed, so I started to dig deep and create a new version of happiness.

Your circumstances certainly don't have to define your future. Grief is such a strange thing. I'm so grateful that the nature of my grief meant I didn't experience bitterness towards friends with a new baby or dread pregnancy announcements. It wasn't anyone else's circumstances which were triggers for how I dealt with events, it was dates and the wondering 'what if?'

It could have been so different. Depression, jealousy and being bitter of other people's family lives could have easily been the path I took, but instead I chose happiness. I chose to love and be loved.

I chose to be grateful for the life we could create and dug deep to create this new life, even to create a new me, because I couldn't allow myself to go down the bitterness route. I knew it would have literally sucked the life out of me.

During this time of soul searching I decided that I didn't want to be sat behind a desk counting down the days to my retirement. I didn't want to chat about last night's Eastenders, or be part of the office politics. I realised it was draining the life out of me and I was turning into someone I didn't want to be, so I decided to make another choice. I was going to follow my heart.

Photography has been (and always will be) a passion from a very early age. I was always the one with the camera, getting everyone together and capturing the moment. Taking pictures made me happy, it made my heart sing and I came alive when I had a camera in my hands. I still do.

It wasn't just about creating pretty pictures. There was something deep rooted in me that wanted to create happiness and memories for people to cherish for a lifetime. It was about capturing the beauty of fleeting moments in a time capsule, so that these happy moments could be remembered forever.

You know that feeling when you stumble across old photographs and you sit there smiling because you realise how special that time was? That's what I wanted to capture for everyone, because it's just so special. In fact it's priceless.
It became my purpose to encourage people to document the happy times, see the beauty in life and to capture these moments as a special keepsake for future generations to enjoy.

I felt confident that people needed what I was offering, so I decided to turn my overwhelming passion for photography into a business. There was no self-doubt this time. It was something I felt passionate about and looking back it was probably the perfect therapy for my own situation at that time.

I didn't know how I was going to do it, I just knew it was going to happen.

At first it didn't go down too well at home. Andy thought I had completely lost the plot, but he supported me on the understanding that I had to take a wage straight away in order to replace my existing income because - reality check - we had bills to pay. I saw this as the perfect challenge and promised that the day I couldn't pay myself, I would return to full time employment.

I never looked back.

When the day came to approach the subject with my boss, her reaction instantly rattled me, because I thought she was being rude. She said 'Sarah, you will always do well in life because you're full of self-belief'. Looking back I have no idea why I took this as an insult, because I now know it's actually a HUGE compliment and exactly what you need to be as a female entrepreneur.

Belief becomes your reality so yes, I am proudly full of self-belief and so should you be. You know what they say?

"Believe and you will achieve."

When the day came to hand in my notice, I was petrified. I say petrified because I had no job to go to, no pension, no regular clients, no stability and no regular income.

People asked where I was going to work next and it felt scary but exciting to say - 'for myself'. I was speaking with such passion and conviction about my plans to become a 'Professional Photographer' that I gained three or four clients even before I'd worked my notice period.

I felt sick and shaky going to my first photoshoot. I felt like a fraud. My head kept questioning myself, 'how dare I say I'm a photographer when I don't have a degree?'

I don't know why I was so hard on myself because the moment I stepped into someone's home, I felt at home. Comfortable, confident, and happy to capture beautiful images.

Guess what? I didn't get asked if I had qualifications and I didn't get asked if I was experienced enough to take pictures. People buy people. If you're authentic, set the expectation, and be the best version of you for your business – you're onto a winner.

I went on to have 10 successful years building an award winning photography business which has allowed me to travel the world, gain celebrity clients, and a highly acclaimed reputation with my clients who returned year on year.

As my business started to grow and build momentum, I wish someone had told me that it doesn't matter what everyone else is doing, what equipment they have or what the latest trends are. I could have saved so much money by just carving my own path from the beginning.

It's so hard starting out because you want to say 'yes' to everything and everyone. I wish I could have had the confidence to say 'no' more often and stop trying to please so much. I wish I could have ignored the FOMO and not tried so hard to be in the cool gang, because all that did was create competitive procrastination.

I wish I valued my time more. I wish I had respected my own self-worth and invested in a mentor much sooner than I did, as it would have saved me so much time in the long term development of my business.

If I was starting from scratch, I'd find a niche and be confident in my direction. Do what feels right to you and don't get caught up in what others are doing. Be prepared to be copied and smile. Why? If you're always true to your own business roadmap, nobody will keep up and you'll carve your own path in your own unique way.

Remember. People buy people and that's what makes you truly unique. Be yourself. This is the exact approach we had when creating Female Success Network.

The idea for something like Female Success Network came quite a few years ago due to the amount of new mums I was meeting who loved the idea of turning a hobby into a business. Especially at a time when the prospect of going back to work and leaving their adorable new baby literally broke their heart.

Clients and friends were intrigued as to how I'd managed to leave full time employment and create a profitable, sustainable business in such a short space of time. I was often quizzed and asked for help with business ideas and launch strategies, so it was clearly apparent that there was a gap in the market. At the time though, I didn't think much of it, until most of my photoshoots also became mentoring sessions.

Although I still had so much love and passion for my thriving photography business, I started to think that I was capable of more. I wanted to help women create what I had created.

Via my in-person workshops and the subsidiary business I had created called The Online Classroom. I started to share my top tips for starting out or starting over in business. I provided guidance and advice on what had or hadn't worked for me, and it felt incredible that I was able to help these ladies turn their ideas into a business.

It became very apparent that there was a need for a support network for women. That's where my soulsista comes in. Meet Abigail. Successful in her own right, we had worked together previously and we were completely aligned in our vision, values, goals and impact for women wanting to pursue their version of success.

Female Success Network was created as an natural amalgamation of ideas, content and learnings, along with knowledge and expertise from Abigail's corporate and entrepreneurial background and my 24 years work experience, lifelong learning, and self-employed business knowledge.

We came together with a vision to create a movement for women. To create a community of like-minded female entrepreneurs; to offer a safe place where they could learn, self-develop, feel supported and enhance their success in life, business and career.

I couldn't be any prouder of what we have created.
We chose collaboration over competition so that women could rise and shine together. A quote I always refer to is…

"Alone you have power, together we have force."

This is very true in our case.
Collectively we brought a diverse mix of skills, experience, and knowledge, but living at opposite ends of the country meant we had no idea if this could, or would work. What we did know was that we had so much to offer, had nothing to lose and so we went all in.

We very quickly invested in a success coach and booked onto a retreat which took us to the Hollywood Hills in LA, where we masterminded, planned out our strategy, and spent quality time on our new business.

Our launch campaign was 6 weeks of valuable content, showing up, and working strategically to spread the word about our mission to help women around the world. Within those 6 weeks, we created a community of over 6,000 women and a tribe of 1,500 who joined our live webinars through our private Facebook group.

Upon opening our doors we very proudly created a six figure business within the first 6 months. Quite an achievement I'd say.

The most surprising aspect of our launch was that our exclusive mastermind was the first sell out. This was a very last minute decision to add to our launch strategy, but certainly the best decision we made.

Little did we realise that those ladies who invested in their future are now sharing their story alongside us in this beautifully inspiring best-selling book to celebrate their own incredible success story.

What a difference a year makes.

Looking back over these past 12 months is nothing short of epic! I'd be lying if I said it's been easy. When you create something as incredible as FSN, it inevitably brings major challenges. Copycats, competitiveness, and people who show their true colours when jealousy gets thrown into the mix.

However, seeing the impact we have created in such a short space of time only fuels our momentum to find even more ways to help women shine bright and have the confidence to turn those dreams into reality.

It still blows my mind that with the right people, hard work and a bit of grit – you can achieve anything you put your mind to. Even if it does feel very daunting at the time.

If you're feeling inspired to turn your idea into a business but haven't yet because:

- You don't have the time.
- You don't know where to start.
- You don't have the money.
- You don't have the experience.
- You don't have the confidence.

STOP!

The best piece of business advice was from a business friend and inspiration, Hayley Parsons OBE. Hayley knows her stuff. She's a hugely successful entrepreneur and investor who is most notable as the founder of British financial services comparison website, Gocompare. Her advice to me was - "Sarah, there is no secret sauce in business. You've just got to put your big girl pants on and go for it!"

The simplicity of this really hit home for me because I had always been "searching". Searching for the perfect roadmap to success. The reality is we create our own success. The word "success" will be different for each of us depending on individual values and goals. It has different meanings to different people so the best advice I can give anyone is just get out there and pursue YOUR version of success.

If you could take only one thing away from my story, I would say it is this:
"There's always a way"
There's always a way to survive hardship.
There's always a way to overcome adversity.
There's always a way to learn something new.
There's always a way to change your circumstances.
There's always a way to pursue your version of success.
You just need to make a choice and take action.

My personal secret to success and sustainability has been through finding balance in every area of my life. Making happiness a priority also created a happy home. It also gave me the passion, enthusiasm, freedom and headspace to never stop learning.

Surround yourself with people who encourage your personal growth and have your back. With the right people by your side supporting you and a positive mindset, you can become UN-STOPPABLE!

Watching how our un-stoppable mastermind sisters have had so much success and seeing our community grow every single day, just goes to show that it CAN work! I also know it's only the beginning for each and every one of us. You, too.

So, as we celebrate our first year of Female Success Network, the launch of this book, the graduation of our founder mastermind members, our monthly members and our ever growing community; it seems the perfect opportunity to thank everyone who has supported and believed in us along the way, THANK YOU.

The next chapter.
Lifelong learning and self-development continues to make my heart sing. This passion beautifully compliments our mission to help our clients work to their unique strengths so that they can create impact, fulfilment, happiness and success in every area of their life.

In addition to this, we're really excited to launch our strengths based coaching programme where we can also help our clients optimise their peak performance in life and business. Going through this process myself, I feel this is going to be a total game-changer for whoever we work with.

We're going global! I know that we already have lots of amazing clients all around the world but Female Success Network will now also have a base in New York. It's such an incredible opportunity for the business to expand so I'll be moving there with my husband and flying the flag for everything we've created, raising the profile of our clients and creating even more impact on a global scale.

The decision to make this move to the USA was not easy. There are so many people and 'things' we will miss but at times like this when you've got a hard decision to make, I think you need to ask yourself what is really important to you. Then you need to believe. Have the courage, commitment and conviction to build your life around that answer. So, that's exactly what we're going to do!

The future for Female Success Network is very exciting! In celebration of our first birthday and all the success we have helped others create, we have combined all the best bits of training, advice and resources to create a dedicated 12 week certified program, Success School. Helping anyone wanting to create a business whilst also becoming certified in 'Business Success' at the same time.

It doesn't end there. It's time to inspire the girls of our future! We're honoured to be The GoGirl Academy's global ambassador which promotes confidence, self-esteem, and wellbeing for girls aged 9 – 16. Our mission is to provide scholarships so girls can attend summer camps and to inspire the girls of our future, something I'm deeply passionate about.

Finally, something to share with you which will probably be one of my proudest accomplishments in business so far. With great pride, on Women's Entrepreneurship Day in November which celebrates, empowers and supports women in business and helps to alleviate poverty, I will be representing Female Success Network & The GoGirl Academy at the United Nations.

Who'd have thought that within 12 months of starting a new business we'd be creating this much impact on a global scale in such a short space of time. Was it expected? NO! Is the future looking exciting? HELL YES!

To say I'm grateful is an understatement. I feel like the luckiest girl in the world to be surrounded by people who light my life and inspire me to inspire others.

However, I can promise you that I wouldn't be who I am today or sharing this with you without the endless love, support, and belief from Andy, Abigail and of course my biggest cheerleader, my mum. I love you and will continue to make you proud. Thank you for always believing in me.

So from the girl who left school with no qualifications and very little to aspire to... **I DARE YOU TO BELIEVE.**

There's always a way so take every opportunity.

Shine bright and **GO FOR IT!**

About Sarah Stone

Sarah Stone is a heart centred mentor to women in business, female entrepreneurs, and creative souls. She is also Co-Founder of Female Success Network, Co-Founder of Authors & Co and Award Winning Professional Photographer who is a certified NLP (neuro-linguistic programming) master practitioner, qualified Strengthscope® practitioner and global ambassador for The GoGirl Academy.

Sarah is passionate about sharing her 24 years business knowledge, work experience, and creative expertise to help others thrive in life, business, and career.

As a successful Professional Photographer, Sarah's work has featured in OK! magazine and national newspapers. Her greetings card range has been stocked in WH Smith, Boots, Tesco's and many more high street stores. She has also attracted a number of celebrity clients and global photography commissions which have taken her to Barbados, Los Angeles, New York, and Singapore.

Her mission is to help others succeed using the tools, skills, and solid framework that has helped her create a variety of successful businesses not only for herself, but for so many of her clients too.

CONTACT:
EMAIL: sarah@femalesuccessnetwork.com

WEBSITE: www.sarah-stone.co.uk / www.femalesuccessnework.com

FACEBOOK: www.facebook.com/femalesuccessnetwork

INSTAGRAM: www.instagram.com/sarahstonephoto/

PINTEREST: www.pinterest.co.uk/sarahstoneonline/ / www.pinterest.co.uk/femalesuccessnetwork/

LINKEDIN: www.linkedin.com/in/sarah-stone/

TWITTER: https://twitter.com/FSNTribe

Alison Goodwin

Do you remember your childhood? For some, childhood memories are cherished and for others they are locked away in vault never to be reopened. What is certain is that your childhood memories play an important part in shaping your individuality.

Memories and experiences carve a part in your soul and they help shape what you are to become.

I share this because I come from a middle class, hardworking family where both my parents worked long hours to provide for my sister Rachel and I. Our childhood was happy and filled with laughter and love.

They taught us important lessons about hard work and the rewards you get if you 'knuckle down'. It was my mum that first incentivised me to do chores to earn pocket money and my dad who showed me that working hard is important in life.

There are days I look back and remember the dreams and aspirations of a child full of innocence and eagerness to go out into the world. A time in my life when limiting beliefs simply were not there and the word 'can't' was not in my vocabulary.

One of my earliest childhood memories is being taught in primary school and being told by my teacher that I couldn't sit at the desk I wanted to. It was next to my best friend.

I remember that day vividly. The desk was medium oak coloured with a lift lid and an inkwell that had pen marks scratched into the wood from the many children that had passed through the school.

SHE WHO DARES

I still remember my answer even now - 'there is no such word as can't, Miss' and I remember her response as if it was only yesterday, 'you're right, Alison. Go on, you can sit there'.

Even then I was determined, a trait that is still with me. We all have experiences that set us on our path and this is just one that has helped influence the person I am today. Without a doubt, it helped build my character and the values that make me unique.

So, let me take you on my journey.

I was always the girl that didn't quite fit in at school. Now, don't get me wrong. I had lots of friends but to quote my friend's much older brother, I was 'far more mature than other girls my age'. You see, I was always focused, analytical, and process driven. I'd question anything and everything.

I formed friendships easily, I knew my own mind and I wasn't one to follow the crowd, I hated gossip and I was incredibly direct. I think it is fair to say that I was quite proud of the fact I made my own decisions, though I'm sure my parents would at this stage be quite happy to furnish you with stories about my teenage years and the trouble I caused them.

At high school I was a decision maker and it was here my entrepreneurship first started to show. In the 'good old days', or should I say 'when I was a girl', it wasn't like it is now. They didn't watch what they served for school dinner (for fear of allergies, additives or other such things).

They served up great big dolloping portions of chips and gravy, and a lovely snack at break called chocolate crunch or chocolate brownie (truthfully, it was only ever labelled crunch when they had over cooked it but no one really cared because it was the best thing *ever*). It was the chocolate brownie that everyone loved and they always ran out.

So, one day I simply asked my favourite dinner lady for the recipe and to my surprise she handed the holy grail over. I costed the ingredients, worked out my portions and started to bake.

I started to sell them, undercutting the school by a whole 5p and I remember feeling like a proper business woman. Even after all these years, I still remember that feeling. My 'first business' was an overnight success and I had my first real taste of entrepreneurship. I'll let you into a secret that was 25 years ago, and I still get asked now to make the school brownies.

At school I was academic, I studied hard so the choice to move to University just happened, it was what everyone did if they wanted a good career in the 1980's /1990's and I just went with the flow. What did surprise my friends and family though was my ability to multitask, its something I still do to this day. I was perfectly capable of holding down several part time jobs whilst I studied and managed somehow to have a really good social life. Looking back now, I am amazed at how I ever managed it all.

I worked as a waitress and a pot washer in a restaurant, worked for the local pizza parlour, as a bar maid, in event management, outside catering *and* during the Christmas period one year tried my hand working at a well-known department store. Have I mentioned when you are at school you seem to get a *lot* of holidays?

It taught me a *lot* and I made a *lot* of mistakes along the way like agreeing to work Christmas Eve for double time. I remember going in for my shift and telling them half way through that I was going home for a family event. I insisted that I had told them all about it.

The truth was I had let my friends talk me round to going out. The 'in' place at the time was Discotheque Royale in Manchester (how many of you can remember that place?). I boarded that bus knowing I'd let myself down, filled with regret but what a night and what a hangover. It's amazing how priorities change as we grow older.

What I am most proud of during my academic years is that unlike many of my peers I was able to fund my own college fees, without the need to ask for help. On leaving high school, I had saved enough to buy my own new car which I did just after passing my driving test in Guernsey where I had spent a year on placement as a trainee Manager for my University course.

To this day, my best friend Diane insists they were wrong to pass me. Something about going around a roundabout the wrong way and mounting a kerb in Sainsbury's car park but that is a story for another day.

Little did I know that it was the experience I gained working in my part time positions and my University placement that would secure me my first real job. This was to be Training and Personnel Manager for a Group that provided conference banqueting and accommodation facilities across the UK. As the youngest management team member to have ever been recruited, I dealt with disciplinary, grievance, training and appraisals, for over 250 staff.

I was recruited and trained to provide HR and specialist recruitment experience and provide support to the Operational Team. In addition to being responsible for the entire site, I was expected to work twice a week as a Duty Manager. The job was a *big* step for someone just out of University and I jumped at it. Reflecting now, I see that I've always been a 'doer' even if something seems impossible, I'll agree and work the 'how' out.

Instead of seeing the negative, I always try to see the positive and so I've always believed 'there is a solution to every problem'.

It wasn't an easy ride and I quickly found out that a young girl fresh out of University was fair game to the very staff I was supposed to be leading. So, I did the only thing I could do and that was to dig deep and earn the respect of the people I was there to lead.

If my shift started at 7am, I made sure I arrived at 6am. If we were short of staff, I rolled up my sleeves and would get stuck in. I would not ask someone to do something that I was not prepared to do myself. I observed each department head in action and took the bits that worked until I had something that worked for me.

All the while focusing on the job but aware of the impact leaders had on the staff, the consumer, and the business. I wanted to learn as much as I could from everybody I encountered and that's still something I do to this day.

There are two beliefs I have: 'lead by example' and 'treat others as you would like to be treated', something I see a lot of leaders failing to do.

Recruitment became my niche almost by default. I remember being called into the General Managers office and being asked if I would consider taking a more active role in recruitment. Headcount was down, attrition was poor and it was going to be one hell of a challenge but I readily agreed. Slowly but surely my work paid off. The praise had started to roll in and retention was on the up. Hires were staying, not falling off, and positive feedback was rolling in.

I loved my job. I loved the people I worked with, but then something happened to burst my perfect little bubble.

I was attacked by a guest one morning. Fortunately, it was nothing serious but I decided there and then that the industry was no longer for me.

I found myself in a position yet again where I didn't really have a clear direction on what I wanted to do. For a few months I freelanced, providing training, recruitment, and support for local companies. I was then approached to go back into event management which I did but I also started to cater privately for events. I catered for some of the UK's top sports people and loved every minute of it.

What I haven't shared until this point is that I love cooking, baking, and everything 'kitchen'. They say you should have a hobby that relaxes you and this is my 'happy place'. At one time, whilst at University, I thought that would be my career. The truth is it just doesn't pay anywhere near enough to warrant the time spent doing it and for that reason I stopped catering and chose something else.

So, here is a good point to give you a little bit of advice:

#1
Always dedicate yourself to continuous learning. You never know what is going to happen, you have to be able to change and adapt.

I always remember the following quote:
'It is not the strongest of the species that survives, nor the most intelligent, but the one most responsive to change.'
Charles Darwin

It was shortly after this that I attended an interview that would literally change my life. I was approached to interview for a role in sales. I got the job. It was not the job that I went for, but in fact the position above. Now, at this stage I want to point out that I had never worked in this sector and it was a steep learning curve. Nobody warned me about what was to come.

I think you will agree when I say sales people sometimes have a bad reputation and from experience I can honestly say that it is the few that spoil it for everyone else. I learned very early on in my career that your customer experience in sales should be of the same standard whether you are working with an individual or a corporate client, and that transitions through into any industry.

Now, I'm not going to lie. It wasn't always easy. When you are in sales you have targets and you are constantly reminded that 'you are only as good as your last deal'. You live on 60-70 hour weeks, have constant phone calls, and you simply don't have a balance between work and life (or at least I didn't).

But do you know something? I can say hand on heart that I loved my job, my clients, the relationship building, and my team. I was *very* good at what I did and I was compensated very well for doing a good job.

I achieved promotion after promotion and I was a regular on the winners trips that took me all over the world. My reputation was for my no-nonsense approach and I delivered an exceptional service to everyone I worked with simply through building long term relationships on trust and a solid business understanding.

I took pride in building teams that were motivated, focused, and driven.

However, with the peaks also come the troughs. They came in the form of a new manager and I'm being honest when I say we just didn't click. My health started to suffer, my love for the job began to wane and as a result my business began to decline.

Then, one day, I received a call that still haunts me to this day. It was a call to say that one of my team members had tried to take her own life and that she would not be returning to work. I broke down, in the middle of the office. Not for me, but for my colleague.

Every emotion possible was running through my body. I just couldn't understand why.

So, I had a choice take the easy option: leave and put it all behind me or pick myself up and look after my team. Which option did I take?

I chose to pick myself up and protect my team as much as I could from the pressure of the industry. I attended a meeting with our company's director and HR team and I told them *everything*, but that was little comfort as my colleague had not returned to work and left the business shortly after. To this day I still don't know why but I was adamant that nobody else would ever feel that low or that desperate.

That year I qualified for salesperson of the year and won an all expenses trip to South Africa. My qualification letter reads *'Amazing comeback, Alison. You're one of the best sales people we have. I'm so pleased for you'*.

My advice to those of you who are in employment and in a similar situation would be:

2

Always be aware what is going on around you. Sometimes it's the little things you miss that matter and morph into something big. Don't ever let anyone be disrespectful to you. If you wouldn't take it at home then you shouldn't take it at work and NEVER be afraid to stand up for your own truth and speak out. If you are in management, my advice is simply to let your people grow, learn to work with them not against them. That is what will make you an awesome leader.

With new management, I stayed with the company building a new team. I loved my job again and I was earning five figures a month but deep down I had lost a lot of respect for the company I worked for. I had a team I was proud of and a combined target of £1 million but I was going through the motions, then life threw me another curveball.

I had an accident at work that required surgery and this is where my story really starts.

I should have returned to work within eight weeks but something was wrong. I can't describe in words how I felt but whilst my ligaments were slowly healing, I had developed a long term chronic pain condition that affected my entire body. This condition was to later be labelled Complex Regional Pain Syndrome (CRPS) and not long after that I was diagnosed with Fibromyalgia.

Now, the toughest thing for me was getting a diagnosis. It was knowing something was very wrong but being treated like it was in my head. This battle went on for years. As anyone with a chronic pain condition will tell you: it is tough, it is invisible, and it is so hard to live with on a daily basis. I can honestly say it was one of the toughest, if not THE toughest, time of my life.

It just kept coming, though. Work had stopped calling, I was suffering from depression and anxiety. I was struggling. Then, I found out that my colleague had succeeded in taking her own life and I turned into a virtual recluse. I lost every ounce of fight I had in me and lost all belief in myself. I realised I needed to work on my health and my mindset.

I found myself in unchartered waters and I had to face the real possibility that I may never return to the job I loved or (if my specialists were to be believed) any full-time job again. With help from my friends and family, I made a conscious choice to ignore what I was being told and I started to look to the future.

The 60-70-hour weeks driving up and down the country were a thing of the past but I could still help others. I suffered from chronic pain and some days were unbearable but I had my limbs and I was semi-mobile.

There are so many people in much worse positions who despite their circumstances continue to inspire others. People like my friend, Nicola, who sadly lost her life to cancer but not before she left a legacy for her family and many others.

Talking about her always inspires me. She formed KMAC whilst ill and raised millions of pounds shortly before she died. Her legacy lives on in her charity KMAC and through her brother Gregg who now heads it up.

It certainly put things into perspective and gave me the courage to carry on.

It is at this stage that I tell you, even in my darkest hours I try to remain positive. I honestly believe it is that mindset that has kept me going and moving forward.

I have needed to focus on the positive even recently. I was told on Christmas Eve 2017 that I had what they thought were cancerous tumours within an 18cm x 10cm cyst on my ovary and that it would need removing. It was urgent and there was a chance I would need a full hysterectomy.

I don't have children so you can imagine my dilemma. In my head, though, I was not ill and in January 2018 I had the surgery.

So, let me give you a little advice from someone who has been through a few struggles and lived to tell her tale.

3
"Your happiness depends on your mindset and attitude." Roy T Bennett

It seems strange to be writing about my illness and injury in such an open way because usually I am such a private person, but it has been part of the journey that I have been through and has made me the person you see now.

I started to think about what I could do and less about what I could not. I started looking at what I could offer people and slowly but surely not one but two business ideas formed in my mind, I just lacked the courage to do anything about it. Then, fate intervened and the lady that was later to become a good friend Abigail Horne came into my life along with the Female Success Network.

I remember the day that we first spoke. It was a cold wet day in August on top of a fence in the middle of a field in Anglesey. With rain pelting down on my face I made the call to Abi that would literally transform my life.

I was drawn to the honesty and openness of Female Success Network. Coming from the 'corporate world' and from companies where competition is rife, it was so unlike anything I had ever experienced.

If you're reading this and wondering what made Female Success Network stand out to me, it was one simple phrase, **"collaboration over competition"**.
This was later to become something very poignant to me.

When I joined the Mastermind group it was with a seed of an idea (well, two, and an idea I have yet to patent and prototype believe it or not). I watched from a distance to see if the 'group' was for me and if I could put my trust into people again. Instead of competition, I found myself surrounded by a group of women who openly supported and encouraged each other but didn't just speak empty words. They did what they promised.

Women who are now so connected, I honestly think we are unstoppable. We pick each other up and support each other in ways that I can't even describe and we are led by two very beautiful, honest, heart led co-founders.

I can state with my hand on my heart that without Abigail Horne and Sarah Stone, Female Success Network would not be what you see today and would certainly not be what it is about to become.

Both Abi and Sarah have become like family. We laugh, we giggle, we enjoy each other's company, and we celebrate every success, all whilst working together as strong business women. Who can truly say that they get to work with a support group who are there 24 x 7 no matter what?

Each of the ladies in the Mastermind will no doubt give you their version of what Female Success Network means to them. To me, it's helped me drill down exactly what I wanted to do with my business and it has helped me to micro niche. I wanted a business that would challenge and excite me, something that wasn't just person to person but business to business, too.

Having seen the potential in the corporate sector, I wanted to build something that was scalable but a service that would always be needed in our ever-changing society.

My strengths are in Career and Business Strategy and that is the building block of each of my businesses. I've always been the person people come to for advice and already have one successful business under my belt.

Over the years, I've helped hundreds of people find the right career for them. If it has not been a career I have helped them with, it has been to help them set up their own companies or to coach business strategy. It seemed right to use these skills in a new business.

This leads me nicely on to my next piece of advice.

4
I realised very early on in my career that business is not about profit but about helping others. If you can help others genuinely with a problem or service, then profit will follow.

That's exactly how www.alisongoodwin.co.uk was born. A company that helps individuals, small businesses, and corporate clients with everything career related. Individual coaching, business strategy, recruitment,and *so much more*. I live and breathe working with people, serving those that truly have lost direction and need guidance.

Working with start-up companies that need a structure, a business and marketing plan, and a map to see them through to profitability. Working with the large corporate clients that need help with business process outsourcing, career engagement, behavioural change, candidate screening, coaching, recruitment, networking strategies, and everything in between.

But I could also see that career advice and guidance for the youth of today was sadly lacking. With the removal of government grants, local authority funding, and lack of help in the education sector it was becoming increasingly clear to me that our next generation were going to slip through the net.

I set up www.yourfutureself.academy to help address this problem.

A company whose sole purpose is to help young adults looking for additional advice when choosing GCSES, A Levels, or University Courses. We bridge the gap between the parent, the young adult, the education provider, and the onward passage to working life.

We offer exam coaching, group and individual coaching, and soon will offer larger workshops and retreats. We work with young adults aged 9-23 and help them choose courses that will give them better career choices in later life.

Often when choosing GCSES or a University course, they do not know what they want to do so options are often chosen based on likeability not suitability. We help guide them to make choices based on the latter. With the average student ending a 3-year degree course with approximately £23,500 debt but almost 60% of UK graduates working in non-graduate jobs, it's clear the system isn't working and they need our help.

What makes me happy is the collaborations that are due happen very soon with people I met in the Mastermind group, people I'm privileged to call friends. I'll be collaborating with Susan Hughes on projects, so head on over to www.theartisanboutique.co.uk for announcements.

I'll be partnering with my fellow Mastermind member Laura Warren www.laura-warren.com on a project that will be unlike anything anybody else has done but involves sporting personalities. I can't say anymore but watch this space. There are so many other collaborations to talk about. The friendships we have formed are lifelong and I just can't see us all ever not being in touch.

The businesses I have started have not 'happened by chance'. I firmly believe that everything that has happened in my life was to bring me to this point and for that I am actually grateful. If not for my accident, I wouldn't be doing what I love. I even found my partner, Steve, in the middle of all of the trauma so it's not all bad.

With both companies, I know that I can make a difference and provide a service that is better than the competition. That comes down to the faith I have in myself and a rock solid business plan.

This leads nicely to my next piece of advice and a quote that always sticks with me,
"By failing to prepare you are preparing to fail." Benjamin Franklin

5
Always have a plan and always do a business plan.
So many new and existing individuals and businesses skip this step and it really is the most critical. You must understand your customer avatar, who they are, what they do, etc. Your business plan will also help you focus on cash flow which is the life blood of every business and cash flow management will help you stay on track and avoid any unpleasant surprises.

For the life of me, I just cannot understand why anyone would miss this step.

My next piece of advice would be:

6
Make sure you have multiple income streams.
It is certainly true what they say about not putting all your eggs in one basket, but that's not all having multiple income streams does for you. It allows you to branch out, to practice new skill, and it also opens your business to collaboration for partnership opportunities.

In today's digitally driven age, multiple income streams are common whether it be an eBook, an affiliate link, products, services, or simply that you licence your ideas. If you're serious about making your business work, make sure your income stream reflects that.

To do better you must understand that it is not just about your customer. You must look at developing business strategies, marketing, selling, customer interaction, and admin such as bookkeeping, payroll, and invoicing. Becoming a business owner means you must wear multiple hats. It's like a right of passage.

But it does not have to be difficult. My next piece of advice is for anyone who feels the overwhelming feeling being a business owner can sometimes create:

7
If you can't do something, then outsource or automate the bits you cannot do. If you can't afford to outsource, then my secret hack is to skill swap your way to it. Just remember that there is always a way.

I will let you into a secret, I *hate* technology. But I acknowledge that and so I outsource it to my partner. It is highly likely that someone in your circle can help. For me, I'm eternally grateful to Sarah Stone who started my website and to Steve who finished it. You just need to ask.

What I will say as an entrepreneur is that without Female Success Network it would be lonely, so if you are thinking of starting a business or even if you have a business already, then you must connect with likeminded individuals.
If you surround yourself with people who are there to cheer you on and not to drag you down, you will notice a difference.

The people that help to raise you up will support you in your journey and will help to eliminate the negative thoughts that often come when starting something new.

I let fear and uncertainty stop me starting my businesses for years. The fear of failure, the worry about mistakes, the uncertainty of succe, and now I look back and think 'why didn't you do this sooner'.

Yes, the odds are stacked against me. Let's face it, most businesses fail in the first year they start. But I certainly do not intend to fail. However, *if* I did, so what!? I would pick myself up and learn from my mistakes just as I have up until this point in my life with the support of my family and friends.

We teach our children *'if at first you don't succeed, try and try again'* but as adults we rarely do.

So, my advice would be to go out and make as **many mistakes** as you can because that is the only way you are going to learn. Then, and only then, are you are ready to become an entrepreneur.

"One thing is certain in business. You and everyone around you will make mistakes." Richard Branson

When it comes to my businesses, I'm an OCD freak. Everything is structured, blocked out, and prioritised. I adjust my schedule on my bad days and micro manage my time so that I still achieve everything I need to do. Flexibility is key.

My goals are not small, and my client's goals are not small but that doesn't scare me. What scares me now is mediocrity, settling for settling sake. Staying productive is about setting big goals and striving to reach them. It is about having a list for the day and doing what you need to do.

I have to say, I've found the whole experience of becoming a female entrepreneur liberating. It's the real things in life that matter. I'm talking personal growth, mindset, love, relationships, friends, family, and of course work.
I'm finally happy.

It has been a cathartic process, something that I truly wish I had started years ago. If you're reading this and you need help, guidance, or advice on anything I have covered then I am here for you as Abi and Sarah were there for me. Always remember you will find a home with Female Success Network and the team of female powerhouses they have created. We will 'have your back'.

On a personal note I would like to thank my friends and family for their support. My dad, who drives me crazy daily, you taught me that hard work pays off and you really are my best friend. My partner, Steve, who has spent countless hours helping me with the 'tech stuff'. My best friend, Diane, who is my sounding board and my 'unstoppable business besties' Laura Warren and Susan Hughes, you girls really are like family.

More importantly, my thanks and gratitude go to Abi, Sarah, and my unstoppable mastermind sisters. I couldn't have done any of this without your support and for that I am forever grateful.

With Gratitude and Love,
Alison x

About Alison Goodwin

Alison Goodwin is a Career and Business Strategist from Cheshire in the UK and a self-confessed learning junkie who is trained in Life Coaching, Career Coaching and Neurolinguistic Programming (NLP).

With 25 years business experience Alison has worked in a variety of industries such as HR, Training and Event Management as well as high pressure, target driven environments like Recruitment and Sales.

It was in these latter areas that Alison excelled placing thousands of people and winning numerous awards. Always one for pushing herself and getting the best out of others Alison rapidly became known in her industry as the consultant that everyone wanted to work with.

Then, suddenly out of the blue, Alison found her career on hold for health reasons and she found herself undergoing extensive 'rehabilitation'. Already an entrepreneur with a successful business under her belt, it was during this period of reflection and forced rest that Alison decided to refocus.

Alison now runs two successful companies.

The first www.alisongoodwin.co.uk specialises in helping individual clients define new career paths, whether that be helping them navigate the everchanging workplace or helping those looking for a complete career change.

Her company also offers a range of services, such as coaching and business strategy to smaller SMEs and start-up businesses, through to training needs analysis, redundancy services, bespoke workshops and individual, executive, group strategy coaching to major blue-chip companies and corporate bodies, all looking to gain that competitive edge in their market place.

Alison's latest company www.yourfutureself.academy was set up to help young people age 12-21 to transition into young adults by building solid foundations for their future, using proven strategies to help them map their goals. Her mission is to make career advice accessible early in life so that our next generation are inspired to do more and to be more.

www.yourfutureself.academy liaises with local education authorities and provides help for parents and young adults looking for additional guidance and support when faced with GCSE or A Level options, college choices and future career decisions. Her company provides services such as option selection, coping with exam pressure, structured revision planning, coaching to achieve grades and confidence building.

All of which are becoming less available through schools and local government, be that through funding withdrawal, lack of resources or staffing capability. Alison's workshops and summer camps focusing in these areas with team building activities for young adults are due to launch soon.

Her ultimate mission throughout her brand is to "provide the tools that empower people to unleash their potential and fulfil their career and business goals".

In her spare time Alison volunteers for the local RSPCA and enjoys walking in the Cheshire countryside with her two dogs Bella, (her day blind black Labrador) and Bailey her over excited black Staffie . She also manages a small international property portfolio.

She believes if you truly want something then nothing will stop you, after all there is no such word as can't.

Contact:
Email: letstalk@alisongoodwin.co.uk and letstalk@yourfutureself.academy

Website: www.alisongoodwin.co.uk and www.yourfutureself.academy

Facebook:
https://www.facebook.com/profile.php?id=1392444520

Instagram: https://www.instagram.com/iamalisongoodwin/

Linkedin: http://linkedin.com/in/alison-g-4286023

Caroline Strawson

As a child, running a business was never something that we ever discussed in my house. I grew up in a very traditional middle-class household with my mum, dad and two older sisters.

Education was everything to my parents and although never discussed, it was assumed that I would do my GCSE's, A levels and then go onto University and get a degree. It was all about security and getting a profession to then have a secure career for life. My mum wanted me and my two older sisters to all get a vocation so that we would always be independent and never have to rely on anyone.

So, I was captain of all the sports teams and a model student gaining 10 GCSEs and 3 A levels and then I went to university and obtained a degree in podiatry. I had always loved anything medical as a child and loved helping people heal.

My mum and dad had always led me to believe that if I put my mind to anything, I could achieve it and I truly believed this but in the confines of what I was led to believe by my parents who wanted me to get a "job" as this was security in their eyes.

I was a high achiever and put an enormous amount of pressure on myself from a very early age to be perfect at everything. Little did I know that this was a constant battle that I was to have later into my adult life but at this stage, it was the norm for me as I was the archetypal model daughter following the ideals of my parents as they just wanted the best for me and I did not want to disappoint.

So after I obtained my degree at just 21 years of age, I worked for the NHS but I wanted to travel, so very soon I joined the UK's second largest airline and had an amazing time travelling, doing promotional work for the company and appearing in national newspapers and magazines.

I was taken to one side during my training course at this airline and told that they saw great things in me. I think I was always seen as a nice person, diligent but with a fierce work ethic. I don't think I have ever met anyone that could out work me!

I even met the boss man himself at the airline parties and promotional assignments many times, and he is definitely one of my entrepreneurial idols and inspirations and I wish I knew then what I know now as I would have quizzed him even more!!

Being super ambitious and still wanting to strive to be the best of the best, I then applied and got a job with the UK's largest airline and stayed there for 9 years. I loved travelling and meeting new people all the time and was even specially selected from 12,000 cabin crew to be VIP cabin crew for the then Prime Minister Tony Blair and traveled with him to many destinations including New York following September 11th.

This trip changed me forever as I realised that life was precious, and life was short. In the time following September 11th, the airline offered unpaid leave and so I took 6 months unpaid leave as I had been approached to work for the UK's second largest shopping channel as a presenter on their live shows.

Again, I was always someone looking for opportunities but opportunities that came my way rather than actively seeking them out myself, as this was probably due to confidence and my upbringing as a secure "job" was always the main focus.

No risk just security! Scared but excited, I worked for this shopping channel for 6 months and whilst I absolutely loved the adrenalin rush of live television, I was away from my husband as he was also cabin crew, and so I went back to flying.

All the time that I was working for the airlines and shopping channel, I still always ran a side business with my podiatry as I wanted to maintain my qualification. In 2003, when I fell pregnant with my first child, I realised I did not want to return to work flying as I couldn't bear thinking that I could be in Australia if my baby became poorly. But what actually transpired was I actually ended up taking the airline to a tribunal for sex discrimination which was settled before it reached court.

Again, if I feel something is unfair, I will fight to the end because I am such a believer that it can take one person to change something for the good of so many more, and I could not sit back and accept what happened as did not want what happened to me to happen to any other woman. Complacency is definitely not one of my traits!!

When I had my son, this is when my entrepreneurial flair started to really show itself more readily as I was pulled in two directions of wanting to be a mum, but also having a fierce ambition. When I look back prior to this, my entrepreneurial spirit was always there and even my sisters say now that it was always there but I think as my parents were both so traditional, it was never nurtured or explored simply due to their view of what secure meant to them.

Wanting to earn some extra money as a mum, I decided to set up a business doing PediPod parties. This was a word that I made up and created as a brand which were my take on mini pamper parties for 6 women, where I would give them a pedicure and a podiatry treatment in one evening. These became so successful that the following year I was wondering how I could maintain them, when one of my friends became my business partner to help me as she had

previous experience in beauty and actually hated her current job. In fact, she has now gone on from this being the start to run her own beauty business based on the back of my PediPod parties.

I went on to have my daughter in 2008 following a really tough time and having four miscarriages, and it was at this time my life was really starting to change. My marriage was breaking down and my best friend, my mum suddenly passed away in 2009.

I was completely devastated as she was my rock. Then in August 2010, my marriage broke down resulting in me becoming a single mum to my two children.

During our divorce, we had accumulated over £70,000 worth of debt and over the coming months, I kept sinking more and more financially and was suffering with depression, anxiety and self-harm. In fact, each day would start on my bathroom floor having a panic attack and self-harming.

I felt a failure because my marriage had ended, and I felt like I had let my children down. I was running a podiatry clinic every Friday to try and stay afloat as I was struggling with debt and money worries. I felt like I was in a dark tunnel with no way out.

Even within my podiatry business, my entrepreneurial flair kicked in as I wanted to be a podiatrist with a difference and offered a range of other treatments that not many other podiatrists did.

But this was not earning me enough money and it was capped, especially as I had to factor in my debt and childcare costs. Also, as I was self- employed, if my children were poorly and I couldn't work, I simply did not get paid so I would feed my children and I would live on rice crackers.

Life continued to get worse and I would get bills coming through the door that I didn't want to open for fear of them asking for money which I simply did not have. Every time I went to a petrol station, I only dared put £10 in my car for fear of needing the money the next day.

Then in April 2013, I had my family home repossessed. A very dark time for me. I had truly hit rock bottom as felt ashamed, lonely and a failure. However, this became the catalyst for change for me especially as I hit 4o in the June and realized I could continue playing the victim or take back control and do something about it. I knew that there was only one way to go and that was up now! My destiny was in my hands and nobody else's.

I started to look around to earn some extra money around my podiatry and my two children and so I started a home-based business in network marketing. I was super sceptical but the business ticked all the boxes for me with low investment and low risk and I simply at this point, did not have a plan B. I had an ambition and a need to make a change and a thirst for learning, and if there was one thing my mum and dad had taught me, was that whatever I put my mind too, I could be a success at.

So in October 2013, I started my business, initially because I wanted to earn an extra few hundred pounds which I did very quickly. Due to my anxiety which was still plaguing me, I needed an easier way to build my business and my laptop and Facebook became my best friend! I could run my business from my smartphone and laptop and use Facebook.

Initially I did this in the pockets of time I had without having to leave my house every night and in pockets of time in the day and once my children went to sleep.

Over time, I invested in my own learning so that I could learn the ins and outs of Facebook and I loved it as it was like a science to me. I spent hours and hours working on myself and my mindset and being the best student I could be. This was when my love of positive psychology was born.

If I was to make a success of my business, it was only me that could make it happen. I genuinely believe that investing in yourself is the very best investment you can ever do, because if you know you are ambitious, then it's a sure thing.

Within 6 months of starting my business from home, I had doubled my podiatry salary and so I gave up being a podiatrist and became an entrepreneur full time. I was loving being in control of my own destiny, and my fierce work ethic was standing me in good stead.

I decided to fully invest my time in building my business and was loving every second. It was nerve wracking that it was down to me but also empowering because it was in my hands, my success. I had never had that as I had always had a "job" with a boss. Within 2 years of starting my business, myself and my team were turning over £1 million worth of products. I was able to pay off all my debt and enroll my eldest son into private education and my daughter will follow when she starts secondary school in 2019. I was the mum I wanted to be, but the business woman with a fierce ambition in control of her destiny. I had the absolute best of both worlds.

I put my head down and for four and a half years, I was laser focused on my business and went on to build a secure income for myself and my family, achieving all the incentives on my companies' marketing plan including over $25,000 in bonuses and 6 free holidays to date.

My children were thriving, and I was teaching them life skills that you can hit rock bottom but you can decide to make a change and if you work hard, you cannot just bounce back but bounce forward. In that time, I also got remarried and have 3 beautiful step daughters too.

My husband was running his own business as a mortgage and protection adviser but kept asking me to help build his business as he saw how I had built my home-based business with such success, but life insurance did not excite me.

However, the policy we had actively rewarded us for staying healthy and the concept was genius, but life insurance?! There kept being a niggle in my head that said how could I make life insurance sexy because every one of us should have it but so many don't, and I have seen both sides of that coin with friends struggling financially to cope after the death of a loved one.

My network marketing business was at the stage where I had a huge team of over 2000 people and a regular passive income coming in, so I decided to help my husband and build a brand called 'Active Life Rewards and Life Insurance For Mums' to help people get protected, more active and save money each month.

I felt like my confidence was growing as a female entrepreneur and I was allowing myself to open up my mind to concepts and ideas that I would previously have not, due to my upbringing.

It was at this time, I decided to embark on something I had always wanted to do. I am someone who loves learning and I truly believe that the best investment is in yourself. I have invested thousands of pounds over the last 4 years in courses, trainings, events, books and CD's, because I will only stop learning when I am no longer breathing, because I believe that life is a journey and you are constantly learning.

I am definitely not the sort of person who simply expects good things to happen to me. You need to see your opportunities and seize them with both hands! With this in mind, I had always had a passion for the subject of positive psychology which is the science of happiness, because I loved the fact that positive psychology looks at what makes people flourish and thrive rather than what makes people miserable.

I decided to go back to University to study for a Masters in Positive Psychology and Coaching Psychology. My kids thought it was hilarious that their mum was a student, but again I was teaching them all these life skills along the way that circumstances and age are no barrier!

In September 2017, I joined Female Success Network as felt I needed a mentor, and I work so much better with a coach as I like the accountability and having someone to bounce ideas off. Due to me never running a traditional business, I thought FSN could help me and I joined their mastermind group.

I became part of a group of just 25 other women also looking to build their business. Through my life, I have had challenges with other women with jealousy, bitchiness and bullying, because unfortunately some women feel that if you are successful, this means there is less success for them to have.

This of course is rubbish, and when I see any woman succeeding, I will shout and cheer because I know how hard they will have worked.

I created an idea for our life insurance business which was different from any other on the market always with our customers in mind. I wrote a business plan with the help of FSN and created a time line for the business.

I am someone who has a constant flow of ideas and sometimes I wish I could turn the volume down in my head, but this is where FSN and the mastermind would guide me.

I looked at all the competition in the current market place, and my mission was to help the UK get better protected, more active and to save money in the process, and this is exactly what we do, with each of our customers saving on average over £1000 every 6 months but having the peace of mind that their loved ones are protected should the unthinkable happen.

My husband was loving all the leads I was bringing in and the business thrived.

As the months progressed, our customer base was growing, and I was loving being in a group of women that supported and shared ideas to all help each other succeed in whatever each of our businesses were.

Whilst I was loving sharing the message and getting the help from FSN, I felt like something was missing and I could not put my finger on it.

Our business was going from strength to strength and we were one of the top companies in our network. My network marketing business was thriving with many successes within my team, but I still felt like something was missing.

When I joined FSN, it was to get coaching about building my life insurance business, but as the weeks and months progressed, I was watching others in the group who were coaches really make a difference in peoples' lives. I was enjoying my positive psychology masters and one of the modules was all about positive psychology coaching and this is when I started to think, could I use this skill to help others?

But who and how? I have always believed that I am on this planet to leave a footprint and make a difference, and maybe this could be my opportunity to do just that? I had coached business in my network marketing business for 4 1/2 years and absolutely loved helping my team achieve, and the more I thought about it, the more I realised that I loved seeing people transform before my eyes.

To go from having zero confidence and belief in themselves, to flourishing and thriving and living a more fulfilled and happy life. I was now running two successful businesses and being in FSN had really opened up my confidence to pursue my dreams and my passion and purpose in life.

This gave me the confidence and belief in myself to dare to dream to set up my own coaching business to help others. I am fiercely ambitious and if I do something, I want to be the best I possibly can be, so I started to look at what kind of coach I could become. Resilience coach? Success coach? Online Facebook Coach?

Business coach? All of which I felt I had experience in but whenever I networked locally, there seemed to be so many of them around, and everywhere I looked online, I saw these coaches. I wanted to stand out from the crowd and really make a real difference.

I brainstormed and kept coming back to people who had been divorced. Women just like me! People who had lost themselves, maybe lost their identity, lost their direction and had hit rock bottom like I had. I wanted to help them completely overhaul and transform their life just as I had transformed mine.

I wanted to help women who did not even know where to start in the divorce process, so I trained to be a McKenzie Friend, which means I help people file for divorce themselves saving thousands of pounds in the process rather than having to appoint a divorce lawyer, as I can assist in all the form filling and accompany them to court for moral support and advice.

I trained to become one of the UK's first accredited Divorce and Breakup Coaches, so this means I can literally see people through the whole process of divorce from the legal aspect to the emotional and practical support. I wanted to become a one stop shop for women going through divorce.

Alongside my positive psychology, I wanted to help people not just bounce back following a divorce or breakup but bounce forward.
I wanted to create an environment where I could help coach someone through the emotional roller coaster of divorce and be their light in their darkness and hold their hand every step of the way.

I had been through my own divorce so had the experience and had been coaching for over 4 years and been a counsellor previously too. I wanted to use positive psychology to give people a toolkit to transform their lives and in 2018, I will be one of only a handful of accredited divorce and breakup coaches in the UK.

I was full circle back at a business idea where I could help people but use my entrepreneurial flair to build a successful business both on and offline, with free downloads, paid courses, one to one coaching and a free Facebook community group called Divorce and Breakup Support Group For Women, which as I type has over 2500 women in where I give free advice, live videos and tips on a daily basis and help many women within the group move forward by creating a safe, private and secure free community.

There is so much support and friendships growing within the group. I also want to create workshops and retreats both in the UK and abroad, to create a social environment with practical support and exercises to move forward, so that women realise that they are not on their own and life need not be any less than you deserve.

Two of the services that I decided to offer came from learning from my own experiences, and that is a High Conflict Middleman Messenger Service and Paramedic Divorce Coaching where my clients have unlimited access so they need never feel on their own, as I know first hand how lonely the divorce process can be and I want to be the strength for these women.

My mission was to become that I wanted to help others see that divorce could also be their superpower as it was definitely for me. I wanted to eradicate the stigma attached to divorce and single parenting that has such a negative connotation with phrases such as "broken home".

I had rebuilt my life after my divorce that had nearly broken me, but it had in fact actually made me stronger than ever. I have learned so much and one of the biggest lessons is to value people and always be true to yourself and be authentic.

I have come across many people who seem to think that your success means that there is less success to go around so I have faced negativity along the way but when you believe in something so strongly, nothing can stop you when you know that something is your true purpose.

This has been a huge challenge for me because when I see people working hard and succeeding, I absolutely love that because it shows me that as humans, we have so much potential if only we all realised it.

I have had failures along the way, but what I have learned is that these are not failures because I choose to think of life as a series of learning experiences and I am a student of life not a victim of circumstance.

I could have quite easily carried on being a podiatrist, having no money, getting tax credits and barely surviving because for a while that's exactly what I did do. I was waiting for someone to rescue me and then I realised the biggest gift I could give myself was to rescue myself. I was once told that why should I not be successful?

Why should I not shine my light bright in fear of making others feel inadequate around me? This was from my amazing sister as she quoted me Marianne Williamson's quote of which I have on a canvas.

I definitely realised that along the way, I have played down my success which I had worked so hard for as I did not want others to feel disheartened about their life, but we all have choices in how we live our life and I feel gratitude every day that my parents brought me up to believe I could do or be anything, and this is exactly how I am bringing my two children up.

Being in FSN has allowed me to thrive and flourish and really strive to reach my own true and authentic potential because this is encouraged, supported and championed. Being in a mastermind group with other driven, ambitious women made me realise that you need to be very careful who you surround yourself with. I have become great friends with everyone in the group and we are like a sisterhood that all help and support each other and champion each other's successes and are equally there to pick each other up.

There is no competition other than with ourselves each day, to continue to strive to be the best we can. We are there for the good times and the bad because this is life and we all have our down days, but we all pick each other up and share ideas and successes under the guidance of FSN.

I am now on a mission to help women recover from their divorce emotionally and financially. To think I started in the mastermind group to build my life insurance business, I am now creating a divorce coaching business with big plans to help as many women as I possibly can around the world, because I know firsthand how low and lonely you can feel at this time and it is my absolute passion and mission to help as many women as I can.

I think my drive and determination to give my children a better life after we lost everything keeps me driven, as I know that there will be women right now feeling like there is no hope and their life is over, and I want to reach out to them all.

I see hitting rock bottom as a gift now because I can now go on to help others recover quicker and see that life may be in a different direction now, but you can go on to be more whole, more in control and happier and more thriving. It is merely the end of one chapter, ready for the beginning of a new and even more exciting one.

Every Sunday, I plan my week ahead with my meetings and all my social media activity, as this is a huge part of getting my message out there via Facebook and other platforms with live videos and free content to help people, so please find me on Facebook and connect with me.

I feel I have now found my true purpose in life and see that through my darkest times, I can now help others through theirs. Joining FSN and the mastermind group has enabled me to grow as a person in so many ways, and I feel so happy that I can turn my passion into a business and see myself doing this forever as it certainly does not feel like work!

Getting messages from the women I have helped to tell me that my coaching has helped them in more ways than they can say, really brings me so much joy and I can't imagine doing anything else.

I started FSN with one successful business and I now have three successful businesses, one in network marketing that I built 80% online, one in life insurance for mums as I had no protection following my divorce and know how important this is so my children are cared for financially should anything happen to me, and finally my true passion and purpose in life, divorce and breakup coaching.

I am even writing a book about my divorce in the hope it will help and inspire others to see that there is light at the end of the tunnel, however dark it may seem.

FSN have helped me to do this with their sister company Authors and Co and this has made the book writing process so clear and easy and my book is called Divorce Became My Superpower and will be out in September 2018.

If you can relate to anything I have said about divorce in this chapter, I have literally only scratched the surface about what I went through, and it will be available on Amazon to purchase.

Again, I would never have dreamed I would be running three businesses, having a chapter in this book and my very own personal story in a book on my divorce when I joined Female Success Network.

It just shows that if you surround yourself with the right people, follow your heart and turn your passion into your business, you can live a fulfilled life both mentally, physically and financially.

I could not be happier right now and the fact that I have multiple income streams gives me peace of mind and security and anyone else starting out in business, I would encourage them to learn their business inside and out, always be on the lookout for opportunities and find yourself a mentor to guide you and keep you accountable.

If you would have said to me 5 years ago I would be where I am now, earning what I earn now, feeling the happiest I ever felt with two balanced, grounded, happy and healthy children, I would not have believed you.

Life can be a roller coaster but if you work on yourself everyday like I do, you absolutely can be where I am now.

I look in the mirror now and the woman I see is unrecognisable to who I was after my divorce. I did not even look in the mirror for 6 months following my divorce as I felt so ashamed and such a failure, but I refused to let it define me. I am in charge of my destiny and I can choose how I react to external circumstances.

You may not be able to change the reality of a situation, but you can reframe your lens in your head of how you

perceive that reality. This does not just happen overnight, and it takes time, just as you could not get a six pack by not going to the gym. You will not get a strong mindset by doing nothing but talking about wanting to be successful or earning more money, it does not just happen by chance.

I am so excited to help as many women as I can with my divorce coaching as I want women to realise that divorce can just be the start, and I feel such gratitude now about my divorce experience as it drove me to create the life I now lead.

I actually feel like a truly successful business woman now, a female entrepreneur who can open her mind up to possibilities that she would never have had the courage to follow. I get to make a difference in peoples' lives guiding them through the initial instigation of divorce, to helping them recover emotionally and practically.

From thinking should they stay or go, abusive relationships, co- parenting, how to handle divorce with children all the way through to getting out dating again and finding love. Being part of Female Success Network has allowed me to grow, learn and flourish and I have made some of the best friends that I know I will have forever.

About Caroline Strawson

Caroline Strawson is one of the first accredited Divorce and Breakup Coaches in the UK. She specialises in empowering women going through divorce with practical and emotional support using Positive Psychology. She uses her experience from her own divorce where she had over

£70,000 of debt and her family home repossessed. Her personal journey to not just bounce back but bounce forward quickly turned into a mission to want to help other women through the trauma of divorce and breakup especially from abusive relationships which then turned into a business.

Caroline now owns two successful businesses that she built from scratch and is a self taught Facebook Strategist. She has spoken in large arenas of over 3000 people sharing her personal story to inspire others. She is building a name for herself in the Divorce Coaching world as an expert in her field.

Caroline has had an interest in personal development for over 20 years and has a medical background prior to her divorce and is currently studying for a Masters in Positive Psychology and Coaching Psychology.

Caroline is on a mission to help women all over the world see that divorce need not define them and can be a catalyst for change and that divorce can be their superpower.

Caroline is currently writing a book called Divorce Became My Superpower to give others hope that life continues post divorce and that you can live a happier and more thriving life.

She has a vibrant Divorce and Breakup Support Group for Women on Facebook with over 2500 women in there where she gives free advice, tips and a heavy dose of positivity in a safe, private and secure environment.

Her mission is to eradicate the stigma attached to divorce and single parenting and take women through the whole divorce process with her Positive Psychology Coaching and proven strategies to design a new and exciting future.

Contact :

EMAIL : hello@carolinestrawson.com

WEBSITE : www.carolinestrawson.com

FACEBOOK : https://www.facebook.com/carolinejstrawson

FACEBOOK GROUP : https://www.facebook.com/divorcebecamemysuperpower/

LINKEDIN : https://www.linkedin.com/in/carolinestrawson/

INSTAGRAM : https://www.instagram.com/carolinestrawson/

TWITTER : https://twitter.com/CSdivorcecoach

YOUTUBE : https://www.youtube.com/c/CarolineStrawsonTheDivorceBreakupCoach

Chelle Shohet

Its 6 pm on a Thursday evening in April 2014 and I am standing in a poorly lit changing room in a London department store with my 10th distraught client of the week.

This woman is beautiful inside and out, intelligent, successful and from the outside, she has it all. A husband, children, great career, she is well respected in her field of expertise and has lots of friends but behind closed doors, it turns out she feels more like a swan treading water.

This story was one that I had recanted to me in some shape or form by the majority of my clients that week, and out of all of them, this lady is the one I least expected to hear it from.
But then that's the point! We never know what is going on behind closed doors or below the surface in this world of ours!

With the influence and filters of the "everything is perfect" Instagram and Facebook world we now live in, how much do we really know about one another? Moreover, how connected are we to ourselves and our feelings, our thoughts, our emotion's and our bodies?

For me the journey from a disconnected individual who once not only disliked but despised her own body has not been easy. It has not been straightforward or uneventful. I have been to breaking point and back; it has got as dark as it can get and yet I have also been blessed with the brightest sunshine too.

My choice to become an entrepreneur and be my own boss has been eventful, it has had its up's and its downs, and I do not doubt that it will always be that way as I and my business develop and evolve. Do I regret that decision? No way! Not one little bit!

Back in the changing room that evening with my client, I found myself wondering if there was something in the air that day, or if there was a cosmic happening that was the reason my clients seemed to all be falling apart at the seams. I knew, deep down, this was exactly what I had asked for in my dreams, a way I could grow my business and start to work with clients that needed me.

You see a year or so before this I was working with the complete opposite client, I was working flat out but not enjoying what I was doing one bit.

On a conscious level, I had set up my business as means to an end. If I am totally honest with you and myself for that matter, at that point in time, I was not dreaming big or thinking big my only ambition was to pay the bills. Some would say I set my business up on a whim, but this isn't true at all.

Reflecting now. I realise I was always destined to be my own boss. I had never been a very happy employee however high up I got in my career, because I always had my thoughts as to how things could be improved, I could always see new opportunities and possibilities. Some employers love this some do not, I have had my fair share of both over the years!

The time came for me to take the leap and set up my own business when I was made redundant overnight. To make things worse, I was 7 and a half months pregnant with my first baby at the time.

I was just about to start IVF treatment when he was conceived so we call Dexta our little miracle. With the shock of the company going bust and a few other family dramas around the same time, I was terrified as I went briefly into early labour. Luckily, he decided he wasn't ready to enter the world early and everything calmed down, but this didn't stop me from worrying at every little pain from then on in!

So, returning to a corporate role in the big smoke wasn't something I could even consider. So, I settled into my little bubble focusing on my baby and me. 9 or 10 months went past and it was in 2012 that I realised I needed something for me, I wasn't just a Mum, I needed something to get my brain going and awaken my creativity once more.

Do not get me wrong there is nothing wrong with being a Mum, I absolutely love being there for Dexta but it is tough. I struggled with postnatal depression for most of Dextas early childhood and I really didn't want that to be my whole story. I had also struggled with numerous bouts of depression in my early 20s, just as my mother had suffered from depression for years during my childhood.

By this time in my life, I had learned that I needed three things to support my mental health a creative outlet, exercise, and connection. Being at home alone with a new baby, a life revolving solely around him with no external stimuli was not good for my mental health or for Dexta. I could feel myself becoming obsessive and fear starting to set in. I knew I needed something else to occupy my mind and get my creative juices flowing once again.

At my corporate job and within my social circle, I had always taken people shopping and I was always asked for advice when a particular outfit or a new look was needed.

So, it was one night while settling a cranky teething baby, feeling frustrated and alone that I came up with my business idea. I would start a personal styling business, it would work around my baby boy and I would be my own boss. It would solve all my problems. It would give me a creative outlet, keep me active, and it would get me connected to the things I needed to validate me as a woman, a mother and a business woman.

Looking back, I wish someone had told me, or instead shown me that being my own boss would be like having another baby. Don't get me wrong I don't regret it one bit, but my god it's hard work.

Moreover, you don't really understand how much hard work or how different things will be until you are in the thick of it doing it for yourself. Just like being a first-time mum you must master juggling a million jobs all at once, from accounts to sales, marketing to customer service, business planning, and scheduling and that's just for starters!

I remember getting my first client and it was like seeing Dexta smile for the first time. Signing a contract with an experience day company was as exciting as Dexta taking his first steps. Whereas doing my accounts was almost as scary for me as Dexta experiencing his first allergic reaction. Copywriting, websites, and marketing were like having a cranky teething baby.

It was a whole new ball game on so many different fronts. Being an employee even at the senior level, managing a team, involved in business planning and business growth, did not prepare me for starting my own business.

It was only when I was reflecting on my progress some three years later, while on a personal development program, that I realised that I had not stopped to think about what was involved.

I had not thought of how I was going to get a consistent income, or what I needed to learn to be able to do things such as accounts or social media. No one told me that as fast as I could learn to master one platform or system, that those same systems would change and the learning would start all over again.

I know this on a logical level, and we all get that feeling when the new PC update gets released, or a new Smartphone becomes available, but somehow in the world of business, it's a whole different ball game. It is not just one system or platform changing at a time, it is several and all at the same time as the law or the data protection legislation and VAT rules get updated.

I probably would not have learned or have grown as much as I have, had I stopped and thought about it. I might not have actually taken the leap and followed my heart.
So, on reflection, I am glad and grateful I didn't stop and think on this occasion. That's not to say I have not made mistakes or bad choices because I have on balance perhaps, for me, it was best to simply.... DO.

People, some fantastic people, tried to warn me what I was getting myself in to and how to navigate the ever-changing business landscape. Some tried to scare the bejesus out of me and encourage me to abandon my dreams, but I was adamant that I was going to not only start my business, but I was going to be a raving success. You know one of those seemingly overnight successes that were making five, six even seven figures within a year.

Crazy I know, but as a first-time mother whose life had fallen to pieces in the last trimester of her pregnancy, I was on a mission to create the life and experience I wanted not only for me but my precious son too.

So, in hindsight to be honest, I am grateful really that I was deaf to all the advice at the beginning, because just like having a baby you really do not understand or comprehend what's involved until you are in it and doing it and by then it's too late to turn back and give up. You're invested whether you like it or not.

Don't get me wrong I am so grateful for those that did try, and did reach out to share words of wisdom. They have become some of my best friends as a result. Those individuals that worked so hard to scare me and put me down. Break my dreams, well some of them turned out not to be as good a friend as I might have thought and that's ok, it's more than ok because life is for the living and not for regret.

Starting a business will undoubtedly show you as it has me who your real friends are and who would rather you stay stuck!

On the surface when I set out in business, it was purely to pay the bills and to be able to work around my family. However, as I have reflected and evolved over the years, I can now see that my choice in business is far more connected to me and my personal journey and experience.

Yes, I wanted to help women to make shopping and dressing a pleasure, but unconsciously there was a far more powerful reason than I had ever realised or could have even comprehended at the beginning.

After that evening shopping session, back in April 2014, I found out just how deep my connection to my business and the services I offered was. I was asked to interview with a lady based in the USA who wanted to do a spotlight feature on my work. She had heard how unlike some other stylists I was.

That I was very holistic and in her words I "had a knack of getting under the bonnet of a woman's feelings and views of themselves and their bodies" in doing so I was able to help women to recognise and overcome fear and anxiety they had around their body. I could help them fall back in love with their body as well as fall back in love with themselves. You see that was precisely what I had done myself in my journey back to colour and back to life!

Rewinding to 2009 and I had not long had emergency surgery that changed my life and my body forever. I went from a carefree 20 something living what I thought was a carefree life. Burning the candle from both ends and really not taking care of my health at all on many fronts.

I would bounce from highs and lows mentally dependent on relationships, I was highly judgmental and critical of myself, my appearance and my abilities in anything, I genuinely believed that I was "good for nothing" and was always living in fear of being found out as the fraud I truly thought I was. Then this emergency stopped me in my tracks. Turned my life upside down and made me sit up and listen.

During my turbulent recovery, I learned how to stop judging myself and stop being so critical of myself, how to trust, embrace and ultimately love me inside and out. That was a true breakthrough.

So, when my business initially took off and I began working with the experience day company, I was booked back to back, I had a constant flow of clients, but I was exhausted and however great the money was, the work was not as fulfilling as I had hoped.

It was varied, but overall, it was repetitive, and I felt I had so much more to give. So, I had managed to fulfil my first ambition to pay the bills and work around my family but at the cost of my happiness and my personal fulfilment leaving me questioning if it was worth it!

One day a client who had become a regular shopping and styling client approached me to ask if I could coach her. Help her to up level and become the woman she wanted to be not just on the outside but inside too. At that moment, the words of an old mentor popped into my head "Go for it!

What's the worst that can happen!" after all she had come to me! She could have her pick of coaches and mentors through her work and network, but she wanted me. I had the skills from my time in corporate so why not combine them.

She told me much later after she finished working with me as a coach, that I had helped her believe in herself and love herself through our shopping and styling sessions, and when she struggled at work it was my voice and my words that would come to mind and help her stop the fear and anxiety in its steps, allowing her to regain her confidence at that moment and move forward. That was the reason she asked me.

Working with this first coaching client and countless others that have followed. I have discovered and developed my own style of coaching. I use the styling, clothing, and shopping to help support women to open up, to support their learning and step in and embrace the best version of themselves so that they can grow as a person, grow in confidence and bring their dreams to life.

Following that client, I started to share my success and attract clients that wanted more than just shopping and styling services. They wanted to look and feel amazing and not just now, and then they wanted to feel this all the time inside and out.

By April 2014 the women I was coaching, styling and shopping with were women who had a vision, had gifts and messages to share. They were women who felt stuck in a rut emotionally as well as in their relationships, their wardrobe's and their style.

Their confidence, their view of themselves and their bodies were all affected. How they showed up and interacted, their relationship with themselves their loved ones and colleagues were also things that needed addressing. So that's why I was on my 10th distraught client that evening.

I naturally attracted the clients that needed my help and support to become their best selves, let go of the negative self-talk and hate that they were often plagued with and see themselves in a favourable light, with love and compassion and bring that best version of themselves to life.

These women were for me like looking in the mirror because I was that woman staring back at them just a few years before. I had felt stuck, worthless, dumb, disconnected, ugly, unattractive and insignificant.

I had no energy or get up and go, I had very little self-respect and very little value for myself or my body. Putting myself last on the list, always caring for others or putting others and their needs ahead of my own. I was physically, mentally and emotionally exhausted and I could relate to them all.

This had become a reoccurring story in my life at this point in time. I knew having been in the same space, with the same thoughts and the same energy at least twice before, I knew I had to make a drastic change if I didn't want to repeat the story word for word again, especially as the time before this had taken me to the brink both mentally and emotionally.

Leading to both self-harm and contemplating suicide, had it not been for the kind and loving words of one kind person on a stormy night in Miami I might not be here to write this now.

Previously the situation and my thoughts and feelings had been amplified by some bad choices and some very negative and controlling relationships. As a result of some of the worst decisions, I have ever made. But through those bad decisions and exceptionally difficult relationships, I have grown, I have discovered the power of gratitude, positivity, and joy.

Those experiences and lessons learned through unbearable pain, discomfort, even self-loathing and hate has given me life. It has awakened me to the deep pain that a person can feel as well as the tremendous highs, the dark lows, and the deep heartache a person can withstand.

The immense love and joy and the complexity of a person's heart. It has given me the ability to understand and empathise with how a person can have such a different view of themselves and their body to what I or anyone else sees.

How deep a wound can run and how the stories often re-run throughout our lives are often in different guises but yet the same story, we are just deaf to the lesson due to our world and culture that is built on the need for instant gratification.

When all we really need is to make ourselves happy, to realise that is our only job, our only mission, and our only lesson.

When I realised this and truly got this, it was like someone had switched the light on.
My life now made sense, my ability to see where a person is in pain now made sense.

The connection between our mind, body and soul all made sense. My mission to help women and girls change the way they view and treat themselves and their bodies inside and out became so clear, just like an old teacher had told me it would when it finally lands and finally shows itself.

During that very laid back interview with a female business owner from the USA, a whole new connection for me and my work, my passion awakened. So out of the darkness come the most beautiful blossom of energy and light. Now that might sound very wishy-washy but its grounded in some very basic, fundamental practices that I have had to master, to be awakened.

Just as I shared back then, on that interview back in 2014. If I had to share any advice with you reading this now. When it comes to starting a business, or achieving your version of success whatever it might be. My advice would be: -

Take care of you because no one else will. Make sure you know what you need to thrive on every level physically, mentally and emotionally.

Its so important to build solid foundations from which you can then build on. Just like being a first-time mum trying to work out what your baby needs to settle when you are exhausted and overwhelmed its hard work trying to work it out after the fact.

Believe me, I have been there, I know how it feels, and I have about a dozen T-Shirts to prove it. However, with a good solid foundation I have worked hard on I can pick myself up and get on, I can see and think outside the box and always grow and evolve.

However, today some four years later I would also say surround yourself with positive and empowering people. People who will help and support you when the chips are down, people who will help you see the wood from the tree's and find your way.

People who will celebrate you and your successes. It is important that you celebrate every… little …thing …. Whether it is big or small, celebrate it. Do not forget this step because if you do not recognise the successes however small, then the journey will become challenging, exhausting and harmful.

The act of celebration is invigorating, it gives you a boost physically, mentally and emotionally. So, surround yourself with people who will celebrate you and celebrate with you.

The people you surround yourself with as I know only too well can be so important!

In business, they can support you to bring your dreams to life, see past the obstacles, and have faith in you when you have none. In life, the people we surround ourselves with are just as important and I have had occasions over the years where I have had to consciously change the people I have surrounded myself with.

I have left toxic relationships, broken negative friendships and distanced myself from people even family who have consciously or unconsciously chosen to take a negative path. Life isn't easy but for me, my business and my mental health it has been the best choice. Sometimes the only choice.

That isn't something that everyone will understand, and some will not want to know because they are comfortable right where they are, however tricky their circumstances are they are comfortable because they know where they stand, they know what to do, how to react and this gives them some certainty and that's powerful.

I know because that was me.

That woman, looking in the mirror not seeing a bright, vivacious, kind, creative, spirited, loving person. Instead, I would see a drab, dumb, stupid, fat, ugly, worthless, selfish, inconsequential, inferior the list goes on.

My choice on that night while nursing a cranky teething baby to start a business to solve my problems might have been a very naive decision in hindsight, but from that, I have discovered myself, I have found and connected to my creativity and my values, I have recognised my strength and my passion.

I cannot explain to you the joy and excitement I feel when I open messages of thanks from clients. Some are for the way they look and feel in the new outfits we have put together and the fantastic compliments they are receiving now that they are walking taller, now that they are exuding that new-found confidence inside and out, entirely comfortable in their own skin.

Sometimes for the very first time, with a style and look that truly reflects them and their personality. Other times the messages are around the new daily, weekly or monthly practices that countless other clients and I use every day.

I am always eager to share these practices due to the excellent results I personally get. So sharing them and encouraging women to use my proven methods, incorporating them into their life is a joy. They can help them grow in confidence, eliminate stress, anxiety and overwhelm of life in general.

My wardrobe planning exercise is always a great tool to help any busy woman. It often becomes a tool that helps them keep the whole family organised too. So, let me take a moment to share this with you too. On a dedicated day, you should give yourself some time to review the week ahead.

Taking time to decide on your intentions for the meetings or activities you have in your diary. By doing this ahead of time, you avoid the emotions and feelings that could cloud your view if you do not think or plan ahead.

This also allows you to choose what energy and attitude you want to show up with. This, in turn, will enable you to plan your wardrobe so that the outfit and style you wear not only matches the energy and attitude you desire but also works for you rather than against you.

This can save you so much time and energy on the day. Eliminating the need to change countless times or the stress and anxiety that can leave you feeling exhausted and even heartbroken before your day has even begun. So that you can start your day in the best mood, with the best intentions and the best energy.

These messages bring me such joy. The legacy is not just for one woman but also trickles down to her kids as well as friends and loved ones. For me, this is when I know I am making a real tangible difference in the lives of women. Adding to that fantastic feeling inside and out.

When I left school regardless of my grades, I didn't think I could write yet here I am writing a chapter in this book. As well as writing my own book too, I genuinely thought I was not good enough to make anything of myself because I had been surrounding myself with the wrong people, I didn't know I had any talents, I felt lost, lonely and at times worthless.

This was my life though it was interjected with good periods, where I found some confidence, right the way up to meeting my husband and the birth of my gorgeous boy and the birth of my first business. I have taken the skills motherhood has given me and implemented them into my business as well as my life as a whole and vice-versa too.

I have put myself and my needs first, and I now have the confidence to recognise when I am not doing that so that I can take steps to fix that and regain my balance. I no longer look externally to meet my needs or work out how I feel because I know the answers are all within me. I now trust myself to work it out, I trust my gut my instincts and my intuition.

All things I would have found any reason to discredit before, because I believed I was "good for nothing."

I am now meticulous about those I surround myself with. Having been used for my talents, my energy and enthusiasm and for my ability to think outside the box. My life in business has been exciting, to say the least, but when you do find your tribe and do find a group of people who can support you, are just as excited for your wins as you are, are just as invested in your success as you are, then you know you are on to a winner.

I have been lucky enough to find that in both Abigail and Sarah the founders of The Female Success Network as well as every single one of my fellow Unstoppable Success Sisters in the mastermind group. We have laughed, we have cried, we have supported, encouraged and collaborated, we have celebrated and we have been each other's cheerleaders.

I for one can say I have made friends for life this year as well as grown my business exponentially with the love and support of these fantastic women and I will be forever grateful!

I have stepped into my power as not only a fantastic coach and stylist but as a leader with a mission to make a significant change in this world.

My mission is to change the way at least one million women and children view and treat themselves and their bodies within the next five years. With their help we can change the way a whole generation views and treats themselves and their bodies, both on the inside and outside, this will then snowball and benefit every generation to come.

So, my questions to you the reader is this..

In reading this powerful book by powerful women, how do you view and treat yourself and your body? Do you do it with love and compassion? Do you celebrate all your win's big or small? Are you connected to your instinct and intuition?

If the answer is no to any one of those questions I'd love you to take a moment, stop and connect, remembering everything you need is within you. Connect to your dream. Connect to who you are and what you genuinely want and take action each and every day.

Discover your style, your confidence, your passion and your mission. Then find your tribe and last but not least have fun doing so.

About Chelle Shohet

Chelle Shohet is The Self Love Stylist, A Certified One of Many Women's Coach, Personal & Fashion Stylist, Fashion Designer, Multiple Business Owner, Co-Author of She Who Dares, Mother, Wife, Sister and Friend with a passion for helping people.

She specialises in supporting real women with real bodies to truly love and embrace their mind, body and soul. Helping them to connect and fall in love with themselves inside and out.

Chelle has a background in fashion design and technology combined with personal development coaching, and in recent years she has further developed those skills becoming a Certified One of Many Women's Coach.

By combining the inner and outer work, Chelle has been taking the sting out of self-love, personal styling and unlocking a woman's inner confidence, making them tangible and achievable for every woman!

By working with Chelle women develop a deep understanding of their physical, mental and emotional needs as well as discover and develop their true style, bringing to life a true reflection of them, their personality, and passions, without them needing to say a word. Working with Chelle is a truly holistic experience resulting in a whole life makeover.

Self-Love and supporting women to embrace looking and feeling amazing inside and out has been Chelle's passion and become her mission due to her personal transformation and the lives she has helped change throughout the years. Chelle knows first-hand all about the effects of low self-esteem, lack of confidence and poor body image. The real results of which have pushed her to the brink at times.

She has also experienced and recovered from burnout during her time in corporate giving her a unique understanding of how today's world and its unique challenges affect women, their minds, their bodies and their soul.

By working on both the inside as well as the outside at the same time Chelle helps her clients to achieve the instant gratification we all desire while also laying the solid foundations that will empower them to build and evolve from robust and unshakable confidence and believe in themselves. Helping them develop and master the art of managing their own energy, balance and emotions. Something Chelle has found invaluable in her own life as well as the countless women that she has supported thus far.

Chelle is on a quest to share her skills and learnings with at least 1million women by 2025. With the hope, they will in turn share them onwards with each and every woman and girl they know.

Her mission in life is to change the way every woman and girl view's and treat themselves! Inspiring women and girls to love themselves, and their bodies inside and out so that they can grow and flourish in this world of filters and social media by being entirely confident in their own skin!

Contact:
Email: Chelle@ChelleShohet.com

Website: www.chelleshohet.com

Facebook: https://www.facebook.com/chelle.shohet

Instagram : https://www.instagram.com/chelleshohet/

Linkedin: https://www.linkedin.com/in/chelleshohet/

Diana Catherine

This is the story of an older entrepreneur who blossomed later in life, but the message in my story is that it is never too late to start.

After having a 25 year career as a police officer, I thought I was done with achieving! As a Police Officer I worked hard. I put myself through university part time, whilst working a 24/7 shift pattern of earlies, lates and nights.

I did all of this whilst being physically, emotionally and financially alone with my babies. I was a single parent, with a full time dangerous antisocial career and as if this wasn't difficult enough I had my university studies too.

Unfortunately there were no family friendly hours in the Police in those days, and therefore I had to think creatively about my childcare and settled on a live in nanny, as childminders and nurseries didn't work nights. This might have appeared to be a luxury to some but for me it meant survival. Expensive, but necessary.

I did what I thought all single parents did, I dug deep and got on with it. Now looking back over those years, I am amazed at what I achieved as a single parent with a demanding career and two small children, and very little money.

My survival throughout this period may have been down to my 'tenacity', as one sergeant wrote on my career review in my early years in the Police force.

I am unsure as to whether my 'success' as I prefer to call it now in my life during that period, can be attributed to my 'tenacity'. I believe my successes in life are more than likely down to pure drive and stubbornness.

The words 'you can't do that!' have always spurred me on, ever since I was a young girl. I hear those words and a switch goes in my head and a little voice inside says "Just watch me!" Firstly it was my father who said 'you can't join the police force!' Whoops, I did.

Later on, it was my male police colleagues and so called 'superior officers' who told me I couldn't be a detective, a traffic officer, or even a sergeant. They said that these were roles for the men, and they said 'No!'

They said that as a woman I was not capable of dealing with potential violent situations and the leadership of men. The 'glass ceiling' weighed heavy on my head as a female police constable in those days and although The Sex Discrimination Act was passed in 1975 it hadn't appeared to have filtered through to the Police Force in the 80's and 90's! I don't believe things changed for women in policing until we left the 20th Century!

I didn't listen to my male colleagues and 'superior officers' I went on to achieve all my goals and more in the Police Force. I appear to believe in the impossible!

Even when the pathway to my goals and aspirations are invisible, and appear almost impossible, I just close my eyes, put my head down and get, on with it. 'Stubborn' my mother calls me. I prefer the word 'focused'.

I continued to achieve my goals and even more in the Police Force. I passed all my police driving courses and became an advanced police driver. I drove the high powdered police pursuit cars in many a high speed chase, pursuing stolen vehicles around the streets of Birmingham. I actually enjoyed the police chases a little too much, and I am really surprised that I didn't stick with achieving that particular goal, as I was having fun. But no I carried on.

In 1998, during the G8 World Summit in Birmingham, I put my fireproof 'riot gear' on, and stood my ground in line as a leader, together with my fellow officers protecting President Clinton and his wife outside their hotel from rioters, who were intent on setting us all alight. My Sgt's stripes were clearly fixed to my overalls, but I stepped up and assumed a higher level of leadership as our communication channels were broken and the senior officers who were supposed to lead us couldn't get to us as we were cut off by the rioters.

We had a goal and a mission and I wasn't going to back down! That was a very tough 24hrs. A situation we had trained for on a monthly basis but never the less it was frightening.
I think that qualifies as a 'potentially' violent situation gentlemen!

I remember going home to the children afterwards feeling exhausted but elated at what I had achieved.

Not only did I become a leader of men and women, in charge of a serial of riot officers on several occasions, I also became a detective sergeant and worked on some very high profile national cases. I actually climbed to the rank of Police Inspector a rank that was impossible to imagine for a woman when I started out.

I saw the sights, the smells and depths of despair that the human race can inflict on each other and yet I still yearned for more success.

Unfortunately my Police career was cut short when I was diagnosed with myalgic encephalomyelitis (M.E), and had to retire early. This was a heavy blow to my self-esteem, as I felt deep inside that I had gone from somebody to nobody overnight!

My aspirations and goals of rising to an even higher rank within the Police Force had been taken away from me. How could I satisfy my hunger for achievement now!

M.E is a very cruel condition. There are some days when I can hardly get out of bed for the fatigue and pain that runs through my body. It can even prevent me from raising my arms up to shower or wash my hair. I can only describe my ME as my sleeping dragon. Wake it up and it can wreak havoc!

If I tiptoe around my dragon, by eating healthily, getting lots of rest, and managing my working hours, I am usually okay. Unfortunately If I get a cold or a slight infection, then this floors me and my dragon wakes up. My goals and ambitions have to go on pause until I have appeased the dragon and it goes back to sleep.

Having ME does involve a great deal of planning. A simple week end away with the girls can mean a week or more in bed afterwards! Although it will never prevent me from doing things, I just have to plan my rest periods carefully.

The worst part of my condition is the affect it has on my cognitive ability. During an ME attack I am unable to read or even concentrate on a video or a conversation, for too long. Watching TV is also impossible. My limited ability to concentrate is worse than the pain on occasions.
How on earth did I ever think I could run a successful business and write a No.1 best-selling book at the same time, whilst managing my condition? 'Pure madness' according to my mother when I told her.

No, it's definitely not madness, just pure inner strength and passion for what I do now that drives me on.

Yes, at times I do become depressed and very down due to my condition. I sometimes feel that I am not achieving what I want to achieve as fast as I had planned to achieve it, and that maybe I am letting people down. The second most important thing to manage in relation to my condition involves managing mine and others expectations of me.

This is the one I find difficult if I'm honest, as I do not discuss my condition with anyone outside of my family, and in fact I am surprised that I have included it here, but if my struggle to manage my condition whilst building a successful business and writing a best-selling business book helps someone else to believe that they can achieve then I'm happy to share.

I was actually talking to one of my business coaching clients a few days ago. I have been helping her develop her cake business for the past 2 years, and I happened to mention my ME in passing .She was truly quite shocked, as she thought she knew me well. She had never suspected that I suffered with ME although she did say she knew little about the condition if the truth be told.

Why should she? I have no need to wear my condition openly as a badge, as long as I manage it, and I am not a very good ambassador for others with ME as I try and keep it hidden. After leaving the Police Force I lost myself in my passion for cakes and cake decorating, and ploughed more time into a cake business I had started years ago when the children were little.

Due to my serious financial predicament during that period, I decided to undertake a cake decorating course at 'The College of Food in Birmingham', so that I could make the children's birthdays cakes. I was a single parent, I did not receive maintenance, and after paying a mortgage, bills, and childcare costs, money was scarce so this was a good way to save money.

I found my love of cake decorating again after attending the course. I had enjoyed baking with my mother, when I was younger and I loved helping her decorate Christmas, Birthday and Wedding cakes for the family, so I suppose it was in my blood.

It also served as a great mental escape from the day to day sites and scenes that accompanied my career in the police force. I could come home from an emotionally stressful day observing how awful life could be, and lose myself in making sugar flowers or baking.

It was and is excellent therapy!

I soon became very good at making the children's birthday cakes. So good that I began to get orders for my cakes, and therefore seeing an opportunity to bolster our dwindling funds I started a part time cake business from home making celebration and wedding cakes.

I was then approached by University College Birmingham, who asked me if I would like to teach cake decorating to their students in the very same class rooms I had learned my craft all those years ago when it had been the College of Food.
I was fortunate that whilst in the police force I had studied and gained my teaching qualification, again part time, through Christchurch Canterbury University, so I was well placed to accept this offer as it involved my two passions teaching and cakes.

I took them up on their offer and once again I felt as if I was somebody again!

I started off gently, teaching part time 2 days a week. I loved teaching cake decorating, but once again my dragon woke up and I began to suffer with my ME and I had to leave after a year.

I felt like nobody again and I still wanted to teach cake decorating.

Therefore, together with my best friend, I started my second business venture and we opened a cake decorating academy specialising in one day modular cake decorating classes. Buttercream & Bows Cake Decorating Academy was born.

Today, we have 5 cake decorating tutors working with us at the cake decorating academy, and have been consultants to well-known names in the cake industry and magazine columnists. We have also been known to make the odd special one off cake when a celebrity asks us too. !

Then in 2012, as a by-product of teaching cake decorating, I actually found my niche, my ultimate passion, the thing that makes me jump out of bed in the morning the thing that I love. Business coaching!

Whilst teaching cake decorating I was asked by a number of students for advice on setting up their own cake business. I knew the wrong way to set one up, as I had done that many years ago and had struggled as I had little or no knowledge of business when I started out.

I had no idea about business in those early days when the children were little. Looking back now I consider that what I had wasn't a business. It was possibly an expensive hobby in those days. I certainly knew the pitfalls that awaited anyone starting a cake business and I wanted to prevent fellow cake business owners from falling into them. I wanted to help.

All these years later I now had the business skills harvested from many a police project management, performance review and finance courses I had attended.

I had eagerly studied business, branding and social media marketing in order to run our cake decorating academy, so I felt I had the skills and passion to pass on to the students, as well as a teaching and coaching qualification to assist me in delivering this learning.

Therefore having identified a need I sat down and wrote my one day cake business class. The Cake Boss Class. I held this extremely popular class in the Midlands and I not only taught students how to start a successful cake business, I took them on a journey of self-belief too.

My Cake Boss class evolved, and I soon became not only a teacher but a business coach in the cake world too, as my students continued to contact me for help and support in their cake businesses.

In order to provide this further help and support I continued to invest in myself, and went on my own learning journey to ensure that I was the best business coach I could be.
It was whilst on my learning journey I discovered the power of positive psychology and the world of Neurolinguistics programming, NLP.

NLP has not only taken me on my very own personal evolution in terms of my life planning and my happiness, it has also given me skills that I have been able to incorporate in my business coaching.

I continue to mentor and coach many of my 'Cake Boss' students to build and run their successful cake businesses, and it brings a big smile to my face to see them flourishing and enjoying their success. They are my Cakepreneurs!

My biggest frustration though was that I was unable to coach my international students without them traveling to England to see me. I have coached ladies from Jamaica, Nigeria, France and Spain to name but a few places, but they come to England to see me and our time together is very short and this has been frustrating.

I clearly remember talking this frustration over with my accountant, Laura Moss, a couple of years ago, at our coffee meet ups.

Laura knew of my passion for coaching and that I needed to find a way to reach my international students without them or me traveling.

Then in September 2017 the breakthrough came, thanks to Laura my frustrations were wiped away.

Through Laura I discovered Female Success Network. Apart from everything else Female Success Network has done for me, it has opened up the door to a wealth of technology which I can use to coach not only my clients in the UK and but those abroad too.

Female Success Network and its brilliant Mastermind Programme have not only changed my business but my personal life too.

It has been a significant step change in my life and it will be remembered forever.

I am now part of a group a ladies who are like me. We are all different ages and have different businesses but we are one. It has given me the confidence, structure, and knowledge to take my business forward in a healthy and happy way.
I now feel like the entrepreneur that I am!

There are draw backs to working alone as an entrepreneur though.

One of the biggest drawbacks I have found over the past few years is the loneliness and isolation, as my office is at home, and I live alone with my two Chihuahuas.

I found this isolation, in terms of motivation, quite crippling at times until I joined the Female Success Network Mastermind. Now I am never alone as I have contact daily with like-minded women, with different backgrounds, skills and strengths, and we all support each other.

No question is too stupid to ask and I have been bowled over by the support I have received.
Now I am not alone.

As I mentioned at the start, I may be one of the oldest women in the Mastermind at the tender age of 53. As with most mature women, apart from my ME, I suffer from middle age issues such as the menopause and 'empty nest' syndrome!

Both my children have fledged the nest and once again I feel like I have gone from being somebody, a mom and a carer, to a Chihuahua sitter.

Yes I have my freedom to do what I want, when I want, and I have my businesses, but as most of my friends are married, I found it difficult to socialise alone. 'Empty nest syndrome' is real and a very dark place to be and it was time to revaluate my life and decide what I wanted from it.
It was no good building a successful business if I had no one to share it with.

I therefore joined the gym and took up my swimming again, and I joined a social group who go away for weekends. Don't get me wrong I do have a 'boyfriend' but I prefer us not to live together so that our time together is quality time where we actually date. This has worked really well for two years and we are both happy.

Being an 'empty nester' it is sometimes hard to define your day, so I keep myself productive by planning and time blocking. I find this enables me to manage my ME too.
I use a plan, do, and reflect cycle for my business and although it is a simple mechanism I find it is the best. Some call it the plan, do, review cycle but it is exactly the same thing.

Every Sunday I look at the previous weeks goals and tasks in relation to my business and personal life in the review/reflect stage.

I put my goals and tasks through a virtual sieve in this stage, comparing them with my business plan and more importantly my mission statement. Any unaccomplished goals or tasks aren't necessarily carried forward to the forth coming week. If they aren't really going to take me forward in my business and life then I don't necessarily carry them forward.
Next I put my goals and tasks through my matrix.

If there is one thing, one simple thing that has helped me to be successful in achieving my goals it is the "Eisenhower Matrix". It is a tool which I use for working out what is an important task versus what is an urgent task.

Many of these planning tools I learned whilst teacher training but they are great for any business.

I read about this matrix years ago in Stephen Covey's book "The 7 Habits of Highly Effective People" and it changed my life more than any other theory. Basically you divide your tasks up into important urgent, important not urgent, not important urgent, and not important not urgent!

When I first did this exercise some years ago I actually found that I was spending most of my time focusing on the 'not important and not urgent' tasks. In fact my whole life appeared to be in this quadrant!

Not so much now. Particularly, when my time is limited the matrix is brilliant.

The final parameter, or planning method, I try and work with is the 80/20 rule. I know that for 80% of my time I should be working 'on my business' and its goals and strategies, and only 20 % of my time should be actually working in my business, actually carrying out the tasks.

It is very easy to get caught up in tasks which could be outsourced or delegated and not progress within your business as planned. This is easier said than done and I will say there are some weeks when the 80/20 rule was not only aspirational but near impossible.

After my epic journey of learning and self-discovery in 2017/18 I made the decision to follow my passion again and to devote most of my working life to my now first love, business coaching.

I continue to coach my 'cakepreneurs' and other businesses outside of the cake world such as a nursery, quite a few beauticians, and other coaches, the list is growing as this side of my business grows organically under its own steam.

In 2018 I launched I took my Cake Boss coaching to the next level and I launched The Cake Biz Coach. I am now able to support my cake business clients around the world using this technology and the plan for 2019 is to take The Cake Biz Coach on tour!

In 2018, under my new brand The Cake Biz Coach I decided to write a book, to put down everything I possibly could in order to help cake business owners reach success in their businesses and therefore their lives hopefully.

I had been writing my book for over 6 years after I started coaching in the cake business, but in 2018 I actually sat down and wrote it.

On 2nd July 2018 my book 'Cake Biz Success' was launched and reached No.1 on amazon in 7 categories, of which business coaching and food were two. By the close of play, on launch day, my book was ranked no.655 out of 3.4 million books on amazon!

I mentioned the 80/20 rule earlier; well this went totally out of the window whilst writing my book. But I didn't beat myself up about it, I just got on with it knowing that there was a clear date on the calendar when the book would be complete and a near normal service resumed.

My ME still has flare up's, so my next mission is to develop and launch 'evergreen' learning bundles to help my clients in the back ground when I may not be available.
I am now a busy but happy entrepreneur, managing my time wisely but clearly focused on my mission to help others succeed in business. 'Love what you do' is my moto, and then it doesn't feel like work.

About Diana Catherine

Diana Catherine is an international business coach, mentor and No.1 Best Selling Author from the West Midlands in the UK.
She specialises in incorporating a mixture of positive psychology together with her twenty years of business experience and learning into her coaching to assist her clients achieve success.
For the past 6 years Diana has concentrated mainly in her chosen business niche of the cake business, inspiring and assisting many of her 'Cakepreneurs' to find success.

Although Diana's first love is the cake business, she is also an all-round business coach and mentor with clients within the childcare, beauty and coaches arena's amongst her current clients.

Her first book, the No. 1 Best Seller, 'Cake Biz Success' was published in July 2018.

Diana combines years of business experience together with her qualifications as a teacher and coach, studying at Christchurch Canterbury University to gain her Diploma in Teaching.

She has taught at The University College Birmingham, written a regular magazine column, and been a consultant to a big name in the food industry, to name but a few of her recent achievements.

Diana as The Cake Biz Coach will launch her new website, and online learning programs in the summer of 2018, via her new Facebook Page.

Website: WWW.THECAKEBIZCOACH.COM
Email: Diana@Thecakebizcoach.com
Facebook: https://www.facebook.com/thecakebizcoach/
Instagram: https://www.instagram.com/thecakebizcoach/

Demi Price

Rich in Life, Love and the Bank!

I always knew that living a life of mediocrity wasn't my jam. It's the reason I've quit over 30 (yes, 30!) jobs at the ripe old age of 22. My inner battle around life and self-worth held me back for years. So, I guess its best to start at the beginning...

Whilst in the womb... I joke.

Growing up, I went through a fair bit (to put it mildly). My parents going through a custody battle, social workers picking my brain, living between 4 houses, switching schools, a new step-mum and 3 brothers (luckily, their awesome, nothing like a Cinderella story ha!), my mam suffering with alcohol addiction, mental health struggles, poisonous relationships, the list goes on.

There were way more good times than bad, all of my family love and adore me, despite life's challenges. I went on many holidays and had lots of good friends. But I guess it was the struggles that pushed me to become what I have today, so it's important for me to fully let you into my story.

At the age of 17 my mam suddenly died from the alcohol addiction. At the time, I felt totally numb. I felt I had to be strong for my nan, she was everything to her. Looking back, I realise suppressing the grief took a major toll on my mental health. I spiraled. I went from one poisonous relationship to the next. I lost all interest in anything other than getting black out drunk. It got to the point I didn't want to live anymore.

One day, I got into my car; my brain felt foggy. The constant thoughts of being a failure, not being able to be happy, anger and confusion about never being able to speak to my mam again, guilt of not helping her, all of it had left me feeling totally hopeless. I could feel that familiar tightening in my chest.

My head was on the brink of exploding. "They'll be better off without me". I put my foot flat on the accelerator. "If I just smash into the wall, it'll all be over". As the car picked up speed, my family faces flickered in my mind; I slammed the brakes on and burst into tears.

This was the moment I decided to get help from the doctors. I booked an appointment and my gran came with me to the surgery. As I explained about the car incident, I saw her eyes start to fill. This was a turning point, realising I never wanted to put them through what my nan had to go through with my mam. No more funerals. The doctor prescribed depression medication.

After a few weeks, I felt much calmer. At this point I was still jumping from job to job, looking for something that I would be happy in, but I knew deep down I would never be happy being tied to somewhere, told where to be and when, capped income, clocking in and out for a pee! It felt like prison to me.

I suffered from an RSI in my shoulder after working in a printing factory. Spent 12 hours looking for cracks in tubes at another factory (the only thing that cracked was me, I quit after 1 shift). A comment from a "Manager" about my "chest" saw me quit a call centre job after 3 weeks.

Looking back, I would definitely have reported it, however back then, I believed I would be sacked as he was the one with the power. That's how low my self-worth was. The final straw for me, was being millimeters away from being scolded. I was putting myself in danger for a couple of pounds an hour. Was this my life at 21?

Once again, I felt like a total failure to my family. I wondered if I was crazy, how were other people happy in these jobs? Although I quickly realised that most people weren't.

Every job I'd been in, the staff would clock watch, they couldn't wait to leave. Friday was the favourite day for obvious reasons. Monday mornings were a drag, where you could guarantee someone would sigh and say "Monday again".

If I had a pound for every time someone complained about how unfulfilled and underpaid they were, I'd never need to work again. I'm sure there are people out there that love their jobs, but for most people it's seems it's just a "means to get by".

For me, there was no chance I was living my life to just "get by". Losing my mam had made me realise life was far too short. Meeting Sam in 2016 was a catalyst to me finally starting to see a future for myself, I started looking for business opportunities.

I had already dabbled in network marketing, but my confidence had held me back from ever taking it seriously. In March 2017 an opportunity fell into my lap. It was here that I started to come of out my shell. I grew a team and found myself coaching these women on all aspects of their life. Although back then, I didn't realise I was coaching.

I discovered personal development. Firstly, joining a mindset membership. I was blown away by this different approach. My love for self-growth started here. My upline introduced me to another coach, and asked me to attend an NLP event. This event was £60, and investing that was massively scary for me back then. Little did I know this small investment would change my life.

The man running the event looked over the filled room and asked a question. I can't remember what the question was, but I shot my hand up. Despite being petrified, I wanted to get the most out of this day (the power of investing).

He started talking to me, told me to stand up and I was handed a microphone. I felt like a small child, my knees actually started to shake. He asked me to come and stand at the front. 50 sets of eyes were all on me.

He said something along the lines of "fearful Demi is talking to me right now, I want to speak to Diamond Demi" (this was a rank in the network marketing company I was a part of). Next, he told me to roar like a lion. "LOUDER! ".. 3 roars later and I felt exhilarated.

Had I really just done that, in front of all those people? The girl who wouldn't even order her own food at a restaurant? This was the day I felt my mind really switch from the anxious little girl to a woman who was determined to make a life for herself.

From this point, I became a serial self-investor. After the network marketing company I was a part of disappeared over night, I realised my heart was in coaching. The stars seemed to align, and I was introduced to Female Success Network through a friend.

I invested into their highest level program, which was a big leap from the £60 investment. My mind was opening up to the possibilities more and more.

Although at the time, it felt like a huge risk; I see now that it never was, because it was on me all along. I knew it was now or never and pushing myself in at the deep end meant there was no turning back. I HAD to make this work.

By this point, I had taken myself off the depression medication and used self-development, meditation and journaling to keep my mind in check. I was starting to feel like myself again, except a much wiser and open-minded version, Demi 2.0.

I wanted to share what I was learning and inspire other women with my story and so, I set out to become a Mindset Coach. After a few months, I realised this was a passion that was much too close to my heart to charge people. And so, I set up a clothing brand to raise awareness and funds for mental health organisations instead.

Early in the year of 2017, we decided we were going to go travelling. This seemed like a distant dream considering we couldn't even afford to move out of our families homes. Nevertheless, we planned the trip. In November 2017, I quit my job to pursue my Coaching business full time. We booked the flights for January 2018, with no real plan of what we would do. We decided we would just figure it out, because waiting did nothing but waste time.

We sold almost all of our things, cars, electricals, our bed – there was no turning back. On January 17th, we travelled to London to fly out to Auckland, New Zealand. Until this point, it didn't really seem real. On the plane around half way through the trip, my anxiety flared. "What if we cant find a job?" "What if we run out of money?" "What if my business doesn't work?". I quickly reminded myself that this was all a choice. I could do anything I set my mind to. And breathe.

We spent 2 weeks in a hostel before buying a 1980's Campervan, who we called Gypsy. We travelled the North Island, visiting the gorgeous beaches and enjoying the New Zealand Summer. By this point, I had made the shift into business coaching. I loved all things business, the freedom it gave people, being able to do something you loved daily, it became my obsession. But my confidence saw me charging pennies and having 0 boundaries.

And then the day that everything REALLY changed. You would think that I'd have of enough life lessons up to this point to really grab life by the lady balls, but apparently not. On March 3rd 2018, whilst Sam and I went jumping off waterfalls in the mountains, a group of men broke into our Campervan and stole everything (of mine).

My phone, laptop, bank cards, jewellery, all of it, gone. The crazy part being, that was the only time I had left my things in the Campervan in the 2 months we had been there. Go figure. The feeling in my stomach when we saw the window wide open, I can't even begin to explain.

I felt like my world had been ripped from under my feet. Anything of any monetary value, they had taken. How would I run my online business? I went into a dark place for a couple of days. My family, Sam and The Mastermind girls were my rock. Luckily, they hadn't taken Sams phone and laptop so I could still communicate with everyone.

They all reminded me of the things I had been learning and preaching to others. "Tell me 5 things that you are grateful for?" Sam said. I tear up as I write this. He was right. I replied, "You, My family, My life, My health, My friends". They may have taken my stuff, but what really mattered was all around me. My dad leant me the money for a new phone (so grateful), and I started taking huge action in my business. I used Sams laptop to create my course and get myself out there.

This experience taught me that I never wanted to feel that hopeless about money or myself ever again. I invested the last of my money into a Sales program. After working on my boundaries, self-worth and sales skills, I took my business from 0 to $11K in a week.

I was gob smacked.

I continued to go deeper on my mindset as I realised I was suppressing so much and never fully facing up to my past which was completely taking over my present. I discovered that having all these self-worth issues was holding me back from having the life I truly wanted. I took full responsibility and continued to do the scary, ugly-crying, brain work. My self-worth was a direct line to my net worth. I was allowing myself to be on the struggle bus.

All at once it was like my purpose was revealed to me. I was here to help other women get rich in life, love and the bank! By working on their self-worth which automatically increased their net worth. It was like my whole life had led to this moment, from randomly having the pull to take Psychology at A Level to now getting burgled and realising money was a catalyst for so much. Maybe this was the universe literally slapping me into my purpose, that's how it felt!

I started working with clients on Money Mindset and Sales Strategies. Everything from Start up to Scaling. They ended up leaving jobs, blowing up old businesses that they didn't actually want to be doing, signing high level clients, having $20K+ launches! But the best part, they were free of the stress and worry that comes with not having enough money. They could be at home with their babies and not bite their partners head off about the extra £5 they spent at the shop.

Seeing the emotional transformation was my favourite part. One of my clients sending me a voice note saying "I'm a Queen" lit up my day. This gorgeous soul had come to me with no self-confidence, and was now hitting it out of the park in the business world!

When it comes to Money/Sales, it doesn't have to feel icky and it shouldn't! If you are struggling with money right now, or even if you're not but you're not where you want to be; do the following task:

Journaling Prompts: Use these questions to dig deep into how you think and feel about money, find where these beliefs came from and really challenge them. Brainstorm what actions you can take that will change this pattern in your life. Finally, write an opposite new belief and repeat this as an affirmation daily.

- When I think about money, what thoughts come up?
- Where do these thoughts originate from? (think of your earliest memory of where this belief may have come from)
- How can I disprove / think about this differently?
- What action can I take that will change this pattern?
- What affirmation can I use daily to re-write this belief?

You may be surprised at what comes up! You can repeat this task anytime you feel yourself hitting that money wall or having self-doubt around money. Moving onto Sales, again its all the same. We do not (and should not) feel like selling is a hassle. When you are confident in the service you offer and you are selling it to someone who genuinely needs it, know that you are helping someone.

You deserve to be compensated and they need that attachment of investing to take action. No one takes action when they are comfortable.

For more on all things Money/Sales/Business, you're welcome to join the community on Facebook, search "The Driven Entrepreneur" in groups.

During this rollercoaster of a journey, I've learned so much about myself and the business world. It takes resilience, determination and belief in yourself, that you will make it, no matter what. One of the pinnacle moments that I urge you to do in your own life, was surrounding myself with women who understood my drive, struggles and dreams.

The FSN Mastermind was more than just business advice. They held me up through times I could have crumbled and helped me see a light in myself that I didn't realise was there. They are truly lifelong friends and the sisters I never had. I will forever be grateful and hold love for every single one of them.

I want to highlight, that I experienced a lot of the negative sides of business too, which you probably have/will. Including the "you're crazy" for investing, "you'll never do it". That my dreams were unrealistic. If you take nothing else from my story, please just take this: the only limits in life are those we put in our own way.

People may tell you you're crazy, but that comes from their own fears and limiting beliefs. It doesn't make it true for you. You can do anything you set your mind to, take action, commit, don't quit.

I don't recognise the girl I was a year ago.

The growth in such a short time is incredible and I really hope this lights a fire in you if you are at the start of your business journey. I always get asked, "how did you do it?"; the truthful answer being, mindset work daily, investing in myself (even when it feel ridiculously scary), and doing what I love. I feel like it's a super cliché thing to say, but you really do need to fill your own cup first.

I no longer believe in excuses. I used to be full of them. Of course, life still throws curve balls, but we get to choose whether they're excuses not to move forward or reasons to push us even harder than before. I bring this into my coaching because I lived in excuse land and it kept me broke and miserable.

Today, I am a Successful Business Coach specialising in Money Mindset and Sales; for driven Female Entrepreneurs who want to fulfil their desires and create impact on a global scale. I open the door for all women to see that completely changing your life is so possible.

I'm here to show you that wanting and having everything you desire is what's best for you and the world!

The vision for the future of MDP is to increase the impact on the world outside of entrepreneurship, helping many causes close to mine and my families heart, including Noah's Ark Hospital, Cardiff; and charities for Mental Health, Alzheimer's and Cancer.

I am also passionate about helping the homeless and have plans for the future, to build and sustain centres to help them get back on their feet. I believe everyone deserves a fair shot at life and I want to be the change I wish to see in the world.

The best advice I can give you, is to remind yourself daily that you get to live a life that lights you up inside.
Reminder: The only limits are those we impose! ... And then take action on that!

I want to take this chance to thank my family, my partner Sam, his family, my friends, my clients, my community, my team, Female Success Network and everyone else in my life that has supported me throughout my journey. I love you!

About Demi Price

Demi is a Business Coach for Female Entrepreneurs, with levels of support from Start Up to Scaling to multiple 5 figures and beyond. She specialises in Money Mindset and Sales Strategies. Helping women to live their fullest life by empowering them to achieve and receive everything their hearts desire, unapologetically.

Demi started her business journey in the network marketing industry, but soon realised her passion was in coaching the women through their struggles and blocks. After receiving coaching herself, she quit her 9-5 and jetted off to New Zealand to start her travels.

It was there that she discovered and worked through a lot of her own money blocks which saw her take her business from 0 to $11K in a week. Realising the freedom that came with no longer stressing over money, she knew her purpose was to help as many women as she could, to create the freedom she now had.

Demi is a certified Life Coach, NLP Practitioner, EFT & TFT Practitioner and CBT Practitioner. She is a self-confessed learning junkie and loves expanding her knowledge, which she believes enables her to help even more people.

Demi is on a mission to change the way women think and feel about money and to help them create and grow businesses by sharing her strategies, learning and guiding them to living a life they truly want to live.

Email: hello@missdemiprice.com
Socials: @missdemiprice
Website: www.missdemiprice.com

Donna Davies

I AM MORE THAN A MUM

I spent many years working up the corporate ladder to the Senior Management team and my role centred around Learning & Development, Business transformation and HR. After both children, I returned to work and found the experience quite traumatic.

After my maternity break from my second child, I returned to a changed team, changed manager, changed job role, in fact, nothing was the same as when I had left. I found it very unsettling especially as none of this had been communicated prior, they were not ready for me and provided no direction.

I quickly realised that while the company said they supported working mums, their actions didn't quite match that expectation and I found it difficult to get the right balance. I worked long hours, travelled on a regular basis and found the office to be a stressful environment. As a new mum, I was already feeling vulnerable, and the added pressure of work compounded this, leaving me feeling exhausted and emotional.

Speaking to colleagues about their experiences of maternity leave, I found I wasn't the only one that felt this disconnect with work and home life. I know it's a familiar feeling, when you're at work you feel guilty about home, when you're at home you start fretting about work. I wanted it to change but wasn't sure how.

People struggle to get back into action after two weeks holiday never mind 9-12 months off work, and having experienced the most significant mind-blowing life event that leaves you feeling like an entirely different person. Isn't it crazy that this is not recognised and that more help is not supplied, as standard, to all women returning to work, across the board?

Yes, we don't want to be viewed as different from other colleagues, but the truth of the matter is we are different and do need a settling in period when returning. Sleep deprived, stressed and anxious is not a great recipe for a productive, happy employee. Not that easy to be black and white and leave personal life at home to do a job

In 2017, about ten months after I returned, I decided to go, I'd had enough of trying to juggle everything, and it was affecting my home life more and more. My choice was made quickly, without any clear vision of what I wanted to do.

However, I did know that I wanted to carry on helping people as I'd worked with lot's of mums and I had seen how difficult it was for new mums from a personal perspective and a business one. I also wanted to use my learning & development experience and qualifications as it's an area I'd always enjoyed.

After a couple of months, downtime spent with the children, and lot's of time to think about my future the More than Mum Network was born. I knew I could help mums through the transition as they returned to work and I could make a positive impact by working with organisations to change their procedures for mums.

Furthermore, I could help them find their identity and remind them that they are more than a mum. We have so many professional goals and ambitions before children, and I'm always saddened to hear from mums who have stopped pursuing their aspirations.

Having children should not be a barrier to you achieving your goals, it should be the reason why you want to reach them even more.

Mothers are important too, their children are their priority, but they are also women in their own right, who deserve to work towards achieving their dreams, to live their lives to the fullest and to achieve happiness. It's my absolute passion to help as many mums as possible achieve success in their personal and professional endeavours.

My mission is to help Mum's get back out into the working world after maternity, in a way that reduces stress, anxiety and overwhelm. It stems from my personal experiences and passion for helping others where I suffered, to protect mums and bridge the gap with HR and to empower employers to be more 'mum friendly'.

Helping mum's regain their confidence and supporting them through the transition as they return to work after maternity gives me a tremendous sense of fulfilment. Supporting mums, who are struggling with anxiety, worry and overwhelm and seeing them transform is fantastic.

Whether it be about how they will manage returning to work, they want to start a business; they want to find a great work/life balance., sometimes it just takes someone to guide them through the options, and I provide that.

My support is two-fold, working directly with mums to support them through the transition but also working with and championing employers to help them provide better returner programmes for women. I feel organisations should be aligning their processes with what their people need, not the other way round.

In my role in HR, I saw a female colleague arrive at work

stressed every day -she was usually about ten mins late, having battled with young children, the school run and rush hour traffic.

She looked like she'd nearly killed herself getting to work every day as she screeched into the car park. I suggested she start work 15 minutes later each day and make the time back at the end of the week. A small change but it made a difference to her.

She was a different person, less frazzled, much happier, more productive as she was much more ready to deal with the day. As a mum, I knew exactly how she felt, but others, managers hadn't seen it - all they saw was her being late. A nod towards flexible working and looking at an individuals scenario can help mums. Its essential managers see the bigger picture of staff wellbeing.

I want to see the development of mums networks within corporate organisations become more widespread and am campaigning for this movement, alongside that of a trade union for Mums. I want mums to have access to information about their rights without the stress of talking to their HR department, so they don't feel judged and can make informed decisions based on their situation.

I started my business without much knowledge on where to start. I didn't have much experience with marketing, writing contracts, networking and lot's more. However, I did know that I was passionate about my idea. Over time I thought about the possibilities, and I'd feel excited, eager and determined.

No amount of objection from those close to me was going to stop me in my tracks. I felt free from the corporate world, my health, mentally and physically had dramatically improved and I wanted to make a change. I had my mission, I was prepared for the hard work, and now I needed the tools and knowledge to help turn my ideas into reality. While the adrenaline and excitement of starting a business can keep you going for a while, there are a few things I would have found useful to know before taking the leap.

I wish I had known about the importance of time and taking action before starting my business. I spent months thinking about the vision for my company, researching, watching hundreds of webinars about setting up a business. I learnt about e-mail campaigns, building lists, setting goals, creating an audience.

I spent all my time learning and not taking action. Before I knew it six months had passed and I hadn't launched a product or service. I was so frustrated and panicked about if this was ever going to work. In reality, I'd spent six months putting off taking any action because I was scared. I had a fear of failing, fear of peoples opinions, fear of becoming visible and sharing my story.

I thought by learning about everything I was building a solid foundation for my business, but I just created a pile of notebooks filled with notes that I probably won't ever look at again! So I wish I had appreciated how fast the time does go, if I'd of spent that six months taking action rather than being fearful, who knows where my business would be now.

It's a lesson learnt, and I'm now very conscious of how I spend my time, I make myself accountable for every minute, and I've slowly stopped feeling so fearful of everything.

Starting a business is a huge life lesson. Your ability, your strength, your resilience, it's incredible how much you learn about yourself. Take as much as you can from each experience, they will make you a better person in life and business.

I've learnt many lessons throughout my career, but I think the biggest one was don't try to be something or someone you're not!

I know a few people that portrayed themselves as authentic, genuine leaders but behind closed doors, they were narcissists. Everything was great as long as it went their way and for a long time, they were revered, almost idolised.

However, you can't keep an act up forever, and cracks soon started to show. The fall was indeed quicker than the rise, and it caused a lot of upset for people, not least themselves. Why did they fail so spectacularly?

Because they weren't authentic, they were putting on a mask, an act. They had very high opinions of themselves and would do anything to make people believe they were these wonderful leaders. It gave them a sense of power, authority and high-status.

It showed me that we often talk about been authentic and genuine to ourselves but how many of us are? How many of us wish we could be or act like someone else? At times I did look at these people and I wanted to be in their position. It soon changed when I saw their true colours.

I realised then that I didn't want to be them, I didn't want that position if it meant I had to be this awful person. I knew I could do a better job by showing compassion, empathy and following my heart rather than the paycheck. So the lesson learnt was first to be careful who you look up to, things aren't always what they seem.

Secondly, be genuinely faithful to you. Don't emulate someone else, don't put on the mask and try to be something you're not. It's not sustainable; the mask will slip. Instead be you. You're unique, and you have a way that nobody else does so use that to create your path.

Along with the lessons learnt, I've also received fantastic advice that has helped me in business and life. I think the most important was don't ever give up because you never know how close you are to a breakthrough. I believe this is true in lots of life scenarios.

Parenting, work, business, relationships…we go through tough times with all of them, but we make it through. There's always light at the end of the tunnel. It's so right that without the struggle you won't discover your real strength.

How many times have you thought about the worst case scenario happening and you wonder how you would ever cope? Then it happens, and you have no choice but to carry on. It's difficult, upsetting and stressful but you come out of it that little bit stronger. Giving up is always the most comfortable option, but more comfortable isn't necessarily right to keep going.

I was also advised not to compare myself to others. It's easy to look at competitors and wonder how they are getting all their clients, creating amazing content and building a thriving business. You could spend all your time panicking that your services or products are not of the same quality, value or you're in an over-saturated market.

However, it won't move your business forward, and not everything is always as it seems. Your competitors may be thinking the same when they look at your company.

Remember to stay in your lane, keep focused on your destination and enjoy the journey.

So after all the lessons, advice, learning, how do you ensure you stay productive? If you are in business, productivity = turnover, it's what we work every day for, but how do you ensure you're productive rather than busy? (there is a difference). Staying focused can be difficult, especially if you work from home as there's always something to distract you.

For me, I treat my business as if I'm going to work every day. It hasn't always been this way, and it took me a while to get into a routine of turning my laptop on and working rather than catching up on the latest news. I'm very easily distracted, so if something on the TV caught my eye or someone rang me, I could quickly lose a few hours each day. I'd then wonder why my to-do list was never completed! So I now make a point of sitting at my desk by 9 am, I plan in my lunch, and I don't finish until 5 pm, just as I would if I still worked for someone else.

I switch all notifications off my phone and put it on silent. I know if I start scrolling through social media I'll waste time so now I put the phone away and focus on the task at hand. I have dedicated time each day to check notifications, update my social media pages and read emails.

Find ways to separate your work and your home life. If you're working from home, having a separate office may not be feasible but at least have a desk space which you can use for your work - and from which you can walk away at the end of the day.

Keep strict office hours. It can be so easy to put things off until later and then find yourself working on through the evening which is not a great idea. Set yourself office hours, and aim always to complete your work within these times, and then "clock out" and enjoy your evening. This is an excellent idea for combating work stress too; we all need downtime. Similarly, you should still allow yourself a weekend.

It doesn't have to be on Saturday and Sunday if you'd rather not, but two days out of work to be you, can work wonders for your creativity and focus. If having set office hours is not possible, give yourself time each day that you will finish work and take time for yourself.

Dress for work. This might sound a bit silly since one of the significant benefits of working from home is not needing to "look the part" in smart office clothes! But getting dressed for work can have a positive effect; it's a ritual that tells us: Now it's time to work. Try it out, and see if what you're wearing affects how you work.

Set boundaries with friends and family. When we're working from home, others can see this as code for "I'm free any time; pop round when you feel like it." While working from home can give us the flexibility to meet friends for coffee when we feel like it, it doesn't mean we should suddenly operate an open house where people are forever coming and going.

Communicate clearly to friends and family alike that you are working from home and as such not available for visitors during the day. It can be hard to enforce to start with, but if you stick to your boundaries, people will soon get the message.

Find an organisation/planning tool that works for you. For some that will be Google Calendar; for others it's Evernote, and others will swear by a paper diary. Try out different planning tools until you find the one that works, and then use it religiously to plan out your days - and to schedule downtime for yourself.

On a Sunday evening, I plan my week, so I know what days I have appointments, calls and deadlines. I then look at my unplanned time and schedule content creation, writing, admin tasks and anything else on the to-do list. I'm also conscious of planning in family and house time. I know what days I'm doing the school run, family assembly, family commitments. The house time is chance for me to do the chores, so I don't feel like I'm spending the whole weekend cleaning.

My partner doesn't work on Fridays, so I limit how much I plan in, this gives us a day together to catch up as he works away the rest of the week. If I look back at the schedule and the balance doesn't seem quite right, if I've hardly any time for family or I have a deadline and need more time to complete the work, I'll move things around until I'm happy with it.

I have a to-do list, but some weeks I found it so overwhelming that I didn't make any progress. So I took it back to basics and decided to focus on one fundamental task per day. It may be writing a blog post, filming a short video, reaching out to someone I would like to work with. I spend as long as it takes on this one task and once complete I'll move on to something else.

There's that old saying that 80% of our income comes from 20% of our efforts; figure out where that 20% is that brings in the money, and focus on that. Be prepared to drop the things that take a lot of time and effort but don't bring rewards or enjoyment - and delegate where you can.

Now you have your workspace, a weekly schedule and an action plan, it is essential you don't forget about working on you and your mindset. I think it's vital for business owners to develop good habits or rituals.

Google routines of successful people, and you'll see everyone from Oprah to Richard Branson swear by a method to help them. I have a morning routine, and although I can't say I'm consistent with it every morning, I do notice a huge difference in my energy, productivity and mood on the days I complete it. My routine includes exercise, meditation, reading and gratitude. It's not always possible to do it all if the children are up early but I try as much as I can.

I know the value of self-development from both a corporate and business perspective. I read a lot of self-development books, and favourite ones include Kyle Gray, Louise Hays, Gabrielle Bernstein who talk a lot about Law of Attraction and raining your energy.

I've taken part in quite a few interviews, and I'm often asked what piece of advice I would offer to someone thinking about starting a business? My opinion is to do it because life is too short. At the end of the day think "What's the worse that could happen?"

Here are a few more tips I share.
Be passionate about your idea. You will spend a lot of time focused on your business so it has to be something you love or you'll start to resent it.

Understand and know your customer inside out, and who they are what problems they have, where they hang out and then make them feel like number 1. The customer experience should be paramount to everything. Think about them not you, talk about them and what they need and be authentic about it.

We talk about putting the customer first, the same can be said if you are employing staff. Engaged, happy employees will help you grow your business, increase revenue and ensure you deliver excellent customer service. Colleague and customer experience should be at the forefront of everything you do.

Happy employees + happy customers = Great business!

Stop signing up for every checklist, webinar, power call or anything else that promises to give you the magic formula for a 6 figure business. All it's doing is wasting your time and stopping you taking action, which is the thing that will make you money.

Review your overall business plan often, at least every quarter…and change it when needed. If the numbers aren't adding up, work out why and find a solution. If somethings not working don't keep hoping that it will correct itself, makes the changes. You can always go back if you need to, a lot of figuring out your business is trial and error. Marketing strategies, pricing, offers…you have to do a lot of testing to find what fits you and your business.

Lastly, never quit. Even if your first, second or third attempt at business doesn't succeed, don't look at it as a failure, see it as a learning opportunity. What can you do better next time? Who can support you? If you feel you need guidance with strategy, planning, mindset, maybe look at the possibility of a coach.

After quitting my job and deciding to start my business, I did have huge confidence issues. I had the vision for More Than Mum Network but no idea how to go about starting it. Initially, I invested in a coach but quickly realised that they weren't the right fit for me. Their programme lacked direction and was too generic for what I wanted to achieve. It was heartbreaking because it cost so much money and I didn't gain anything concerning business strategy or learning from it.

I then found support from a women's online community, Female Success Network and joined the Mastermind. Driven on by other inspiring female entrepreneurs, and coached by leading businesswomen, one of whom was a working mum, they gave me the strength and determination to launch More Than Mums Network.

Everyone in the Mastermind is now a friend. We cheer each other on when there are achievements and celebrations, we console each other when we have a terrible day, we guide one another through the overwhelm and uncertainty, and most importantly we know we've got twenty women watching out for us and wanting us to succeed.

It the best decision and investment I could ever have made. What I've gained in confidence, skills, ideas, strategy, personal development plus the friendships....It's been worth every penny and more.

ABOUT DONNA DAVIES

Donna is a mum of two boys, founder of the More Than Mum Network and author of the book Don't Judge Me. A qualified HR management professional and a mother who's endured negative experiences of returning to work after maternity.

Donna has now built a career around her passion, after the corporate world failed her. Her mission stems from her personal experiences and passion for helping others where she suffered, to protect mums and bridge the gap with HR and to empower employers to be more 'mum friendly'.

Having always been ambitious and wanting to make a difference Donna spent 15 years in the corporate world - climbing the ladder and achieving success, yet she didn't feel fulfilled.

She was working in a very male-dominated environment, and as much as she did, she didn't feel able to make a big enough difference. She did, however, gain many valuable skills in this job. Learning that customer experience was improved by employee engagement was something she would carry with her into her future achievements.

Being a mother herself she struggled to strike a balance between family and work life. After battling with anxiety, depression, sleep deprivation and overwhelming responsibilities during and after her pregnancies she felt under tremendous pressure, and when returning to work, she felt broken. Working with a predominantly male leadership team, she felt there was no understanding of her needs and knew this needed to change.

In her HR capacity, she often helped new mums, providing them with support when she identified them struggling. The HR policy for returners in place at Donnas workplace was strictly for legal purposes. She soon realised it wasn't designed to help people; it was apparent it was only there because it had to be.

After realising that in this particular company she could do no more, Donna decided that to make an impact she had to leave and start her own business. She wanted to help other Mum's struggling the same way she had, while also assisting organisations to improve how they treat new Mums. A few months later the More Than Mum Network was born.

Donna now offers a range of services to help new Mums get back into the working world. The broad range means there is something to suit everyone. She launched at the start of this year and has already supported many mums.

As well as helping women returning to work, Donna also coaches women who feel they indeed can't return to their corporate lives and instead want to embark on a business of their own, to create their desired work-life balance.

Contact
Website: www.morethanmumnetwork.com

Email: Hello@morethanmumnetwork.com

Facebook: https://m.facebook.com/morethanmumnetwork/

Twitter: https://twitter.com/Donna_Joanne_Co

LinkedIn: www.linkedin.com/in/donna-davies-more-than-mum

Instagram: https://www.instagram.com/more_than_mum_network/

Jennifer Barnfield

Believe in yourself, Become Unstoppable.

January 2001, I was 18, six months off finishing college and homeless. That's where my journey of being an adult started. Three months after my 18th birthday I ended up in a hostel. I had to move seven times that year and was finally housed in a hostel for teenagers.

I had a three-year relationship which saw me become a mother at nineteen years old. All which should have been a happy experience from the start, however, instead I experienced serious domestic violence for just over 3 years which then resulted in becoming a single parent aged just twenty-one.

Now at the tender age of twenty one years old, I was getting to grips with being a mum, becoming a single mum to my son, Tobey, and trying to understand how to care and support ourselves as the cost of childcare was almost 90% of my monthly income. I had a mixture of income which started from being on benefits whilst I finished college and applied to university, becoming a waitress, working in Marks and Spencer's lingerie section and training as an optical assistant in Specsavers.

I always tried to make sure that I worked darn hard to make sure my son never wanted or went without.

Throughout all the craziness of becoming a single mum and working to support him, I had returned to my lifelong passion of figure skating in 2003 and my son, Tobey, was only seven months old.

I had started skating at the tender age of three and now, aged twenty-one, I had thrown myself back into training. That was the start of my understanding of hard work and knowledge combined with the right attitude to achieve goals and dreams. My training regime consisted of three to four hours on the ice, five to six days a week and two hours in the gym five days a week. Off-ice training was mainly a varied selection of two-hour gym workouts per day.

After only one year of training, I received an unconditional offer for a Primary school teaching degree at Manchester University. Tobey was two, I felt it would be a great career as a mum, however upon deciding to further my skating dream, I deferred the start date for one year. There just wasn't time to concentrate on my primary school teaching degree which required full-time attendance.

I immediately hit the competitive circle once again after being absent for around six years. This first season, my return season, I respectably placed within the top two or three across the country in qualifiers for national championships and placed a respectable third at the 2004 British championships and furthermore, I won the Welsh Ice Dance Championships too.

I wasn't happy though, I desired more, I felt I had to prove myself to all those peers who had knocked me down at school. Tobey turned three and I had to make a huge decision. Do I carry on skating and go for gold in the next competitive season, or do I take up the more sensible option of starting a primary school degree which would prepare myself for life as a mum with school holidays free from childcare costs and arrangements?

I chose the former option. Tobey started at school, I had to plan my training carefully around school hours.

It was the best decision, a risky decision and probably the most nerve-wracking decision I had ever made.

The training paid off. In just less than 2 years I was crowned British Ice Dance Champion, British Adult Ice Dance Champion (over 21's), twice Welsh Ice Dance Champion and Scottish Ice Dance Champion.
I had done it! My success, my dreams became reality, I had never taken my eye off the goal.

I had done it!
I Had Won!

As a figure skating sportswoman who ended up going from homeless to competing at National and International level, only knowing how to eat, sleep, train, repeat and love what you do, whilst being a mother, little did I know this was the epitome of being self-employed.

Being self-employed requires a huge amount of planning, patience and productivity. As well as a thick skin. I wish I had known how to create and plan a business and just how important a business plan is. Also, how much willpower is needed, especially when there's rejection every which way you turn.

Just as becoming an ice dance champion was no easy feat, being self-employed is not an easy journey. Just like in ice-skating, being self-employed you are open to judgement and opinions. The very responses that started to knock my self-belief shortly after winning my titles.

Even though it has been a bumpy ride, it has most definitely been worth every emotion experienced.
I was nearly twenty-two when I set up as a self-employed professional figure skating coach both on and off-ice and later as a personal trainer.

Throughout my 12 years of working as a self-employed adult in the big grown-up world, this brought by far the greatest learning achievement. Learning and development included licence updates every year and the paperwork that went with it, diary and time organisation, customer service, working alongside other coaches who are all competing with one another for the same business – in the same ice rink, accounting, advertising and marketing, lead generation and all the politics too!

I can honestly say becoming self-employed was the best decision I ever made. It has allowed me to be at home with my son when he needed me, to be flexible in being able to watch assemblies, attend sports day, help the PTA (Parent & Teacher Association) where I was made chairman and learn new skills along the way to work on my own terms.

I have spent the last 12 years teaching figure skating, coaching mindset & self-belief and working alongside hockey referee and CEO of Ice Aid LTD - Tony Boynton during the Christmas season, running and coaching at outdoor ice rinks.

Ice Aid LTD is a company which constructs outdoor ice rinks, provides staff for on-ice marshalling and off-ice services such as skate hire running, ice skate grinding on-site including training courses and certification, maintenance, engineering to run the rinks 24/7, first aiders, pop up cafés for the rinks and 24hr security.

To be able to thoroughly enjoy every moment teaching figure skating to many people, in an environment of my choosing, with people I enjoy working with is epic!

Why? because I have been fortunate enough to coach people of all abilities. Including a blind man, who skated freely to the sound of my voice, a ninety-six-year-old lady who had it on her bucket list, and various dancing on ice celebs too.

Seeing the fear people tell me they have and it eventually transform into excitement, happiness and joy of being able to ice skate is incredible. I love to use the word 'FEAR' to mean 'Face Everything And Rise'.

It's not so scary then. It is an incredible opportunity to teach one of the most difficult and most 'feared' sports in the world – standing on a half centimetre piece of metal and being expected to stand up and glide.

I have learnt a great deal from teaching others about what it takes to learn, develop and achieve your goals. The ability to achieve only comes with the right mindset.

Fix the mindset, further the ability.
This is probably the most important lesson I have learnt.

The method I use to teach ice skating and coach people individually outside of skating, has now transformed from a verbal way of teaching to an official documented method known as The PEPP™ Method.

From seeing and realising those learning to ice skate, I understood they needed more than to be just taught the technique of ice skating. They needed to find self-belief again.

I found that to ice skate confidently the following is vital:
- overcome fear and be positive,
- increase one's inner belief,
- find one's confidence,
- place trust in me as their coach,
- be confident and feel empowered by the knowledge they gain.
- Understand the intricacies required for a new skill outside of their comfort zone, so they can begin to feel powerful and in control over themselves.

- Utilise their trust so they can believe that they are in complete control of their ability to be productive.

Sounds just like life.

While this method began as a way to teach ice skating, I quickly realised that it was much more adaptable.

Teaching ice skating the way I do is like discovering and learning a life lesson of self-belief and confidence. The method is completely transferable to any area of life, and that is what makes it so extraordinary.

We must overcome fear, be positive, find our confidence, trust ourselves and those we take advice from, allow ourselves to feel powerful in our best self and utilise everything. If we feel in control of and have belief in what we are doing, we are then in a place to produce something incredible. Something I like to refer to as our Genius Self.

I put together the principles on which I base my ice skating teaching upon. These were;

- To teach with positivity, in a way people forget their fear and overcome it with laughter.
- To empower each pupil, instilling self-belief, self-trust and build up their confidence in trusting themselves.
- To give my pupils the power to decide that having allowed themselves, with my help, to empower their decisions (in learning to skate), that they have the power deep within to learn and grow in any capacity they choose.
- Finally, to create productivity. Using their newly established positive outlook upon their self-esteem, confidence, self-belief and trust, I supported people's learning journey through focusing on how their mind functions to overcome the initial 'I Can't' fear.

The results are just extraordinary!

Results such as, confidence within people, the growth of self-belief people developed when in trying something new, teenage rugby players whom I have coached strength and conditioning to and many more – most of my clients have taken onboard The PEPP™ Method and share it with their family, friends.

Upon completing The PEPP™ Method course they found that they could try something new, such as a new sport, career change or business growth, or simply learn to cook when before they didn't. People find their inner power and can say yes to stepping out of their comfort zone. They become more productive in their job, family and general life by becoming organised, decisive, secure and happy in their choices. Seeing growth in a person who has learnt this method is incredible.

This method of teaching also developed further based on other life experiences beyond skating. In particular, an experience I had in my late twenties with my son.

Tobey was 10yrs old he was told that he'd never be good enough to succeed in anything and to give up because they no longer believed in his ability.

I'll admit, he was a spirited, happy, excitable young boy. He had a passion for rugby, football, cricket, swimming, tennis, athletics, in fact, anything that involved a ball and/or running around outside, getting sweaty and laughing! Sitting in a classroom wasn't his ideal, however, he did try hard and he was very capable.

Some people just didn't seem to understand him, which led to them becoming frustrated and they would put him down. He lost pretty much all his self-esteem, confidence, self-belief and many other negative thoughts crept in. It is very easy to internalise such negativity from others.

I saw my son change from a fun, loving, happy young boy, into a shadow of his former self, full of negativity, frustration and upset emotion. Having been bullied for seven years, I felt totally crushed as a mother as I was told nothing could be done. I often refer to my children as excitable puppies! If you show them love, loyalty, treat them as you wish to be treated yourself and maintain a high level of discipline, you won't go far wrong!

After all, I have raised my children to become confident, respectful, useful members of society, but not doormats who will allow societies opinions and comments to impact their own self-belief.

Having experienced this heart-breaking moment and various other moments equally as upsetting, it has given me the determination and huge passion to help support the current and next generations. I support them by increasing self-belief, self-esteem, confidence, positivity, empowerment and show them how to be happy, successful and productive in their own way.

Success is not measured by a letter or a number, but by heart and head full of happiness, dreams and goals achieved, and how you grow in inner greatness along life's journey.

In order to explain another reason why I am so passionate about self-employment, I need to backtrack to my employed years. I remember working at several prestigious health clubs and spa's, at one, in particular, I had a highly sought-after position.

Now, being a mum, working shifts that fitted around my son's school life and around my husband's job was perfect. Well at least that's what I thought until I logged in one day and up flashed the message;

'72 hours registered on the system for the last 7 days'
This meant I was working too many hours, within a 7-day period, and was a warning on our computer login system showing us to time manage more efficiently.

I was being paid for 40hrs of work. No more, no less, no overtime, no time back. Just the expectation that I would work my 6am -2pm shift and stay on afterwards to help with other staff members who were new to the health industry. Week after week this kept happening and the final blow was when I returned to the bus stop, 45 minutes late, in the pouring rain, to find my son, huddled up, under the nearest tree, writing out his non-verbal reasoning homework. I was absolutely heartbroken.

I felt so pressured to work late and there was very little concern for my family and responsibilities outside of my work commitments.

Yet despite all of this, I continued to exceed my targets, maintain staff happiness and I even ended up taking on some membership sales too. But this was not good enough. I had been told I wasn't putting in enough hours and safe to say I ended up leaving.

The final straw though was being demoralised as a female member of staff by being finally told that if I had more children I would become a financial risk to the business by requiring maternity pay.

Words fail me and I have no idea how they got away with this.

I had heard and experienced enough, I didn't feel that I or anyone else should be subjected to such sexist opinions against female employees and such a lack of family's consideration and importance.

The lack of flexibility, understanding and compassion of such employers really stayed with me.

I couldn't bear to think that the narrow-minded employers in the world get away with this and treat their employees in this way. This is not how any working environment should be. What a learning curve. When life throws you lemons, make lemonade and add gin! That was my lesson, take the bitter with the sweet and make it into something good.

Having previously felt that I couldn't succeed and being made to feel like a failure in the workplace, I discovered the difference between failing and failure when I met Julie Britton, a life coach in October 2015.

Failing - that is something we call fear. However, I truly believe that we should only experience failing, never failure.

Failing is to be unsuccessful at something, in particular, it is part of a process where learning is gained and we can always move forwards.

Failure is more final. It is the neglect or omission of expected or required action.

The difference between *failing* and *failure* is huge. *Failing* is learning that something you tried isn't or doesn't work and being open to suggestions, alterations and amendments.

Failure is completely giving up. It's never trying again, turning your back and not learning through mistakes and learning curves.

'Success' truly derives from the repetition of failings and bouncing back as quickly as possible whilst maintaining an open mindset that can grow. Known as a growth mindset.

How do you look at it? How do you change? If you're failing then it's rectifiable, fixable, do-able. You can bounce back and learn from what didn't work last time. Everybody fails, it is those that learn from their failings, reflect upon them and think about how to move forwards. If we never learn to see our failings, this is a signal of failure.

My biggest failing in business was my naivety which, looking back, made me defensive and reactive.

I was brought up, to be honest, truthful, respectful, kind and considerate, amongst other values too. I couldn't understand why so many adults had few or none of these. I learnt to see that everyone had different morals, judgements and ideas in life.

By seeing how people perceived a situation so differently, it enabled me to understand and move forwards with my communication. By learning and developing a more intuitive communication ability, I moved from failing to communicate to becoming effective and concise.

Having become defensive and reactive to many situations due to constantly being put down, I realised this was a failing. Not only in a business environment but also personally.

I needed to find and grow my inner power of confidence, self-belief and ability, I had to start again. I tracked back to what my beliefs are, my core values, those people I surrounded myself with – I made sure they were positively uplifting people. All of these helped me to improve and strive to reach where I am now, my best self and I'm still growing.

The underlying issue was my protective mechanism which I had developed due to the lack of trust in myself and others. I had no self-belief. Thankfully I learnt that if people criticised me this doesn't take away my trust in myself. Inside I will always have the power to allow myself to always be empowered, to strive, to improve and grow.

One of Julie's beliefs is that everyone already has the answer to their own questions. She worked on finding my inner power and helped me realise I already had to answer each question I asked myself. This is one of the best pieces of advice I've had.

When you look deep into your true feelings and desires, only then does clarity emerge. Clarity over what you truly desire in life, clarity in decisions which stop procrastination.

A productivity tip of mine is to stop procrastinating and be decisive. Being a Libra I have previously, truly, met the description of being an 'indecisive procrastinator'. Something I have worked on and still am.

Procrastination is something I have always been very good at, and being indecisive has made me avoid taking on projects or making decisions. I had to make a clear conscious decision to stop and develop an organisational way of living to be my most productive, enabling me to easily make decisions confidently and move forwards.

I plan my weeks by the hour so I know exactly what I am doing and when, but this also allows for my important family time. Having spent many years allowing my working life to spill into my family life, I have now moved into my most organised life of all time.

My diary is clearly sectioned, sometimes colour-coded and always clear. I share an online calendar with my husband and son so we all have clarity on the family's movements and appointments.

I love face to face meetings rather than via email or another text format. I love being able to make true, working connections which are so important to me as I find it creates a genuine and approachable working relationship.
Social media and email are great, but people buy people. You will find me live on social media most weeks.

Let's be honest, every business must make money and when 'people buy people' what better way than to get in front of people and talk. Getting out there and creating those connections is where I have found my success in happiness, business and life.

With coordination now at the centre of my weekly planning, I have found that my ability to network face to face and communicate has increased and improved thus creating a less defensive response. I feel so much more at ease.

Another productivity secret of mine is my daily affirmations. Wow! These are literally life-changing.
I have gradually learnt that the more you say them, the more likely they are to become reality, and it's all about how you say them too. Here are just a few of mine that I say each morning:

I am thankful and grateful for the roof over my head.

I am thankful and grateful for the bed in which I sleep.
I am thankful and grateful for the food in our cupboards.
I am thankful and grateful for the water I have to brush my teeth and wash in.

Other affirmations involve visualising my desires and speaking them in present tense whether they are present or not.

I feel so much trust in myself through my visualisations and affirmations, and am therefore able to create more positive thoughts and visions instead of internally producing negative thoughts. I am no longer defensive and instead able to think positive and be positive towards life through my thoughts, the way I speak and my actions.

The reason daily affirmations and visualisations work is that the subconscious mind believes the conscious minds' decisions and beliefs. The subconscious mind acts upon the conscious decisions and beliefs and therefore 're-wires' your internal self-talk and thoughts.

Here are a few of my daily visualisations:
I am loved and appreciated.
I am a powerful and productive woman.
I am writing a book.
I help 100 people each month to be more positively empowered, powerful and productive version of themselves.
I am happy and love my life because the way it is, is the way it should be.

What is vital to staying within your genius self is the following:

- Being around people who support you no matter what, that must become a habit and a lifestyle. They can be people you associate with through social media, online, in person or across the other side of the world via telephone! It doesn't matter where they are, just don't let the negative ones in.
- Daily affirmations. Say them every day. Strip them back to the bare necessities of life in the hard times and keep on track with gratitude and praise.
- Consistency and planning your week. Organisation is key to a productive and happy life. Share calendars with those you live with, keep a visual board in the kitchen or hallway which could display affirmations, positive words, to-do lists or what is on this day/week/month with each family member. There's a method for everyone, try lots of options, find one which works and maintain it. It's been a lifesaver for me.

The best advice could give is this; with your gut, don't listen to anyone else. Let yourself be led by the trust inside you and never, ever look back.

Remain positive because, as my tagline has always said;
A Positive Attitude Produces A Positive Aptitude.

And that creates a Marvellous Mind!

With a marvellous mind, decisions become clear and one of the best business decisions I made was in September 2017. It was to become a Founding Member of the Female Success Network (FSN).

This network has taken me on an incredible journey. Up until September 2017, I had genuinely never felt so much support in business and personally. The support received being a part of FSN is second to none, even though you may never have met anyone face to face.

From the live training and webinars to the connections we have all made and those connections we pass onto others that are incredible. To have the backing from people who have never met you, yet completely believe in you is a feeling that brings a lump to my throat. From being founding members but strangers to becoming close friends in less than 5 months, that's how much growth can happen when support is unlimited.

It is incredible to think that I never thought I would have gone from being homeless and a single mum to the founder of The PEPP™ Method, providing PEPP™ Practitioner and Training courses, one-to-one coaching in The PEPP™ Method and student well-being programmes.

I give enormous gratitude to Abigail Horne and Sarah Stone for their creation of the Female Success Network with their integrity, honesty, and ability to remain true to their morals. Both bringing together their vast experience of becoming established female entrepreneurs, the corporate environment, self-employment and international business development. Advice flows so abundantly and flourishment is mind-blowing.

Thank you so much to Abigail and Sarah who are the Founders of the Female Success Network. Thank you for helping me to draw upon all the experience in my life and guiding me to the creation of the best version of myself and my business.

As you can see through being self-employed, I have met some amazing people, developed productive working methods and created a fabulous mindset.
Both employment and self-employment are equally as time-consuming, but the reward being self-employed and being able to organise your own timing, working location, those you work with, and what you do is absolutely priceless. The self-belief development is incredible.

My life journey has taken me from having self-belief when competing at both national and international level to learning how to support Tobey having had his knocked out of him.

Then losing my self-belief and confidence, to building up my inner power, self-esteem and belief which is where I am now. Learning a life skill such as how to develop and maintain self-belief, confidence, inner power and create a positive mindset is so important. I realised I needed to maintain applying the technique to myself.

I recognised that when life isn't going in the direction we desire, we have the power to change course.
This is when I recognised the method I had been using all these years and the self-development I continue to learn is so simple and could help so many other people. There is nothing else out there as simple as this, and so The PEPP™ Method was officially created.

The PEPP™ Method is taught through a variety of accessible paths and educational specific courses, one-to-one coaching, online training and top-down coaching for the corporate world as well as staff and students in education.

Not forgetting an online learning to ice skate course, downloadable to your smartphone enabling you to learn to skate at your leisure, wherever you desire.

The overarching theme of The PEPP™ Method is a simple four-step system based on the principals of Positivity, Empowerment, Power and Productivity, which encompasses the ability to trust yourself and believe that you can achieve no matter what. All whilst creating interchangeable thought processes relevant to the situation and creating your desired result.

As we develop in life, we mature into several different people: from the child to the teenager, the adult, the partner/spouse, the parent, the middle-aged, the elderly and so on and so forth. This method is adaptable at any stage of life because you are the fundamental player in the decisions and direction.

My mission is to grow The PEPP™ Method into a globally known method which positively empowers people, with honesty and integrity. They will be given the tools and an understanding of how to increase their inner power and use this to become incredibly productive people. All whilst maintaining their dignity using our empathetic and compassionate manner.

Everyone who works with The PEPP™ Method will always be supported in such a way that they unlock their true potential and increase their inner aptitude because a positive attitude produces a positive aptitude.

My mission on how I wanted to help develop people's mindset and beliefs was clear in 2006 when I started my professional coaching career. My core values, honesty, integrity, dignity, empathy, compassion, belief, attitude and aptitude, all helped form my clear mission.

Every time I read my mission statement I feel so incredibly proud to know those who I mention below, as they have contributed to every situation I have experienced. Without them, this simple and effective method wouldn't exist.

Firstly, my truly incredible children who are the absolute sunshine in my life. Their faces and conversations completely light me up with pride and happiness. Their passion in striving to achieve their best ability in life and yet be at peace with themselves makes me so proud. They open my eyes to seeing life in a different way and I am so blessed to have them.

Marc, my husband. Throughout our journey, we have experienced so much, yet despite whatever is going on in life he has always maintained a steady ship.

Mum and dad, who through thick and thin have supported me, despite the ups and downs, we have always found a way to move forwards.

My peers I knew growing up, who put me down and told me I would never achieve anything or make anything of myself. Thank you for setting me off on the path of determination and positivity.

The negative relationship I had at a young age where I was insecure, reactive, with no self-belief. However, I now realise that this directed me towards the path I then took in finding and developing my positive reactions, self-confidence and belief.

Joan Slater MBE, Mike Fish, Mark Poole, Keith Hudson who were my main figure skating coaches and believed in me when I trained for the figure skating championships and told me never to give up. All so incredible and I thank you from the bottom of my heart for every breath of encouragement given to me.

To the person who told me I would never become a British Champion and laugh whilst doing so, thank you for encouraging me to become that Champion.

Julie Britton who helped me find my strength, overcome broken friendships and realise that life's path is to grow through all circumstances and allow ourselves to be at peace and remember that everything that is happening is happening for a reason. Everything is as it should be at this moment in time.

Laura and Ryan Rafferty who have been the most genuinely incredible lifelong friends through all the good, bad and ugly times. No matter what, they are always there.

Kelly Miller, Emma Logan, Natalie O'Donoghue, Willa Cookson for creating so much laughter, being my shoulder to lean on, the ears that listened and the hands that held me up when times were bad.

Life Church in Sale, Cheshire, !Audacious Church in Manchester and 21st Century Church in Llanelli, who have taught me so many incredible values and life lessons and helped me to create such wonderful connections and friends.

Finally, Ali Wrighton, one of my cousins – someone who has always been there for me no matter what, never gave up hope and trust, always supported my every move and never ever doubted anything.

Thank you, Thank you, Thank you for helping me cultivate the strength to focus on my desires.

You are all incredible and I'm so blessed to know you all no matter what our circumstances have been! Thank you so much.

My final words are these;

**Make every thought, word and action PEPP™ Inspired.
Positive, Empowering, Powerful and Productive.
The dictionary definition of Happiness is,
'The state of being happy,'
Find this and never, ever let it go.**

About Jennifer Barnfield

Jennifer Barnfield is a former British, Welsh & Scottish Ice Dance Champion and an International Silver medallist, now the Founder of The PEPP Method™. She is someone who radiates positivity no matter what, sees the light in the dark and helps others to see joy and happiness in even the worst times in life. Like a stick of rock, she reads positivity all the way through, and as a result, won't give up.

Being someone who lives to give to others providing it will benefit them, Jennifer over delivers each and every time. Her quest is to be a life changer to those she meets and to always leave a positive ray of light behind her.

Jennifer combines her knowledge of over a decade of coaching with a positive & effective communication and studying business & marketing, mindset and mindfulness to produce The PEPP™ Method. She has now helped thousands of people to find their inner confidence and use her knowledge to create their own version of being happy and positive people. Her clients now fulfil their careers desires, uplift their family life and can share their foundations of how to be a happy, positive person.

Having competed at the highest level in International and National ice dance championships, she found that digging deep, believing in your desires and dreams, aiming for your goals and never ever giving up was the only way forwards.

What is her mission now? To change the belief that everyone is worth something and no one is ever worth nothing. Having experienced this personally it caused a spark of passion and drive to create something life changing to everyone, accessible to everyone and for everyone.

The PEPP Method™ is centred around interlinking steps of Positivity, Empowerment, Powerful and Productive steps. All using the experience Jennifer had as a mother, teaching people to ice skate and coaching people how to establish their inner confidence.

Jennifer's wealth of experience has enabled her to work with entrepreneurs, private businesses and with the education sector, all who are looking for simple, effective ways to introduce a memorable method which increases positive mindsets and renews ones' belief system all of which is interchangeable throughout life. This gives Jennifer's PEPP™ method the leading edge with her simple, four-step structure.

Jennifer draws from personal experiences such as breaking down and crying out for help, life coaching and finding faith. These are combined with the science and research of how to achieve a Positively Empowered, Powerful & Productive mindset and state of being; which is unbreakable and unapologetically happy.

Jennifer is the epitome of her tagline "A Positive Attitude Produces A Positive Aptitude." She truly is a positive creator, wave breaker, public speaker, passion maker and motivational shaker.

Let's have a PEPP Talk!

CONTACT:

EMAIL: jen@jenniferbarnfield.com

WEBSITE: www.jenniferbarnfield.com

LINKEDIN: www.linkedin.com/in/jenniferbarnfield

FACEBOOK: www.facebook.com/jenniferbarnfield

Jennifer Stevens

"You deserve the world, even if it means giving it to yourself"

When I was younger I never knew what I wanted to be when I 'grew up'. I was a shy girl that liked my own company, but I was raised to be independent have my own mind, something which although my parents are proud of, I'm sure it has backfired on them on more than one occasion.

But being independent and a bit stubborn, I often felt on the outside as I never followed others, I found school at times lonely, and as much as I enjoyed learning it left me lacking in enthusiasm for it, I just wanted to get it over and done with.

Luckily I thrived in the subjects I loved and I was extremely creative and artistic. When you speak to your peers at school about what they wanted to be, there are the usual Doctor, Nurse, Accountant, Teacher, Policeman, Beautician etc.... Then there was me and I only knew what I didn't want to do and that was a lot of things.

There wasn't much help back then for those who weren't sure, all I got from the careers advisor was, well if you don't know what you want to do, how do you expect me to help? and then I was excused from our session. I just thought "Great! how helpful, no guidance or nurturing just a closed door.

After I finished school I decided to pursue my passion for Art and Graphics and went on to college to do Graphic Design and then on to do a HND in Visual Communication, which used photography design, web design and more and I loved it.

Some of my earliest memories are of me surrounded by crayons and paper to the point where at Christmas or on birthdays my mum would make sure I opened any crayons or books at the end, or I wouldn't bother with anything else I just wanted to draw, colour and read.

So My dream as I progressed through college was to move to London with my degree and work in the design industry. I wanted to live in an apartment in the city, have a great social life and to travel the world.

However life happened and I became a mum at 20. I was also single, so my mission was to provide for us, and right up until I had my son I worked full time and then some in my retail job to provide for us. Which to be honest I loved at the time and I was good at it too, it wasn't long before I was opening and closing myself, had it not been for my falling pregnant I was told that I could have been a area manager within a year or so as I had so much potential.

But having my son changed everything for me, what I wanted was no longer a priority and I put everything on the back burner to dote on him full time. When my son was two years old I married my now husband and we moved to Germany due to him being in the army, being that far away from family it made me start thinking about life differently and for the first time I thought about being self employed.

Having a young family meant I needed a way to earn money but still be a full time mum, so I trained and qualified to be a Childminder which I really enjoyed, and at the time I was the only one in the area which was a nice achievement to have.

By the age of 24 I then had 3 boys in total, for family reasons I had to stop Childminding but I continued to find new ways to make money working from home. I decided to start making my own beauty products which included organic soap, bath salts, bath bombs etc which was a new way for me to keep being creative too. It actually did really well, I was a registered business within Germany and I often made gift bags and hampers for all the military wives parties, at times I was making batches of 2-300 at a time which was manic but not a bad problem to have and It was so much fun doing it all.

In the past I had worked in quite a few different places as you tend to as a teen in college, I'd been a waitress, retail assistant and a nursery nurse. As much as I enjoyed my time in those roles I found traditional jobs suffocating I never had any choices and it just didn't fit with me as a person.

I can't say I ever had a job I really loved but I also never hated one either, I just wasn't suited to it. Also like everyone I had good bosses and not so good ones too but we were all just trying to find our place in the world, mine just wasn't in employment.

However saying that, the best job I ever had was whilst I was living in Germany. My youngest had just started nursery and I got 3 hours a day to myself and worked 15 hours a week at an information centre for the forces families in Germany called the HIVE.

I was responsible for collating all local and national information, plus attractions for Germany, which meant as I spoke the language quite well I was able to write to every company and request information for the forces families and then translate it and put them into information packs.

I did a lot of translating whilst I was there and preparing information for the army housing offices. I was also sending out weekly newsletters with local events, important army notices and more. The best thing was that I had an office to myself as we was only a small town and my boss was a floating manager who I had a great rapport with and she trusted me to get on with my job, I really respected her for that.. I was really sad when we had to leave Germany and move back to England as I knew I'd fell in lucky and I'd never have a job like this again. That job gave me a taste of holding my own, knowing I could work for myself and gave me food for thought for my future.

We moved back to the UK in 2014 and my husband was posted away so we moved back to my home town to be closer to family after being away so long, my husband commuted at the weekends, it was incredibly tough and something we wished we never did as a family.

So again I needed flexible working, and to fit in with the boys I became a nursery nurse at a private nursery so I had similar working hours and holidays to them.

I was fiercely independent and never asked for help or babysitters so I made it work for us. This became really mundane after a while and I was utterly miserable. I never had time, I was always rushing around stressed and it was a far cry from that home work life balance I had previously. I know this is a problem that many many people face but I just wasn't prepared to settle. Life has to be better than that, right?

In my search of finding an alternative and better suited way to work, I stumbled upon network marketing shortly after moving back completely by accident, as i really didn't feel like I could take on anything else whilst I was working at the nursery, but it looked like it could have been exactly what i needed.

It was completely new to me I didn't even know network marketing was a 'thing' so I really got stuck into this new and exciting way of working. It took some getting used too but I really wanted to do well and I had such a great team around me it was such a lovely atmosphere to be a part of. I got caught up in the hype of the industry and I really felt like this was that break i was looking for.

I got a pay rises and promotions and recognition I didn't always get in my previous roles but the better I did the more I was finding myself feeling trapped because I was having to do things that I didn't want to do.

The whole reason I wanted to be 'self employed' was to make my own rules, choices and to do what made me happy, but after a few years I started to lose the spark and passion I once had. I was starting to feel lost again as network marketing was supposed to be my get out of jail free card (employment) and no matter how hard I tried I just didn't want to make it work. You can't force anything when you are self employed, I feel you are either in or you are out.

As of January of this year I decided that I needed to find something that made my soul happy again. Sometimes as mums we lose our identity and having children young I felt like I didn't know who I really was, so I decided I needed some guidance to help me pull these thoughts together and into something I could work with.

In my time in Network Marketing there were a few names I was familiar with Sarah Stone a well known Photographer & website designer and Abigail Horne a Pro Networker & business woman. They created a platform for budding entrepreneurs called The Female Success Network. They'd bring in guest experts every month to teach you something new and it was just what I needed, I needed knowledge fast.

It wasn't expensive to join and every month I was getting hundreds, sometimes thousands of dollars worth of courses and information so it was a win for me, especially as it was the price of a few coffees and a cake in Starbucks. A few courses in, still after all this time I couldn't shake the idea that I was still meant to work creatively and decided that I wanted to still stick with my roots and do something with my background in Visual Communication and Graphic design.

But I just didn't know where to start so I approached the girls that ran The Female Success Network found out about their mastermind programme, then we went from there and put a strategy in place.

I think without the girl's direction I would still be so lost. They listened to my history and I told them what I loved but I lacked direction and unlike my careers advisor they didn't close the door in my face they helped me make a plan. Since my kids have been born I have had some sort of camera in my hand and I have loved taking pictures of them and every place we've visited since.

I have probably taken more than 100,000 photos and I've loved it. I always wanted to do photography as a business but weddings and baby portrait shoots never appealed to me, so I couldn't see how I could make a business of it.

Sarah Stone and Abigail Horne did though, they gave me strategies, connections and they have opened up the doors for me to work with some incredible people.

It's only the beginning for me. I only started working with them in January 2018 and I am just about to launch my own Photography business providing Lifestyle Photography and Styled Stock Images for Females in Business.

Being in network marketing was my real introduction to being self employed and what It meant in terms of hard work and determination to being a true entrepreneur, it opened up so many doors for me along the way.

I have met so many people across the world and it eventually led me to Sarah and Abigail, for that I am grateful for. I now have so many different skills and a abundance of knowledge around females in business.

As someone who has struggled with anxiety and self confidence it's something I've wanted to help others with as going through something yourself you want to help or prevent others going through the same thing.

I am always helping people and network marketing gave me the opportunity to help others create businesses across the world and building their confidence as business owners, spanning as far as Jamaica and St.Lucia. It's amazing what the power of a internet connection can do and what you can achieve.

I love to make others happy so I decided that when I was looking at ideas, I wanted to create a business that empowered other women into believing and feeling confident in themselves, by showing them how they can use the beautiful images I take for and of them, to elevate themselves in confidence and their online presence.

Every woman should feel confident in themselves and in what they do so If I can have a small part of that and the girl power movement then that makes me so happy. Women should feel like the Queens that they are at all times.

I really do have such a deep passion for photography in its entirety, I love exploring nature, it's where I get many new ideas from and where I tend to do all my planning. I have so many many ideas for my photography which will start rolling out this year and even more next year.

It's been incredible so far, I have photographed 2 retreats, a mum and baby fitness retreat and the most recent being a spiritual retreat in Glastonbury, which was one of the most amazing experiences I have ever had, to not only take photographs and capture amazing moments turning them into great memories, but also actually taking in everything that was happening and then there of course, meeting all the amazing people along the way.

It just blows my mind, to make it that bit better I have been booked to do the retreat again but in Greece which is really really cool, as well as talks of going out to Dubai to do photoshoots for another business, so it is all getting very exciting and it's feeling very real now.

My mission is to travel the the world providing Female Business women with beautiful photographs of themselves, their business, the lifestyle they've created for themselves as well as styled stock images for their social media, blogs and websites. I love to support others and I feel I am able to do that by providing them with beautiful photographs whilst also being creative and free. I never want anyone to feel anything less than brilliant and I'd love to spread the love as far and as wide as possible.

As a young mum I always felt like I was wrote off and people thought I would never achieve anything. From my point of view I have already been living my best life raising my family with no regrets and now I get to do something for myself to put the icing onto that cake, I feel so blessed.

I never gave up hope that I was meant to do great things. My mum said to me the other day, I did wish that you finished university then went on to a career that you loved, but you decided to do something different and went down the unconventional route but look at the amazing life you've had so far.

My mum taught me I wasn't meant to follow the crowd, I knew neither was I meant to lead I, was just meant to follow my heart and thats what I have done and will continue to do. Looking back I wouldn't have done anything differently and I would always advise others to never give up on what they want.

Even if you take a different slightly longer route like me, it doesn't matter as long as you get there in the end. I have never been afraid to be different, stand for what I believe in or do what I feel is right. I am starting to think now that I was never meant to be 'normal'. Being a mum is my true calling and my superpower, but I know I am more than a mum, I am also me and I am excited to continually evolve and explore this new part of myself whilst trying to ignore the mum guilt.

Being in the mastermind has been a great experience. I still have till January to continue growing so there is so much more to come which is hard to believe, but I have gained so many new friends and a few life long ones too which means so much.

To have a group of women from all different backgrounds and living all over the place, that we come together as one, supporting each other and our visions for the future. It has really opened my eyes as to what is possible for me now, where with some planning and hard work where I could be in a few years time.

I find it so exciting knowing that I am working towards a career I could have only dream of before, and it's all going to be on my terms. I don't have bosses to answer to only myself. We have an amazing family, we own our own home we have nice cars, but for me that bit that was missing was something to say, I did that, I created / achieved that and even though I didn't finish university with my degree I am still successful and will continue to be.

I want to thank both Sarah and Abigail for the opportunity to share my story to this point in time, on top of everything else they have done for all of us in the mastermind, and to the Unstoppable Mastermind Girls for being simply awesome everyday, and for all of their continued and shared support for one another. I am so glad and grateful I met every single one of you.

To my husband and my boys. Thank you for always having my back, for being a constant support and for always making me believe I can do anything. I love you beyond words.

About Jennifer Stevens

Jennifer Stevens is a lifestyle and branding photographer from the Midlands though resides in South Wales, who specialises in lifestyle images, stock and event photography for the female entrepreneur, helping them to create an authentic and soul centred brand that connects directly to their ideal client.

After spending more than a decade learning in all things creative, she decided to turn her passions in to a business she could be proud of and it's her mission to empower women by photography, showing them that they are beautiful, powerful and worthy of every bit of the success, that they worked so hard to get.

Jennifer is a wife to Michael and mom to Matthew, Oliver, Finlay and Poppy their dog. Away from work Jennifer can be found hiking up mountains, reading books, meditating, practising yoga, doing a spot or two of retail therapy, travelling often and just living her best life with the people she cares about most.

Her skills do not end there though, she has many different rolls of Mother, Housewife, Secretary, Accountant, Referee, Doctor, Nursemaid, Personal Stylist, Interior Designer, Photographer and Chief bottle washer.

CONTACT

Email - hello@jenniferstevens.co.uk
Website - www.jenniferstevens.co.uk
Facebook - www.facebook.com/iamjenniferstevens
Instagram - www.instagram.com/iamjenniferstevens
LinkedIn - www.linkedin.com/jennifer-stevens

Jo Gilbert

Profits are Better Than Wages

For many years now, people I have met or been introduced to have described me as 'lucky'. They would say things like 'OMG Jo you're so lucky to have such a beautiful house' or 'You're so lucky to own that car' or 'Jo you're so lucky you go on all of those holidays' 'You're lucky because you've got a good job'.

I felt I needed to address this perception and share my story of overcoming some extreme adverse events and situations. So, I wrote my first book 'Strength & Power' which became a #1 Amazon Best seller in no less than seven categories on the day of its release in May 2018 and held the top spot for two weeks.

I'd love for you to read my back story, to get an insight into my journey to becoming a successful business entrepreneur. Luck wasn't involved, it was down to a lot of hard work, perseverance and sheer guts and determination. In my book, I share some of the tools and techniques I use every day to keep me moving forwards by taking focused, purposeful and positive action to achieve my goals.

I think from a very young age I knew I wouldn't make a very good 'employee'. I don't like to be anything other than winning or leading, so being employed and having a manager was quite a strange event for me really. I would always give 100% to any employed job I had, but to be honest with you, where ever management in companies were concerned, I recall frequently thinking, I could do a much better job than they were doing given half a chance.

Those chances seemed few and far between really, as the further up the career ladder you go the fewer openings there are. So, inevitably you are left at some point in your career, with the choice of accepting the job you have and settling for going no further up that ladder, or, creating your own business and your own success story, which is exactly what I decided to do in March 2010.

I had worked my way up the career ladder at a large corporate organisation, at the time of my resignation I was responsible for quite a sizable project budget and multi-million-pound project spend. For almost ten years, I had invested quite a lot of my personal time in self-development. I wanted to learn more about the sector I worked in and be recognised as a subject matter expert in a number of areas in the industry.

My employers, however, failed to see the investment I had made in myself and the knowledge I had acquired. Instead they took advantage of me and my giving nature. I was stuck working two jobs for them because they asked me to temporarily step in to a role while the position was filled, but could I retain my own role as well. Sixty plus hours a week I was working, and it took them nearly 18-months to advertise and fill the position I was supposed to cover for 'a couple of weeks'.

It was only after I had contracted sepsis and was off poorly did they actually get me some support. However, it was too little too late and, a year later I set-up my own Business Consultancy and left their employment.

Jim Rohn once said "Profits are better than wages" something quite profound that has stuck in my mind ever since I read it. He was absolutely right!

I have no regrets and have never looked back, the offer of a £10k pay rise and company car payment didn't sway me to stay either, I saw this as confirmation I had made the right decision.

Within two years of becoming self-employed I was earning more than double my annual employed salary every month!

The only thing I wish I had known before I became self-employed was the importance of a great accountant or book keeper. Expenses, invoicing, tax returns, VAT all make me shudder and go straight to the bottom of my to do list. I could've saved myself a lot of time and effort in the early years if I had just brought someone in from the start who enjoyed this type of work and more importantly understood it. If you are considering self-employment or setting up a business, an accountant from day one is a must have.

The reason I chose to become a Business Consultant was twofold really. Firstly, and unashamedly income! The day rates some consultants charge is ridiculously high. I figured I knew as much, if not more than the consultants I had been working with in my employed role from some of the Big Four Consultancies'.

If I could offer the same advice and service but at a more competitive rate, then I would never be short of work. My strategy worked and in over 8 years of being self-employed I have never struggled for clients or work.

Secondly, I had spotted a potential opportunity in the industry. Changes were being implemented to open up competition in the energy markets and it was clear to me that there was going to be an influx of new energy suppliers who would need support in setting up their companies and getting through the minefield of regulation and compliance.

So, I had found my niche, and while everyone else was focused on what was happening with smart meters I was focused on getting known for being the expert in market entry and energy supply company set-up and operations.

That was my mission from the outset, I wanted to be the go to person for market entry. The person who was recommended, and first in mind for service providers or recruitment agents when a new company needed support. I'm not going to lie I was also chasing the income, and the more I earned the more I wanted to earn to see how much I could actually achieve. The income was just a by-product really, when you focus on delivering for your customers the income grows naturally.

As the number of energy suppliers coming to market increased, other consultancy businesses started to appear offering similar services. So, as the waters of my previously blue sea of opportunity began to turn red and become crowded, I once again felt drawn to focus on a new niche.

This fish went and found a new blue sea to swim in. What I didn't expect after returning from a retreat in Bali, was a complete change of direction and industry. I certainly didn't expect to become a qualified teacher in meditation and mindfulness, life coaching and hypnosis, plus many other subjects I have studied in the past year.

I truly believe that people buy from people, they don't buy from companies and brands. Getting to know your clients and ensuring they know, like and trust you, will win you business time and time again.

Having an enthusiastic, motivated, knowledgeable and valued team around you is also really important. One of the greatest lessons I have taken from my time as an employee, has got to be the complete lack of feeling valued, and how negative and mentally challenging that was especially with everything else I was dealing with outside of my working life.

It all came down to the difference between a manager and a leader. I have experienced several line managers, who managed their teams with rule books and work flow, even requesting intelligent grown adults, to sign in and out of timesheets if they needed the loo!

Very few of them showing any qualities of being a great leader or someone I could look up to and admire, someone who made me feel loyal to the company and want to stay. I wanted out of the daily institutional oppression, and to be the complete opposite of the management styles I had experienced so far in my working life and to lead by example.

I strongly believe that the greatest assets in any business are the people who work within it. Without great people, you're left with a logo, a website, product or service and some operational procedures.

It's the people that bring your brand to life, they create the culture, the vibe and ensure your mission, values and objectives are delivered.

People need to feel valued and listened to, they need to know that their contribution, which for fulltime employees is usually at least 8-hours a day, 5-days a week, is appreciated. That's a huge time commitment spent away from family and friends. Everyone in an organisation has an important part to play, it doesn't matter if they are the cleaner or the CEO they all matter and should be celebrated and valued.

Most employees seek leadership from their management team. They need to be led by someone who can inspire them, someone who shows commitment and passion.

They need someone who shows honesty and integrity, someone who is a great communicator and not afraid to delegate and empower their team. A leader who shows great creative skills and innovation. A decision maker who is willing to be held to account for their actions.

Someone who will roll their sleeves up regardless of status or job title and just get shit done! If I'm not willing to do it, then I don't expect anyone on the team to do it either.

I've had some huge lessons these past eight years too and some very expensive ones. For example, in 2011, I decided it would be a good idea to spend £60k on marketing an energy switching service I had created without really completing any market analysis or research.

I used some of the profits from my consultancy work to pay for it but didn't complete any sampling to see if the marketing would work. I just went ahead and blew my £60k profit and marketing budget on radio advertising, posters on buses and leaflet drops and got very little return.

The important thing to note here is, I learnt an expensive lesson, but kept on going, I didn't quit. I didn't see this as a business failure and head straight back to employment. At that time in my business I was wearing every hat a business needs, brand development, marketing, website build, strategy even being the accountant and so on. Most people starting out in business have to wear many hats so it is worth bearing in mind, if you dnt have a particular strength in an area, sometimes it can save you a lot of time and money to out source this.

As I see it, you never fail in business or life, if you keep going, you only learn. It is these lessons which have helped to strengthen my approach to delivering my business and personal goals. Seven years on from losing that £60k, I approach things very differently now and tap in to marketing channels which are very cost effective.

For example, writing my book, guest blogging, video creation, I also now complete 'A – B' testing of any advertising to ensure its hitting the sweet spot with potential clients. The important factor is don't give up, shit happens, learn from it and grow.

I think the best piece of business advice I ever got to be honest with you, was from my best friend and founder of Female Success Network and Authors and Co - Abigail Horne and that was to simply to get on with writing my book. Abi said to me "Jo people need to hear your story, it will help so many people. You can show people that there is hope and light at the end of the tunnel, and no matter what shit they are dealing with they can get through it. Jo your skills extend way beyond gas and electricity bills, you have so much more to offer". She was so right!

You see, the journey I have been on and the skills I have learned over the years are valuable to more than companies or people in the energy sector. Writing Strength and Power took me on an emotional rollercoaster, like nothing I have ever experienced.

It forced me to deal with emotional hurt and anxiety I had buried deep inside for many years. It opened up new learning and development areas and business opportunities, and helped me to see how I could support other industries, people and businesses, not just in the UK but globally.

By combining all the usual traditional business management tools with some personal development tools, such as focused mindfulness and meditation techniques, I am now supporting others to really shine and elevate their businesses through my coaching programme 'The Lift™'.

And it's not just businesses I have been able to support either, on a 1-2-1 basis using meditation, mindfulness, hypnosis, visualisation and many more techniques. I have worked with clients who are dealing with adverse events such as death of a loved one, marriage or relationship breakdown, self-confidence and health issues.

I am currently implementing meditation, mindfulness and hypnosis retreats which will combine with some amazing business entrepreneurs from around the globe to deliver some unique sessions and retreats with a difference – Yoga, Hypnosis, Theta healing, Reiki, Book Writing.

My book has been so much more than me putting pen to paper, it has now given me a fantastic marketing tool, reference material and positioned me as an authority and expert in my field. From this I have created a new niche coaching business which is already proving very popular with my clients.

My productivity secret? Honestly, I would have to say it is having a love and passion for what I do, that always helps.

That and daily practice of gratitude and meditation.

My advice to anyone starting out in business is to create something you have an interest in, something you love doing and enjoy. If it doesn't spark a fire in your belly when you think about it, then it's never going to fully satisfy your desire to succeed, so your productivity will suffer. Maybe it use to, like the energy industry did for me, but doesn't any more, that's ok. If that is you in employment or you in business don't ever be afraid of acknowledging your growth and move on to discover your next path to continued success.

Don't chase money, if you focus on delivering a great product or service, supporting others and just generally being a nice person, the money will flow.

If someone had told me a year ago I would be a #1 best-selling author, featuring in a collaboration book with over 20 other female entrepreneurs and opening a meditation and mindfulness centre in Lanzarote whilst also coaching men, women and business owners from all walks of life on various topics, I would think they were barmy.

I have simply created a business from a personal interest and invested my time once again in self-development to become qualified in so many new areas. Not only that, then moving to another country something I have dreamt of for so long.

I hold complete faith and trust in being present daily and that the right doors will open for me at the right times. When I learnt more about meditation and mindfulness, and learned how to switch off the auto pilot, I really started to see how this was improving my productivity levels and preventing endless hours of procrastination. My social media scrolling addiction has been kicked into touch.

I have basically seized an opportunity to help others in business to do the same, to switch off the auto-pilot, be present and more aware, mindful and grateful of the here and now.

My success habits are driven by 100% self-belief. I am the only person that truly knows my ability, my strengths and my weaknesses. I can push me harder and give me a harder time than any manager ever could.

People have a perception of what you are capable of, but rarely is this a true reflection of your actual ability.

I simply maintain self-belief, focus and perseverance no matter what life throws my way. Listening to that voice in my head, feeling that fire in my belly, trusting my instinct, my intuition and allowing other people's actions and self-limiting beliefs to make me even more determined to prove them wrong.

Always celebrating the whole iceberg of success not just the tip of it that people see and congratulate you for. Usain Bolt trained for endless hours and sacrificed so much for a 9.58 seconds win, is that all we should celebrate the 9.58 seconds? Of course not!

Remember – The Man on the Top of The Mountain Didn't Fall There!

My advice to anyone who is just starting out in business, or even considering quitting employment to start a business would be 'just do it'. If you are on maternity leave currently and are dreading going back to work full time, find a way, find your niche so you can carve out what your days look like with your little one. If you are a mum, dad, grandparent and your children are in day care and after school clubs and you crave for more time with them, find the path, find your niche and don't stop until you have achieved it.

If the self employed, own business, entrepreneur thought has entered your mind and you have had the courage to dream about it, the only thing you need to do now is to have the courage to switch off the self-sabotaging thoughts of self-doubt and the millions of excuses your subconscious mind will throw in your way.

There will also be other people's self-limiting beliefs and reasons of why you should stick with the daily grind, usually coming from nervous family and friends.

Seriously just do it! Create a plan, and begin to take action, get to work and don't let your focus be swayed. Buy into the whole dream and achieve it one step at a time.

"Man's mind stretched to a new idea never goes back to its original dimensions." - Oliver Wendell Holmes Jr.

Remember business is hard, being employed and making someone else rich is hard, you just have to decide which hard you prefer. And if you do find you have critics and nay sayers, simply ask them what makes them so qualified to tell you to stand still and stop dreaming? Why aren't they rich yet and are they are going to pay your bills for you?

If I want business advice, I won't go and ask my uncle Frank who's been employed all his life and accepted annual pay rises and a Christmas gift voucher as reward for all his years of service. I don't have an uncle Frank by the way, but you get my drift.

Neither would I ask someone who has all of the theory but no real-life experience, for example I wouldn't ask someone with no children for parenting advice, probably why I never listened to my health visitor when my first baby was born. She had no children of her own but was trying to tell me how to look after mine?

I prefer to use a more common sense approach. I go and ask someone who has been there, dug the trench, got their hands dirty and got the experience. Someone who knows the stresses of invoices not been paid on time, someone who knows what it's like to pull a contract or business proposal together, someone who knows what the 2am shift feels like when you can't sleep and your to do list is whizzing around your mind.

Someone who has also worried whether or not they could pay themselves this month and put food on the table and pay the bills. These are the types of people who can help you to avoid pitfalls and grow, they have been there, worn the t-shirt and persevered to grow successful businesses!

Surround yourself with people who will lift you up, like the ladies at Female Success Network, connect with all of us in this book, our contact details are in this book for that very reason. Don't be afraid to approach us for support, to collaborate, network, service swap, get yourself out there, start to be seen and heard. The world is one great big market place full of consumers, there is room for all of us.

I've spent a year in the unstoppable mastermind group, with all of the wonderful ladies who feature in this book. It has been an absolute pleasure and one of the most rewarding experiences of my entire life. Watching so many women create businesses from scratch and to now see them a year on, flourishing and doing so well.

The mastermind has provided the support from twenty-four outstanding female business entrepreneurs who were all on their own journeys and supporting each other with the ethos of collaboration over competition. It great to be able to pop in the group and run ideas past the girls or let them know you need support or a pick me up.

They have been there to celebrate every single win, and every single lesson, there have been tears of sadness, frustration and sheer joy, I can't recommend this experience enough. Thank you to each and every one of you, I wish you all continued success.

And if you are reading this book, take inspiration from it, that if we can do it, then you can do it to! Together we can all achieve more.

About Jo Gilbert

Jo has been a self-employed Business Consultant, Coach and Success Mentor since March 2010. She has worked with large corporations, PLCs right down to micro businesses and self-employed business entrepreneurs. Jo's focus has been business creation, business planning and strategy, customer, revenue and profit margin growth, operational and service excellence and customer experience.

Jo is the Founder Shangri-La MMC

In May 2018 Jo became a #1 Amazon Best Selling Author with her first book on overcoming adversity, 'Strength & Power'.

Jo is also an accredited Mindfulness and Meditation Teacher, and certified NLP Master Practitioner, NLP Personal Development Coach, NLP Life Coaching, NLP Self Esteem and Confidence Coach and a Hypnosis Practitioner. Jo works on a 1-2-1 basis with clients to really get to the core of events, thoughts or feelings which can hold you back in your career, life or business.

By combining traditional business tools and techniques with personal development tools including Visualisation, Goal Setting, Mindfulness and Meditation, Jo will help you to create your very own version of success.

FEMALE SUCCESS NETWORK

CONTACT:

Email – jogilbert1971@gmail.com

Website – www.jogilbert.co.uk

Facebook – https://www.facebook.com/jo.gilbert.313/

Facebook – https://www.facebook.com/ShangrilaMMC/

Instagram – @jo_gilbert3

Twitter - @ShangrilaMMC

Linkedin - https://www.linkedin.com/in/joannemgilbert/

Jo Swann

Don't tell me I can't ....

When starting out in 'business' at the age of 25, a 5ft2 blonde with a bubbly personality the world is your oyster....with a business name and brand that attracted attention I thought nothing of standing up to be counted, of putting my head above the parapet and of being seen, in fact I revelled in it.

No-one could tell me 'you can't do that', I never thought about people wondering 'who do you think you are' - it simply didn't cross my mind. I just wanted to be on a level with the MDs, the Chief Execs and the seasoned Marketing Managers who I was pitching to work with - and I nailed it.

Within 1 month of going solo I was consulting with MDs who had been in in business for over 20 years and they were paying me for PR advice and consultancy. Boom!

I called the business Chocolate PR. This was after a brainstorming session in the office of a colleague, the Creative Director of the company I was working at before I left to go self-employed. We created the brand there and then, including the name and a fun, quirky logo.

One of the best pieces of advice I ever got was to connect my brand with my values and create a strong brand character from day 1. So, the brief was make it creative, make it fun, make it repel boring companies I don't want to work with!

To be honest this was more of a 'self-branding' exercise than actually establishing a business as such, but it turned into a brand that was well loved and a perfect representation of the business and its values, as it grew.

The Chocolate PR brand has held me in good stead over the years and I really appreciate Angela's creative skills that helped to launch me.

The logo was a caricature of me - something that was actually very fresh 15 years ago (before the world of the avatar!) -but looking back now all I can think of is wow, that's a bit heavy on the ego! It served its purpose though, with the first round of the business cards being little purple squares with the character on - these most definitely won the best business card game at those corporate networking events I did the rounds of.

The brand evolved but the logo remained until only this year, when a rebrand took place to move the business into the future.

Prior to becoming a business owner I had suffered months of stress and unnecessary tears. I wonder now if maybe some of my working life experiences had given me some of the drive that then helped me to succeed, however some of the relationships I had endured with previous colleagues I wouldn't have wished on anyone.

As a twenty something career driven young woman I was keen to impress. Having jumped out of Uni into my dream job at a radio station where I got to interview pop stars everyday (including Craig David in his hotel bedroom), hang out with DJs and live the party lifestyle, I believed life was on my side and I was going to achieve whatever I wanted.

Don't get me wrong I worked hard here, and committed to a commute of initially 3 hours a day, to then one of over 4 hours per day when I got quickly promoted to a bigger station. But this didn't phase me. Work was fun. I got to feed my creative side, wear 'non corporate' clothes, hang out with some amazing people and listen to music everyday.

It was perfect. BUT it was not to last. My role was a part of the online team, and we're going back nearly 20 years - online was new, and apparently a risk. The big chiefs who owned the network decided it wasn't paying for itself and so they cut the entire online department.

The injustice. The craziness. The fools. We all knew this was a HUGE mistake and they'd just end up rebuilding it again a few years down the line - which they did -but they weren't brave enough to ride the wave. So, my dream job was no more, and I had been made redundant from my first ever career move.

Luckily I had built up some really strong relationships with the rest of the team at the station and the news editor put me forward to a contact of his, the news editor at The Yorkshire Post, a regional newspaper back on my home turf.

It seemed they were feeling braver and were starting up an online team to support the newspaper and provide online content to boost the editorial in the paper, and extend the advertising opportunities for clients. This was perfect as I had actually always wanted to be a journalist, shadowing the local reporters on our local newspaper on work experience when I was only 14. My degree of English, Media and Psychology was focused around me working in journalism, so yes, this would do nicely.

It was a big job - online content editor for a new site that they really had no idea about. They were impressed that I had managed the online content of the radio stations and were looking to me for advice. Me, a twenty something practically just out of uni. They asked for content strategies, content plans, ideas on how to integrate with the rest of the newspaper and the online ad teams.

I had lots of ideas on all this, and a total confidence that I could deliver. I got the job and a nice pay rise. (I remember my mum commenting around me being so bolshy and having no fear, laughing and shaking her head in disbelief as I played the game when negotiating my salary)....where has that relationship with money gone now?? It's not something I managed to hold onto.

This next job was a challenging role, but one I revelled in, and it mixed my journalistic skills with more of a connection to business as I was always looking for ways to make more of the content for the advertisers too. I loved this role too which saw me work closely with the news editor of the papers as well as the online digital teams and my skills grew in both areas.

But alas, groundhog day, and job 2 was axed - once again in a mass cull we found ourselves redundant. Now, this could give you a complex, but actually I kind of revelled in the fact that I had been at the forefront of industries, that were ahead of their time - well they would have been if they'd have seen the projects through!

They chickened out and this always saddens me and it was a mixture of frustration and satisfaction when both media companies re-recruited our exact same roles several years later - to do exactly what we'd been doing (only worse!).

So, onwards and upwards - next I decided it was time to leap into PR - after reviewing my options with risky online businesses that seemed like car crashes waiting to happen, journalism jobs which paid peanuts unless you moved to London and PR which seemed a booming industry and perfect blend of my journalism and marketing skills - PR won hands down, however it seemed getting a job in this field was not so easy.

Still in my early twenties I was determined to find a way in, so signed up with lots of temping agencies who worked with marketing organisations. I had taken typing at school - whilst most of my friends had taken business studies, and do you know that was one of the best moves I made. Not only did it provide me with very well paid summer jobs that saved me working all hours in a bar, it also provided me a way into what I now consider as my industry.

I got a job as a PA to a director of an entertainment agency. I had no actual qualifications for this apart from typing (and my WPM was up there!) - but I blagged my way into the role. The next thing you know I'm spending days with the very flamboyant entrepreneur, driving to Liverpool in his Jag, negotiating with theatre owners on promo deals and newspapers on ad deals.

We were representing a Liverpool singer who was putting on a show and I was responsible for the promotion of it. Press releases were written, local media coverage achieved and I had got the bug for PR.

My boyfriend had bought me a suit for my birthday and there I was a twentysomething going on 40something, full of confidence and bravado, taking on every challenge thrown at me. Yes I was TOTALLY out of my depth. No I had no real clue what I was doing, but I made it work, and it was a huge learning curve - it was also lots of fun as I managed to recruit my friend to help out over the summer and we spent days cutting celebrity stories out of the best gossip magazines (because Barry wanted to represent some of the celebrities and it was all research) whilst dancing around the office singing Mambo Number 5.

This was my entry into PR.

As with all the horses I had backed so far this turned out to be a risky one. An ambitious entrepreneur who loved the finer things in life, but not the person who'd help me get where I wanted to be so the time came again to move on.

This brings me to the job I left to set up Chocolate PR. This job, at a marketing agency, started as a telesales role. I, as most other people on this planet, hated telesales but it was a way into a marketing agency that had a PR department and that's what my focus was on.

It was actually quite a 'soft sell' booking eye appointments for an opticians so not too terrible in that respect - but what was terrible was the unyielding targets, the sheer amount of calls we were required to make a day, and the soul destroying criticism when appointments were not forthcoming. I hated this job, but was totally focused on the bigger picture.

And, the time came. The woman running the PR department announced quite suddenly she was leaving to go to London. Looking back now I can see how this could have happened after she finally snapped and could take no more, but at the time all I saw was an opening to make my mark. Was I qualified for this role. Hell no. Was I going to take it? Hell yes.

As my temp agency knew my grand plan (and were clearly excited about the huge hike in salary from telesales to PR exec) they pushed for me to be tried out. I got the chance and the next thing you know I was picking up where the PR Director had left off, after an extremely rushed handover, running national campaigns, with hefty budgets and lots of logistics to negotiate.

I'm not just talking media campaigns but large scale events run nationally that involved all sort of complexities that were all alien to me. But I learn quickly, and I embrace a challenge and get stuck in. Once again I was traveling around the country with the directors, this time meeting MDs of their longstanding clients, discussing the best route for PR success for them and this was something I revelled in.

I *knew* this was my thing, I could schmooze just as well as the big boys who'd been doing it for years, I could install confidence in business owners when chatting about PR opportunities, because I was passionate about getting the best possible results for them. I enjoyed the success of this role for a while - but it was to be ruined in a matter of time.

My approach to PR is to really work alongside your clients, to get under the skin of their businesses and to be a part of their team, to integrate with other departments and create campaigns that are joined up. This takes time, commitment, and constant communication -and this costs money.

What I didn't know when I joined this business, was that the company was owned by an accountant. And as I was taken more seriously, whether intentionally or not, I was also simultaneously made to feel so small, this was my reality.

Progressing to boardroom meetings was for me something I was excited about, being about to report back to the team on our PR successes for our clients.

Yet, however much success we achieved I ALWAYS got ripped to shreds. Think Alan Sugar boardroom and you're not far wrong. I remember working in the office until midnight on the run up to board reports. I remember being reduced to tears time and time again being told the P&L wasn't good enough on the department because I was 'committing too many hours to clients'.

The business was looking for maximum profit for minimum effort - a sensible approach financially I guess - but actually I wanted to deliver an above and beyond service, and a commitment to clients I could be proud of.

My problem was I wasn't very good at conforming to this dictation and I *did* stick up for myself, even if terrified.

I put up with it for so long, but the truth is I was so unhappy. Lucky for me I wasn't the only one unhappy here and one joyous day during a board meeting myself and two other female heads of department upped and left in a two fingers up signal that enough was enough.

We walked and didn't look back!

I wish I could have told myself earlier than this point "This is just not worth it" "You shouldn't have to put up with this shit" "You shouldn't be broken by being so passionate about your work". I guess as we took the strength to quit these realisations hit in some way but actually I'm not sure it ever really sunk in - I think it was more a case of it was time for flight rather than fight anymore.

At this point I had never intended to go self employed. I most certainly had never intended to run my own business, and it was very early days to be doing either, but the empowerment I felt doing this alongside two other, more established, confident inspiring women is what drove me on, and I appreciate their support so much that got me off the ground onto the path I have now followed.

I think deep down I always knew that I'd rather work for myself than someone else, but this experience really made me take ownership of my career, and so Chocolate PR was born.

With Chocolate PR I rebelled against everything the previous agency had stood for. The brand was more energetic and fun, the terms of working were more flexible, in the clients' favour and the rule of thumb was to over service and never under service, god forbid.

However you may spot a flaw here -whilst the business built quickly and I had some success I most definitely didn't have a head for figures. I rebelled against keeping an eye on my numbers, and I got into debt and this is something I'd warn anyone starting out against, as it takes a long time to dig yourself back out!

I loved having my own business, but with no actual business skills I shouldn't have been left to my own devices really at this point! I hated sending invoices, and always sent them late and my cash flow was a nightmare.

So whilst it looked like I was growing a successful business, what I was actually doing, in hindsight, was growing a successful brand. I was making a name for myself, I was getting noticed in all the key business circles, I loved networking and made some fantastic alliances as I bonded with business besties who would turn out to not only be clients, but also friends and respected peers.

As the business grew and clients expanded I needed some help and this was a big move, taking on staff and moving into an office, and this is when I actually started to take the business seriously, once I was also responsible for others.

I still had money issues but was getting better at managing it - however I know now that I was massively limiting my potential by huge money blocks I was harbouring - and reflecting now I'm convinced this is down to rebelling against the accountant in the previous agency.

I didn't want to work how other agencies I had worked for did my focus had always been the client not the finances. In doing this I went to the extremes of underselling myself and our services, and giving away far too much knowledge and expertise for free.

Money issues aside, the brand however, was continuing to strengthen and over time we worked on some amazing campaigns for the likes of the NHS; women's highstreet clothing brand Whistles; leading fast food giant Yo! Sushi; legendary British brand Timothy Taylor Breweries as well as celebrity brands and charities such as NSPCC.

We also did a lot of work with big corporates and financial institutions. We won awards for much of our work, and this always made me proud, knowing that our innovation had been recognised. In all of this the focus was the clients, never me and my profile. Yes I wrote the odd industry piece or guest PR blog but it was few and far between.

As time went on and the business continued to thrive, I became pregnant. This was a huge mental challenge for me. Being such a career driven woman, to even comprehend how this was all going to work out. I wanted to be a mum but also didn't want to 'drop' everything I had worked so hard to build up, and we were at the height of our success at this point.

I worked up until 10 days before my due date, and managed to make a deal with my mum that she'd help out a couple of days a week, and I'd go back to work part time after just 3 months. This is exactly what we did, and I am so grateful for her, and my husband, who also took a day off a week, who enabled me to jump back into my career so I could juggle work and spending time with Jake.

In all honesty without my career I think I could have really struggled as a first time mum and I'm sure it saved me in more ways than one.

When you start to juggle career and parenthood everything becomes different though. You challenge yourself more in terms of how you are spending your time. You are exhausted and your time is more precious than ever, and working on huge campaigns for large corporates where you feel like you're banging your head against a brick wall just provides unnecessary, if well paid, stress.

Going to board meetings of 20 people, most of whom had no comprehension about PR on often less than 4 hours sleep was not fun and so I started to re-assess what I wanted to spend my time doing.

Work means lot to me but Jake is my world. I needed to make sure my efforts were leading somewhere and that my time away from him had a purpose. It became important that the business I was building and the impact I made when at work was something he can be proud of, and something that would reward us all, in the future.

We started to move out of the large corporate domain and move back into working with smaller business, where there is more passion, more energy and more desire to just get shit done. I relished this and the successes it brought for clients as it reminded me the impact that my work could really make, and if also felt like I was giving the business more direction and purpose.

I was networking with a fabulous group of like-minded women in my village at this time, after my now very good friend Lyndsey reached out to mums 'who liked to work and drink wine!' - I was the first to put my hand up and say I wanted in and now being inspired and motivated by other working mums who didn't just want to talk about soft play, but who were committed to building up businesses they were passionate about gave me another kick up the backside to start making more of a mark.

I was particularly inspired by an amazing lady called Emma, whose story broke my heart, but who is now someone else I consider a close friend, and one of the women I most admire - her support and guidance over the years has also pushed me to new levels as she is very much an 'anything is possible' kinda girl.

Fast forward a couple of years and I'm back in the flow, loving life and work - when my husband is in a life-threatening car accident. I can't count the number of times I have been told by medical professionals he is lucky to be alive, and it's incredible he's not paralysed.

He suffered horrendously physically and emotionally, and life suddenly changed quite dramatically. Throw into the mix a miscarriage that also devastated us a couple of weeks later and this was a true annus horribilis.

However, what this awful time did do was make me wake up. It made me look for others I could help. It made me step up to make more impact as I wanted to make my work count for more. At this time there had started to be what seemed like an epic shift towards female entrepreneurs and I was networking with these women on a regular basis. I was hearing their stories, of how they had ended up doing what they were doing, and I was blown away every time.

These were stories that were untold -but God they needed to be shared. SUCH inspiring women, who by default motivated others, in a very humble way. I wanted to be a part of helping them gain more visibility and this is where my focus on PR coaching for female entrepreneurs began.

Now on a mission to help share stories of female entrepreneurs, globally, through empowering them with PR knowledge, training and coaching, I am revelling in my focus and the impact I am making. For this to work I do need to raise my own profile, something I've not been comfortable with -maybe going back to the awful bullying incident at that marketing agency, or maybe through a slow demise of confidence as I've got older.

However, I know that to help others I first have to help myself so I'm on it. Achievements so far - Facebook lives globally; PR training webinars; guest speaker slots at large events, and blogs and podcast interviews whenever given chance.... for someone that hates the sound of their own voice these are big steps!

One of the reasons that now is the right time to go down this path for me is thanks to Female Success Network, and particularly the Mastermind group, as I know there's a whole 'pack' of women who have my back.

By pack I don't want you to think of a wolf pack, fierce and aggressive, yet they would be had they a need to defend me - what I mean by pack is a group that has mutual respect for one another, who will be there to pick you up when you need it but also are there to cheerlead you on at all times.

I can honestly say I have learnt so much from being around such inspiring female entrepreneurs, always striving to do more and be more and Abi and Sarah really do lead from the front, letting us into the intricacies of their business, so we can learn along their growth path. I know I've found my place and am now excited to really go for it to make my mark here. It's time to stop pissing about and have real impact.

I know I have huge amounts of knowledge to share and now thanks to Abi and Sarah, who have helped me take my business online (something I hadn't even considered 12 months ago - (ironic when I stated out in the online space well before its time!) I now have the platform, faith and accountability to do it.

You could say I've come full circle. Looking back now 15 years later it's really interesting to reflect on who that person was, back in her twenties, and ask how much of her is left, as I now turn the very grown up age of 40. The good news is I know there's lots of her left, but some of her has definitely been in hiding for a while. As I reflect on my successes and failures, I'm now really excited to bring more of her back as I embark on the next chapter of Chocolate PR.

She was tenacious, ambitious, confident, full of fun, passionate, excitable, energised and driven - add to this now what I think my old age has delivered - more kudos, credibility, mindfulness, and focus…along with more of a 'sod them' attitude towards anyone who is not aligned, and I'm starting to believe I can achieve whatever I set my mind to.

I'm excited to tell more female entrepreneurs stories globally, and also appreciate that somewhere along the way I might have to revisit my own.

Finally, if I could give one piece of advice to anyone keen to get into PR, or any competitive industry, or indeed make your mark with your own business I'd say it's not an easy path -but why should it be?

You have to find your way, overcome obstacles and navigate blips in the road - but if you have vision and focus, and you can hold on to some of that fierce grit and energy from your youth, you'll make it.

As time goes on you'll make your path even more personal to become a road that only you have trodden and this is something to be proud of.

You *can* do it, and don't let anyone tell you otherwise.

I'm *ready* to go global - there I said it! So, here's to getting up everyday with the tenacity of a twenty-year old but the freedom of a forty year old - as I make my next Chapter really count!

About Jo Swann

Jo is an award-winning PR Director and founder of Chocolate PR, working with clients globally. She offers PR consulting & PR mentor services, PR Strategy, PR Training and Content Development for both media relations and social media.

Jo has worked in PR and communications for nearly 20 years, as a journalist, online content writer and PR working with big brands and corporates - and now her focus is on small businesses and female entrepreneurs. Jo is passionate about PR not just being for the big boys and her PR Mentor service enables smaller businesses to tap into her expertise with flexible support.

She launched Chocolate PR nearly 15 years ago, after working in media, marketing and PR agencies, to challenge the way PR was being done by the bigger agencies as clients were being served up terrible experiences through ineffective retainers and inauthentic agencies. With Chocolate PR Jo set out to produce accessible, effective PR services using creativity and imagination alongside her journalistic skills to generate visibility for our clients.

An ex-journo, online content developer and magazine editor she understands storytelling from all angles.

She's worked with companies of all sizes including the likes of women's high street clothing brand Whistles, celebrity fashion brands, children's charity NSPCC, training providers learn direct, Dale Carnegie, and British Superbrand Pitman Training, along with creative food brand Yo! Sushi, to name just a few, winning many awards along the way.

BUT in working with these brands the niggling feeling was always lurking with her, that what she lives for is to help small businesses, and particularly female entrepreneurs harness the power of PR. She's passionate about helping making PR work as a cost effective, creative marketing medium.

She wants to help you tell your story and have fun doing it and works with small businesses and female entrepreneurs globally, helping them to do just that. This last year Jo's focus has been on making a bigger impact, knowledge sharing and educating as many people as possible through free webinars, tips and advice via her free facebook group, live interviews and speaking at events and workshops.

She also launched a number of new services to support female entrepreneurs and their teams including 121 and group coaching programmes and her PR- You Can Do It! online courses.

Jo's all about Raising the Bar and knowledge sharing to empower more people to reap the benefits of PR and is on a mission to spread the PR love globally.

Jo Swann I PR Coach I www.chocolatepr.co.uk
www.twitter.com/chocpr
www.facebook.com/chocpr
https://www.facebook.com/groups/PRYouCanDoIt - Free Facebook group full of PR tips
https://www.linkedin.com/in/joswannchocolatepr/
https://www.instagram.com/jochocpr/

FEMALE SUCCESS NETWORK

Kimberley Banner

Never in a million years would I have thought I would be writing a chapter in a book telling you about my journey to Female Entrepreneur. It's been one heck of a journey to get here and it wasn't plain sailing, but life isn't plain sailing. You will be on that rollercoaster. It will break down, it will start back up again. It will never be a smooth ride. BUT…it most definitely is worth the ride!

It was always a dream of mine to become a teacher. I would come home from school each day and reenact the lessons I'd had with my Primary School teachers. I remember looking back I could hear my sister and mum sniggering at the bottom of the stairs as they were listening to me teaching and telling the pupils off in my classroom (the playroom upstairs) and putting them in detention who had upset me that day at school.

Through channeling my passion for teaching and education in the games I played at home, I knew 100% that teaching and influencing young children was something I was incredibly passionate about so needed to make sure that my career was just that.

Growing up at school wasn't plain sailing. I wasn't the "usual" body type. In fact I had tiny abs & a slim frame with the chest of a young boy. I absolutely adored sports, especially swimming and netball. My body type didn't bother those at Primary School - it was when I started at Secondary School where people began to point out that I was "skinny" I had "pancakes" for boobs & I looked like a "twig".

I didn't really think there was anything wrong with my body but that soon changed when more and more people felt the need to identify these things to me.

I get it now - children are cruel and don't really care if they're hurting your feelings. Do you think I want to have a flat chest?! Do you not think I can see that I don't have anything curvy on my body?! I swam every single day after school, sometimes before school started.

I was a great swimmer and even got selected to represent the whole of Central Lancashire as the captain. I was immensely proud of myself with my swimming and sports. I put everything into it and there nobody judged my frame and body. In fact, they probably wanted it more because my slender body glided through the water faster than the rest of the girls I competed against.

At 14, I finally started my period. I was ecstatic - strange emotion to have when you're a young girl but I was the last one to start. I finally felt like I was becoming a young woman. I knew my body would start to physically carry on changing and become more 'womanly'. It was around this time that I decided that my passion also lay with netball after playing it alongside swimming.

Swimming was getting difficult to get to - it was a huge commitment and unfortunately, things change and so do your interests. Luckily for me my interest was still competitive sport. I made some incredible friends and developed great skills. I was still the small frame and for some reason hadn't had my growth spurt...I was still quite short. I'm 5"10 now so as you can imagine I had some time to grow!

Because of this, when I was playing at a higher standard, I wasn't chosen as much. My skill set and ability matched those around me in the same position, it was just a case of not being tall enough. That's what I told myself anyway. I was committed no matter which position I played and my Mum would take me all over the north west to allow me to follow my passion, just like she did with swimming.

I absolutely love to make my family proud. It's what makes me thrive. I love to bring that kind of joy to someone. It's a lovely feeling to have. I knew I made them proud at school. Academically I was bright, although it didn't come super naturally to me. I had to work at it.

Exams scared me so much. My memory isn't great so retaining lots of information isn't for me. My concentration levels weren't brilliant. But get me in the PE lesson and you'd get my all! I excelled at school and I had lots of proud moments including being selected as a Prefect, Head Girl & my favourite, I won the award dedicated to a teacher who sadly passed away - Harry Cartlege. I won his award for being Happy.

This is something I really treasured. Being known as the happy one. I brought happiness to everyone around me. I always wanted to make people smile. Making my peers and teachers smile also brought me great pride. This is something I've kept with me all my life. To have that effect on someone is such a wonderful feeling. It's one thing I most definitely want to be remembered for. The one who makes people smile - and I will. I promise to myself that I will always be the one to bring smiles to the faces of others.

So, school was a breeze other than the body image police wanting to bring me down. College - what a different atmosphere! Completely different to school but a great place! Wearing our own clothes and expressing our personalities through the clothes we wore was an important thing. The workload increased dramatically and the exams got harder. Academically - it's safe to say I struggled with my A Levels.

College life was a stepping stone to uni but also caused me some personal grief…

I wish I knew all about mindset back then…because I sure needed it. I remember it vividly - I was playing GS for my college netball team. We were winning (of course) & I moved quickly to receive a ball ready to shoot. As I did so, the GK from the opposing team went into my right knee…and SNAP - I fell to the floor with sheer panic at the snapping noise. Adrenaline kicked in…I couldn't feel the agony I was in, I was just concentrating on the noise I'd heard. I thought I'd snapped my leg in half.

Turns out I'd badly injured my knee. Without me realising, this was the universe's first signal to me that my career perhaps wouldn't head in the direction I'd always intended.

To cut a very long story short with my knee injuries, I had actually damaged my cartilage & snapped my ACL (Anterior Cruciate Ligament) - hence the snap I heard during the match. This wasn't picked up on my countless trips to A&E - they told me I had a muscle spasm initially. Because there wasn't a diagnosis, I rested my knee for months and then gradually got back into sport and netball. My injury would creep up on me again but I had no idea the impact it would eventually have…

Uni life - wow it was something else! I learned a lot about myself the summer before going to uni. I went to America and did the whole 'Camp America' thing. It was life changing. I learned to be at peace with my own company. I am such a home bird and adore my family and missed them immensely but I grew up that summer. 3 months away from them saw me become an adult.

I made life long friends and memories that I cherish in my heart. I was a swimming instructor and lifeguard. That summer I inspired children to be polite and use impeccable manners, to be strong, confident and positive and to be great swimmers. It was the summer of a lifetime that will last forever. After camp I travelled and visited NYC, Niagara Falls, Miami & Boston - what an experience.

The bonds I had between the children were just amazing. I know I inspired those young girls to be the best versions of themselves and again, knew that becoming a teacher was my path. I was surely destined to become a PE teacher now?!

My time at University was THE BEST! I made life long friends, especially those in the netball teams! I was selected to play for the Edge Hill University Netball 1st team as a 'Fresher'. I was so proud to be picked! It was such a huge honour. During my degree, I had two more operations to "fix" my "biscuit knee".

I was in and out of playing netball and doing my degree. I did most of the practical lessons sat on the side with my crutches. For someone who's so physically active all of the time and going from swimming every day after school to playing netball to a high standard, both training and playing games, it was a really difficult thing for me to experience it all from the sidelines. It's like dangling a bone in front of a dog and making them sit there and watch it…torture for me.

I made it to my third year at uni & was selected as both the Social Secretary & the Joint Club Captain & First Team Netball Captain for Edge Hill Netball Club - a MASSIVE achievement for me and something I'm super proud of. Achieving in sport for me is so important. It's always been a huge part of my life and something I strived to be the best at throughout my school and college years, so for it to be acknowledged at University level was a fantastic feeling.

Not only this but I met the love of my life at University too. I never thought I'd find someone so loving and god damn beautiful all rolled into one! Michael changed my body confidence levels dramatically. He had this air of calm about him and made me feel proud of every inch of my body because he sure was. He made me love myself and my body.

Since meeting him, I never questioned my appearance. It wasn't too much about my weight then - I'd put weight on after stopping swimming and became more interested in the gym and eating better foods. It was my boobs - I literally do not care that I have "no boobs". I love them. They are a part of me. They are mine. They make me me. They suit my frame and they suit me. Nobody else has to love them, they're not theirs. What a great feeling to have right?!

So I graduated from Edge Hill University with a degree in PE - BA (Hons) Physical Education 2:1 to be precise! Despite being completely proud of myself, I had no idea that my dream of becoming a teacher was going to be crushed.

The 'road' to teacher wasn't easy. In fact, if I was aware of the 'Law of Attraction' I would have been understanding these 'curve balls' and interpreted them as messages from the universe that it wasn't meant to be. But me being me - a determined young woman - I would do anything I could to be that teacher.

I had two more operations later in life to fix the mess my knee was. A bone graft operation where they would take out the old screws and fill up the hole they drilled in my tibia to attach the new grafts to…meaning I would be spending lots of time in bed unable to weight bare and wearing a sexy knee brace. Frustration really did kick in.

These operations happened during my two years in employment as a 'Cover Supervisor' which is a permanent cover teacher based in the school to cover lessons when teachers aren't in. I would be supervising the class and ensuring they were all focused on their work the teacher had left. Sounds easy. Trust me - IT WASN'T. Children don't want to sit in a classroom and do boring work set by a teacher whilst someone babysits them. Well, 75% of children don't. The ones that did were a dream. They were me when I was at school - a little angel!

After two years of working the same job in two different schools and between that not getting accepted onto a PGCE at Liverpool John Moores University (with my lovely accessories - crutches)…I felt it was time to hang up my boots. Teaching was NOT for me. I admire anyone who teaches. Especially those in Secondary School.

The youth of today know too much. Social Media and T.V. has created mini monsters. Children now don't respect those older than them. In fact, there's only a handful in each class that have any respect full stop. I'm not saying every child and every school is like this but the experience I had put me off. Not only the children, the teachers too. The environment I was in was completely NEGATIVE.

They were ALL stressed. Stressed because they felt restricted in what they were teaching their pupils. The government focusing too much on things that wouldn't matter in the real world. Putting teachers under pressure for results which took all the enjoyment out of teaching.

All my life I had this vision to create the most amazing PE lessons for girls. I wanted to inspire them to be active, to take part in team and individual sports, recognise their strengths and build relationships with their peers. Some of the best friends I have, all came from sporting teams. The bonds you make are incredible. I wanted these girls to experience it too.

Well - these girls aren't interested. Only a handful are. They're so under pressure with snapchat filters, posts on Instagram and Facebook that they forget about real life and what really matters. They were obsessed with what they looked like. Their PE kit didn't exist - instead they had a Make-up kit. Now don't get me wrong, being interested in make up isn't a problem - my nickname at nursery was 'Lipstick Lil' because I'd apply it without a mirror from a mystery lipstick I stole from my mum.

But when I was at school I was at school, I wore vaseline for lipgloss AND mascara. The difference in what girls look like now and the pressure of what they SHOULD look like is immense. It's something I'm really passionate about changing and I will…watch this space.

So, teaching wasn't for me. What the heck do I do with my life now?! I felt lost. I felt down. I felt sad. I felt like I'd let my family down - especially my parents who funded me through university meaning I entered the real world with no debts. I was and am SO grateful for the incredible upbringing I've had - my family are amazing and are a huge part of the person I am today I will never ever forget the experiences and opportunities I've had because of my family. But I felt sick. Sick to my stomach. What can I do? I can't be a failure. But what else can I be? I've never considered anything else?

I worked in a few jobs before finding myself in Network Marketing. Something that has lead me onto the path I'm on today. I didn't realise it at the time but NM was only ever a bridge to bring me to where I am now. I learned a hell of a lot working for myself. I became my own boss. I learned how to motivate myself and others. I learned how to market myself online. I incorporated every adversity I'd been through in life to use in my NM career.

I'd use my tenacity and determination to get back into sports after my countless knee injuries to drive me to be the best I could be in my business. I built a substantial wage and team of people and inspired them to lead a life where they didn't need to limit their beliefs that they could only achieve success in a mainstream job with a boss and a 9-5 structure. I opened my eyes at the possibility of living a 'dream life' and learned so much about myself.

You are always on a constant journey through life and I learned some very tough lessons in my NM career. But remember - you focus on being you and concentrate on your own life and journey and you will be just fine.

I became so savvy with my Social Media. I'd always had an interest in it. I loved showcasing my life online to inspire others. I used it to my advantage and people began following my journey. I loved it, but quickly learned not everyone did. Not everyone can be bothered with it or have the time/knowledge/understanding of what to post and what people want to see.

"one of my most challenging moments in early Business was having thousands of pounds stolen from me by some one I trusted and as a result, made me lose confidence in myself. I doubted myself. I blamed myself. I would question how and why someone would do something like that to to me. From this experience, I would question relationships I had with people. Would they steal from me too? I didn't know how to act. I lost my mojo.

I didn't know who I was, who I wanted to be or what I wanted to be. It had all gone. But I carried on. I had to be brave. I kept on doing it. I ploughed through. I knew I was forcing myself to do it. I wasn't enjoying this period of my business. I couldn't pick myself up to get up and work. It was tough. I felt battered. I felt bruised. It now makes me question my character and how to be around new people. Although this part of my life broke me, it also grew me. I'm slowly getting to the end of that chapter in my life and know I'll become stronger as a result... One thing that I've learned from this unfortunate experience is that you should always surround yourself with people who uplift you. People who want what's best for you. People who genuinely care about you. People who when you've left their presence make you feel fabulous.

Life is way too short to spend time with energy sapping people. You can protect your energy from people and avoid situations like this. Listen to your intuition. Listen to your gut. Be brave enough to trust your gut feeling. You won't be wrong. It's something you will probably have to learn the hard way - but it will be a lesson worth learning in the long run. Once you've experienced a pain like this, you won't want to experience it again. So identifying your gut feeling and being in tune with it will really help you with decisions in later life and in business.

So now I find myself here. Helping the most incredible Female Entrepreneurs have a kick ass Social Media presence which looks beautiful, is authentic and is completely eye catching and on brand. How did I get here?! I had the idea 12 months before I started. I could see my boyfriend working tirelessly running a gym and didn't have time to post any results his Personal Training clients were getting.

What Michael and his business partner have created with IntensiFIT is absolutely brilliant but wasn't being seen by enough people. I offered to help. I knew how to. I knew I was good at it. I knew his results needed to be shown consistently and knew he couldn't do it without my help. Then he opened a healthy eating cafe. Again, he didn't have time to post about the delicious food and tasty snacks. I stepped in. There was something about helping others that set my soul on fire, especially when it's for those who mean a lot to me.

Then, as if by magic, or as I now know it as…DIVINE TIMING, Female Success Network appeared in my newsfeed - I was FLABBERGASTED (love that word). It was JUST what I needed.

It was beautiful, attractive, completely aligned with what I believe in and stand for and I HAD to know more. I contacted Abi and Sarah having previously worked with them both and being fond of their work and congratulated them on how amazing everything looked. I had to be a part of it somehow.

FSN came just as I was thinking about really putting myself out there as a Social Media Manager. I needed their guidance. I knew I did. I didn't know how we'd work together but I really wanted it to happen and it did. Abi and Sarah saw something in me. They knew the potential I had and the potential my business idea had.

They completely TRUSTED me, BELIEVED in me and filled me with the confidence to pursue my dreams. They helped me create 'Stress Free Social Media'. I have tremendous respect for these ladies. They both had businesses and I knew they had hit the jackpot with this amazing idea to help empower women on their own journey to success.

They knew women like me needed the help, guidance, a gentle nudge and strategy to create a successful business and they attracted them. They attracted every single one of us writing a chapter in this book.

They are completely heart lead females who have a passion for helping others and have attracted the exact same women into their Mastermind. I have learned how to run my business successfully, attract my dream client, go from earning absolutely nothing and having zero self confidence and being shattered by my previous experience, to leading a tremendously successful business with so many exciting future plans to scope and scale it.

They knew exactly what to do to help me transform my life. I felt like they actually injected me with life again. I felt like me. They gave me back my identity. I felt confident. I felt inspired. I felt powerful. I felt I had purpose - this was finally what I'd been looking for. I learned that it's okay to be vulnerable. It's okay not to know everything, it's okay to learn as you go, it's okay to be me and it's okay to follow my dreams.

Because of the Female Success Network and Abi & Sarah believing and trusting in my ability by handing over the reigns of the Social Media for FSN, they allowed me to build my business on their successful platform to show Female Entrepreneurs what I could do, and the benefits of what my business had for those who had a business on and offline but needed an online presence.

I started with one client. I now sit confidently and proudly with 17 clients. 17 businesses CAME TO ME. I haven't advertised. They have followed me via word of mouth and the online presence that I have created for myself. 17 businesses believe in me, love my work and WANT to work with me. Quite literally the best feeling in the world to know that so many people have that amount of trust in me.

For me, the success this has brought me has been astronomical. Everyone's version of success is different. Mine is freedom. I have the freedom to live a life on my terms by helping female entrepreneurs. Helping others sets my soul on fire. I've always felt joy by bringing happiness to others. That's what I'm living each day. The more people I can give the 'Stress Free Social Media' experience to, the happier people will be all round!

The personal development I've experienced and the journey I've gone on has completely transformed me as a person. I've been exposed to some incredible women and learned so many important skills and techniques in how to build my business. I have so many tools to choose from and they're all at my fingertips. I've created life long friendships with not only Abi and Sarah but my Unstoppable Sisters. We are united by rising each other and sharing our businesses with the world.

The future excites me. Every day my business grows and with that, so does my confidence. I would absolutely love to be able to have the opportunity to use my Social Media platforms to encourage anyone, especially females and young girls to escape the world of insecurities and self esteem knocks. You are enough.

You will always be enough and you can achieve anything you put your mind to. No matter what life throws at you, or no matter what names you get called, you can still be successful.

Remember that everyone's version is different, so never compare yourself to anyone, Ever. Promise me? Comparing yourself is pointless. Everyone has a different ruler to measure their progress too - you cannot expect to achieve the same as others because you are not them and they are not you.

Be bold in your decision. Don't hold back. Push yourself despite the adversities you go through. Use these challenges you face to make you a stronger person. Use the "failures" you experience as learning curves. Accept them with open arms. Accept them as a positive. You WILL be a better person from it. Never say to yourself that you can't handle things that are thrown to you, because you will never be sent anything you can't handle.

Things happen at the right time, to teach you the lesson you need to learn at THAT time. Be thankful for the lesson and remain positive. Whatever is meant to be WILL be. Divine timing is beautiful. Thank the universe for the experiences you have and always know that if something isn't working out or that relationship broke down or that friend betrayed you, it's because you needed to make room for bigger and better things.

My final message would be that you should NEVER try to change yourself to be something like what you THINK people want you to be like.

"You Do You."

Short but perfectly sweet. You are you and that is what makes you so special. Embrace your body for what it looks like. Embrace your mind for the thoughts it has and embrace your personality for the traits that you have. Love the skin you're in. Love yourself. Take care of yourself.

Be kind to yourself and never pretend to be anyone you're not. You are good enough just the way you are. Embrace your flaws, your skinny legs, your flat chest and your big nose - who cares if that's what people think?! You can still be successful in life and in your own right no matter what you look like. Ignore those opinions as much as you can. Stop believing those opinions others have on you. You're beautiful. You always have been, you always will be.

I've learned a great deal in my 28 years including how to dig deep and overcome obstacles you're faced with in life. Did I let the injuries and operations I went through stop me? NO. I'm playing netball again. Twice a week! I play for two different teams and feel so strong. I go to the gym and squat and lift heavy weights - yes this tiny slim frame! Did I let my crushed dreams of becoming a PE teacher stop me from still trying to help inspire young people?

No - I will carry my passion with me throughout my life and do my very best to teach and inspire positive body image and confidence and Social Media. All you need to do is believe in yourself. You CAN overcome those moments you feel your life is over. You can transform your life and become anything you put your mind to. You can achieve incredible things. Never give up on what you're passionate about.

I aim to positively influence children, young girls, women, anyone with the power of Social Media. I want to change the way people see Social Media as being a negative influence on how it pressures people to look, act, be a certain way. I will show them that they can be anything they want to and don't have to conform to the pressures of society.

I will maintain my happy mission by spreading happiness everywhere I go, including my clients - that award will always stay with me and I will use it in a powerful and life-changing way to help so many others feel happiness. So think about what your version of happiness is. What's your version of success? No matter what comes your way, you're in control of your own happiness and success so make the decisions for you and nobody else.

Stress-Free Social Media has an exciting future...there are so many ideas I have which will be coming very soon..including workshops, an academy and 1-1 mentoring...just a FEW of the things coming. I'll say it now, I'm damn proud of myself. From feeling like I was a failure to building a business up from scratch with such a promising future is just something else! Since I've been writing this chapter I signed two more beautiful clients - the success keeps coming and there's no stopping me now!

So as my chapter comes to a close, I want to send you all so much love and gratitude. Thank you for taking the time to read my journey. Remember to do you without a care in the world and surround yourself with those who love you and support you... you've got this!

Kimberley Banner
Stress-Free Social Media

About Kimberley Banner

Kimberley Banner, Social Media Manager, Blogger & Social Media Influencer is the founder of Stress-Free Social Media. She uses her creative and linguistic skills to help craft an authentic, enthusiastic and beautiful feed which encapsulates her client's perfectly.

She creates engaging captions to engage the audience of their ideal client and matches that with eye catching and on brand images that are both aesthetically pleasing and cohesive. She ensures each client's strong brand and ethos is at the heart of the content created and produced.

Kimberley has a Bachelor of Arts degree in Physical Education and achieved a 2:1. She has used her experiences in her education and career to date to create a successful business from scratch.

Kimberley values personal development and understands the importance of a strong mindset so practises techniques learned in her entrepreneurial journey in order to create her own positive and powerful brand to inspire people on Social Media.

Her mission is to empower females and young girls through Social Media to be a positive influence and show people the power of using Social Media to spread positive messages about self love, body image, confidence and self esteem.

As well as this she wants to help create a Stress Free Social Media experience for business owners across the globe to show them how to create a stand out Social Media profile for their business.

SOCIAL MEDIA LINKS

www.kimberleybanner.com
www.instagram.com/kimberleybanner
www.twitter.com/kimberleybanner
www.facebook.com/KimberleyBannerSocialMediaManager
www.pinterest.com/kimberleybanner19
hello@kimberleybanner.com

Laura Moss

From the Prison Service to accountancy

My stepfather Rick had asked me to work with him on a few occasions, but I had always said no. I couldn't imagine working in accountancy, especially when my dream had been to work in a Prison and I was finally there. The whole idea of a Prison had fascinated me and when I was about 18 years old I used to ask my husband to drive past our local Prison, so I could have a look. Everyone, including my husband thought this was strange.

Little did I know that my dreams, goals and passion would change when I had my eldest son Charlie. When I returned to work after maternity leave, I was travelling to and from work three days a week but just wanting to be back with my little man. It was an hour commute away and to me that was too far.

Rick asked me again if I wanted to come and work for him. This time my ears pricked up and I really thought about the prospect of retraining and being 10 minutes away from home and from Charlie. In 2014, Charlie had a febrile convulsion one evening when I was putting him to bed. I had no idea what it was at time, so it was the scariest thing I have ever seen.

I now know these convulsions are very common and happen when a child has a sudden spike in temperature.
This was the deciding factor for me. I didn't want to be an hour away from home. I wanted to have the work life balance every parent wants. So, I started attending college one evening a week and doing one day a week working for Rick.

Studying with young children

For the next 3 and a half years I studied two nights a week and during the midst of all that revision, exams, up in the night with a toddler and attending college, I had my youngest son and a puppy. I do not know what I was thinking. I don't do things by halves!

I remember on one evening (quite possibly more than one), having just arrived at college to get some revision done, and receiving a call from my mom. Charlie was upset and didn't want to stay with my mom for the night as planned. I just broke down. I sat in the car crying. I felt torn; being a mum and trying to get my qualifications to start building a different career. No question I had to go and get him, cuddle him and take him home. Revision had to wait.

When Henry was only 3 months old I went back to college two nights a week. This was so tough. The brain capacity you need to study versus the 2 hourly feeds through the night was tough. However, I was determined to get this done so I could have my evenings back, enjoy the kids and not feel so exhausted.

Truth bomb here. I failed quite a few of my exams in the final year. I put a lot of pressure on myself but having to retake several exams again was exhausting. It was like doing the year again. So, in May 2017 when I got the email to say I passed my final exam I was elated. I cried with joy. I couldn't quite believe I had done it.

Does this make me a rubbish accountant because I failed some exams? No. It makes me human. This just shows that with determination you can do anything. When obstacles are put in your way you can overcome them. You must have faith.

Being an accountant isn't just about how much you can cram in your brain and perform in an exam. It's about getting to know the individual behind the business, it's about supporting the individual on their journey of Self-employment which can often be a daunting one. Don't get me wrong it took me a while to think like this. I always criticised myself, my abilities and whether I was cut out for this career. Now I know there is more.

But one of the most important factors here is, you must have a team supporting you; my husband who wanted me to defer my last year so Henry was a bit older, but he supported my decision anyway and was a massive support. Without him I wouldn't have been able to go back to college. My sister and my mom who came and helped hubby to do the nights with the boys.

My step father who believed in me and gave me moral support when I had failed another exam but gave me the biggest congratulations when I had passed. My work bestie Debbie who understood what I was going through and who reminded me to stop putting pressure on myself, to remember that my circumstances were different to most and it was going to be harder for me. Debbie supported and was my cheerleader and I will always be so grateful to her.

Working with family
I would be lying if I told you I wasn't sceptical when I started working for Rick. When I was 16 years old I had worked at his office in the summer holidays and it was a challenge for me. Why? Because I was 16 and I didn't like to be told what to do and especially from my parents! I thought I knew best.

I am pleased to say that joining Rick in my 20s has been the best decision I have ever made. I have grown up and I am also more mature in his eyes as well, and our relationship has changed so much over the years because of this. Don't get me wrong, I still get told off for not doing the washing up in the office, so not everything has changed!

The experience of working with family is a different one. It is amazing for me having such young children because it has given me flexibility and understanding. When the boys aren't well there is no feeling of guilt that you would get if you were telling your employer. Rick understands as they are his grandchildren, so he wants the best for them too. What an incredible feeling. I am so lucky.

There is already a trust. Unlike any other job you don't need to build up the trust when you first start out in a new job. Its already there. He has trusted me with one of the things that is most important to him, his business, and that is an honour and something I will be eternally grateful for. We both have the same goals, the same special people we want to support and work hard to make it happen.

How it all started
In 2014 when I joined Rick at his business, Smart Accountants Ltd, we decided that perhaps there was another area we could explore with accounts. The online world. The world is forever changing, and people are becoming more tech savvy and want things to be even easier.

Smart Online Accountants Ltd was created for just that reason. To reach a wider audience, to make accounts affordable and stress free all online. The idea was that new clients would sign up online, send their paperwork in a prepaid envelope and we would complete their accounts.

Our business still has this vision, but it is now so much more. Our clients have helped us develop and change certain aspects to suit them.

The unsung hero
When it comes to Smart Online Accountants everyone thinks of me. The last thing Rick wants is to be plastered all over social media however I do think it's important to introduce him. To let people, know that without him this business wouldn't have been possible. Without him supporting me in more ways than one, this dream of mine I am living would be non-existent.

Rick has been in this industry for over 30 years and is a fountain of knowledge, but he has let me take the reins and trusted in what I am doing which is incredible. The online world is not something he has a huge part in, but he knows it's something I am part of. The online world is the way of bringing our business into the 21st century which has been how our business has grown. It's not something Rick wants to be a part of but a way that we will survive and compete.

What was my mission? How has it changed?
When we first started the business, our mission was to reach clients all over the country. We wanted to provide a more modern way of completing people's accounts. This has not changed but we have learnt so many things along the way.

My clients are 90% females, which I didn't intentionally target, however I can relate to women which is a huge part of it. Most of my clients are just starting out in business, have never had to pay their own tax or submit a tax return. This brings with it many questions which is great and what I am good at.

Although our mission remains the same, it is also now to try and reach as many female entrepreneurs that we can to reassure them about their accounts. Let them know it doesn't need to be stressful and cause sleepless nights. You just need the right support. A guiding hand. And someone to cut out the jargon and tell you what to do.

Often my clients need a step by step guide on where to start, what to include as a business expense and what the processes are. I love to help them feel more comfortable with where they are at with their accounts, reassure them and allow them to feel like a weight has been lifted. When you run your own business it can be stressful, there are many plates to spin and what we do allows my clients to have some time back (some room left in the brain to focus on other things) and concentrate on their passion, the family and themselves.

Don't be afraid if your mission changes. If your ideal client isn't what you originally thought. Listen to the feedback your clients give you, what they need and make changes when you need to. You and your business will grow so things are bound to change.

My mission hasn't changed dramatically but it has expanded.

I hated maths
When I was at school I hated maths. I know surprising from an accountant. But my step father tutored me through school to help me through my GCSE's. So why am I telling you this?

Because I want you to step into your power like I have over the last 12 months. Katie Helliwell, friend client and coach, helped me realise this. She has encouraged me to tell my story.

Be relatable. All the things I have thought would hold me back in my business have been the things that people relate to. I don't proclaim to be a mathematician, yet people always say, 'you should know this Laura you're an accountant'. Funny enough when I was studying for my AAT qualification I was not randomly asked throughout the exam what 50 divided by 12 was! Rick always said to me 'your job is not to add up but to interpret numbers'.

What I have learnt throughout my journey in being in business, and especially in the accounting industry, is that when people come to you to sign up to your services or ask for advice, they don't ask to see your CV as well. People use their intuition. They trust and get to know you.

This is why I love my job. I love to get to know the person behind the business and learn about their story. How they got started. How they started. I can relate because I have set up a business, I am working part time, I have two small children and I have had a huge career change.

How I grew my business
The only way I was going to be able to grow my business was to get some help and support. One of the earlier things I learnt in my business is that you cannot be good at everything and you certainly cannot do it alone. You need help and support. That is certainly what I found when I decided to make a change.

The start of my business growth began when I decided to invest in myself and my business. I used to look at business coaches and think 'I cannot justify that money' or 'what results will I even see in my business if I invest'.

When you have a business, or even if you don't, if you know things need to change and you aren't getting anywhere fast, take a leap. Trust yourself and invest in making improvements. Nothing will change if nothing changes.

Female Success Network mastermind (my secrets out)
In September 2017 I joined the Female Success Network mastermind group. Not everyone knows I invested money in it, mainly because I didn't think they would understand and may try and talk me out of it. My husband tried.
I now feel so confident in the decision I am happy to shout it from the rooftops. I am proud that I took a leap and it has been an amazing journey.

As soon as I saw Abigail and Sarah had created this amazing space, my gut told me I needed to be part of it. I decided to take a leap, go with my gut, and sign up. It was the BEST decision I have made so far in business. Why?

Stepping out
Abi and Sarah helped me to create Laura Moss and you. A brand that made me step out from behind my Smart Accountants logo and show people the face behind it. I urge everyone to step out. Stop hiding behind your logo; do live videos, tell your story and be relatable.

I didn't want to change the name of our business because I am so proud of how it came about. I am proud that my step father took a leap of faith and asked me to join him. I am proud I can carry it on for him and hopefully do him proud.

But I knew as a female entrepreneur myself that using Laura Moss and you, would be more appealing to other like-minded women in business. This decision was to attract my ideal client. Show people there is more to me than the logo and that I am not in fact your stereotypical accountant.

Investing in me
I invested in myself and my business for the first time ever. And this was the start of realising that I need to put myself first. I am the business and the business will only be as successful as I feel. As my confidence has grown in the last year so has my business. I believe in myself and my business and what it can do for people.

This has helped me with business but also with me, my life and those who surround me. It has led me onto investing in other things which I am soooo excited about.
But one of the main reasons, I now know how important it is to look after me first is because it will then make me;

The best mum to my boys
The best wife to my hubby
The best daughter
The best friend
The best sister

My journey
I have always been a positive person. My mom has always said 'there is always someone worse off than you' and that has stuck with me. Such an important thing to think of when you are feeling down.

However, since I started my business I have learnt so much about mindset, mental health and how this has such a huge impact on your business. I always used to scroll past posts on social media about mental health awareness, thinking it didn't relate to me. How wrong was I.

Our mental health, what we tell ourselves, is crucial to the person we become but more importantly how our children are brought up. This is my biggest lesson so far in this journey and I am determined to ensure my children have all the tools in place to be the happiest they can be.

If I was starting over, what would I tell myself?

Value yourself
When I first started out in business I was charging a monthly fee of £20 per month. I don't regret this decision, but I soon saw that I didn't value myself. My prices were too low. As I was starting out this was a great place to start but by pricing yourself too low can sometimes put people off as well. Why are her services so cheap? On the other hand, you can't increase your prices suddenly so its important to increase prices gradually or at least in line with inflation. This is to be expected in most businesses. It's vital for all businesses to increase their prices otherwise you are decreasing your prices and losing money.

A wonderful lady, Sarah Morgan, recently told me to look at things in a different way. Instead of looking at what service you provide and the outcome your client gets, start to think about how your service has made them feel. That is a powerful way of looking at it and a way that has truly helped me.

When you start out in business you don't often value your services correctly. You don't value your time, the extra support you provide or the impact you have had on someone's life. That is powerful!

Now I absolutely appreciate the affect I have on my client's life. It may sound dramatic, but I have witnessed how stressed someone has been when we first had a phone call. I have seen their face as their brain races with thoughts and questions. But then I have been over joyed at the look of relief at the end of our phone call. Something that once caused them sleepless nights, has now been removed and they are totally reassured that someone has it in hand for them. What an amazing feeling.

In the last 12 months I have increased my prices, twice in fact. It took me a long time to feel comfortable in increasing them. My whole mission has been to be affordable to people. The last thing I want is for someone to be put off from starting their own business due to the cost or stress of completing your accounts.

I was also so concerned about my current clients. I will be eternally grateful for their business, for believing in me and my services when sometimes I had doubt. But for me to offer them the best service I need to increase my prices. It's not sustainable to continue charging such low prices as my clients increase and inevitably overheads increase.

If people around you are telling you to increase your prices, then they are usually right. Those who are your ideal clients will completely understand. They will support you and appreciate that you are now going to be charging your worth. Start to think about how you change their lives. Change the way they feel and help support their business.

You can't serve everyone
In 2014 I remember starting to write down all the types of businesses that Self-employed people had. Plumbers, electricians, dog walkers, beauticians…But I didn't get far. I did not appreciate the amount of industries this covers. And I also thought I could serve everyone.

It is impossible to serve everyone. I cannot reach the 4.6 million Self-employed people in this country, or whatever that figure is now, and neither would I want to (I want a life ha-ha). Focus on what your ideal client looks like and write a list. This helps you focus and makes you feel ok when someone decides not to use your services.

I would often feel a bit deflated when someone decided to go elsewhere. I would wonder what I was doing wrong, what I could have said differently. This can come across as desperate though as well. But also, they were more than likely not your ideal client.

I have now realised that I am not for everyone and everyone is not for me. And that's ok.

Don't compare. Be inspired.
I was forever comparing myself to other accountancy practices. Why are they doing so well? How did they get so many clients? I am so jealous of their branding. They look so professional.

I remember reading a quote a while ago that really resonated with me. 'Don't compare your chapter 1 to someone else's chapter 20.' How true is that. We are always comparing our journeys to someone else's, but they are so different, so they aren't comparable.

Not one business is the same. No other business has you in it and you bring something different to it. I hated maths, I am no good with my own money and for ages I brushed those little facts under the carpet. But now I own it. I appreciate that it makes me different, relatable and real. I am so happy to have stepped into my power, show others they should to. Someone will relate to you and be inspired by you doing what they haven't yet had the courage to do.

Social media has been amazing for me. I wouldn't have the business I have now if it wasn't for social media and the wonderful technology we must reach clients across the country.

However, it also makes it even harder not to compare to others. It's always in your face, but don't forget, people post what they want you to see. Don't compare the outside of someone's business and what they show you to the inside of your business; the nitty gritty, the figures and the money.
As soon as I stopped comparing myself to others around me my business flew. I was able to concentrate on what I was doing instead of watching what's going on around me.

Remember what success looks like to you
One of the first things that really stopped me in my tracks when I joined FSN was that success is different to everyone. One person's success could be measured by a large house, an expensive car or luxury holiday. Another's success could be happy children, feeling fulfilled and happy. No success is right or wrong, its personal to you but just don't forget it.

So, when you are looking at someone on social media with their brand-new car just remember that may be their version of success but is it yours?

To me I will feel successful when I am financially independent. When I can treat the ones I love to holidays, meals and gifts. Success to me is brining up my children to be kind, happy and the best version of themselves. This leads nicely into….

Remember your why
My why is not to be a multi-millionaire. Firstly, my why is my children and my family. I want to provide a comfortable life for them but to also be able to save for their future. But I also want to support my step-father and my mum. To treat them to holidays as they done for us over the years. Their happiness is my why.
My why is also to prevent stress and overwhelm when it comes to accounts. So, if I see something that I am doing that isn't in aligned with my why, I stop and rethink.

The best is yet to come
Now that I am armed with all these new lessons and tools I can grow our business even further. Don't get me wrong I have learnt and am still learning many lessons as my clients have over doubled. My processes need to be tighter, I need to outsource more work and I need to be strict with my time to prevent overwhelm and continue to have the work life balance I want.

The future for me is continue my self-love journey. To study more into the Law of Attraction and how that can help me lead my happiest life plus learn more about the spirit world and how they can guide you in all areas of your life.
My main drive in life is my children. Teaching them to lead their happiest life, have tools throughout my life to help them in times of upset/fear or worry. And to teach them that they can do ANYTHING.

Smart Online Accountants will continue to grow, I have no doubt. I know there are more women out there that I can help. More women that need to feel supported and know there is another way. But I don't want to make my millions through this. You think I am crazy I am sure, but my passion and aim is to provide affordable accounting and to get to know my clients, their story and support them. To ensure I create this dream of mine, I don't want so many overheads that I must increase my prices, I lose focus and I don't know the people that are supporting me in my life.

I feel like I have more to give in this world. So, watch this space.

About Laura Moss

Laura Moss is an accountant supporting female entrepreneurs across the UK with their accounts. She specialises in changing the feeling of stress and anxiety often related to accounts to feeling like someone has their back.

After graduating from University with a Law degree she always thought her journey was set out for her. But her career path changed dramatically when she became a mum in 2012. Her priorities changed, and she wanted a better work life balance. That lead onto to her finding her passion and creating her business Smart Online Accountants Ltd with her Stepfather 4 years ago.

In 2017 Laura completed her AAT qualification and as her confidence grew so did her business. As she launched Laura Moss and you, to show everyone the face behind the business, her business rocketed in 2018 because she stepped out and told her story. Her passion shines through as she supports her clients in not just accounts but in other areas of business.

Laura is on now mission to support more female entrepreneurs; reducing their stress, preventing sleepless nights and cutting out the jargon to create an better understanding of the complex world of accountancy.

Email: lauramossandyou@gmail.com

FEMALE SUCCESS NETWORK

Website: www.lauramossandyou.co.uk

Facebook: www.facebook.com/lauramossandyou

Instagram: www.instagram.com/lauramossandyou

Laura Rhian Warren

Did I ever grow up thinking I was going to be an Entrepreneur? A Business Owner? Not at all!

In fact, I remember the day that the idea of being a business owner was put to me. I had just completed my time as a Lacrosse Sport Scholar at the University of Maryland in May 2004. I was twenty-two years old. A month after coming home to the UK, I jetted off on a round the world trip, partly on my own, partly with friends, mixed in with visiting my Australian family and Australian Team mates who had shared the American College experience with me.

We were visiting Fremantle in Perth where we randomly walked past a little shop that was offering 'Readings.' My friend Zoe and I had a chuckle and went and gave it a go, and to this day I cannot believe how accurate that lady was in her reading. I was told that I would be owning my own business by the age of twenty-six. At that point all I knew was that I would be returning to the UK to complete a PGCE in PE. At the time I thought it a waste of money and thought nothing more of it.

Eighteen months passed, and I was working at a 'Curves' ladies' fitness centre to finance my spot on the Welsh Lacrosse Team for the 2005 World Cup in Annapolis; Id just completed a PGCE in PE and an NQT year. Then on 8th October 2007, two days before my 26th birthday, (yes you guessed it), I became a business owner. Myself and partner Simon became Franchise owners of Curves Ladies Fitness Centre. We went on to own a second one the following year.

I spent from 2007 until the day before the birth of my first son Louis in October 2012, working almost every waking day in our gyms. I absolutely loved it! I didn't really do any of the admin and money matters, I took care of the fitness and 'Member experience' side of the business. That is where I learnt my first business lesson. You need to have a product and a solution that people want to buy; but people also buy into the person offering that product.

Without blowing my own trumpet, I'm genuinely one of the most modest personalities you will find; when I was working face to face with the members the club was busy. People were coming in because of my workouts, and the way I made them feel. So, it doesn't matter how much competition is out there, you must be YOU!

I myself have experienced a situation where our unique concept and business was for want of a better word 'ripped off' and duplicated within a close proximity of our gym. At first, I felt angry that we had been used to get our knowledge and system.

However, we spoke with a mentor who knew how unique my personality was, and she said to keep offering my positive energy within my club and that the copycat club will not make it past two years.

So, we kept our focus positive by serving our members with our uniqueness, and our club flourished and thrived. I actually did feel sad for the lady in question as I always want people to succeed, but proud that we had not given in.

That leads me on to another value I follow. Excuse my language, but when shit happens, I let it be just that. The first thing that comes into my mind is "that sucks but right, what do I need to do to either amend this, improve this or get the hell out of it?" I won't moan or blame, I just find a way to solve it. Next I think "this has happened for a reason, I may not know why now, but I trust and believe I will know soon."

I am still unsure if I believe whether there is someone out there watching over me, signs, and the other world. But what I do know is that thinking this way has worked and has allowed me to deal with things that most people would not be able to deal with.

So, as I mentioned, Louis, our first-born arrived in 2012, five years after we opened the Clubs. They were five years living and breathing everything to do with the Clubs and because of that they were very successful. I am so thankful that Louis is here as he has changed my life for the better, he is the one reason that my routine changed, and I stopped 'living' in the Clubs.

After Louis arrived, I took a short two and a half months off before I returned to work three days a week. Not only was I working the Club, I was also trying to train to get fit for a Lacrosse International Tournament and a World Cup. Louis was aged three months and eight months at those two events. With trying to do it all I felt massive 'mummy guilt.

I wanted to quit everything because I felt like I needed to be with Louis 24/7. Thankfully the Welsh Coaching staff were incredible and allowed me to take Louis on tour to America with the team and to the World Cup. I could write a book on just that experience alone!

I remember sitting in my Manager's car in freezing, snowy, ice-covered Princeton watching my team mates warm up. Louis wanted a boob of milk and I was the only one with a boob full of milk! I remember taking him off when he had finished, shoving him to the Manager and then fleeing off to play with basically no warm up. I remember having a mental breakdown on one of the game days as we were trying to leave the hotel. I was so exhausted from feeding in the night and then having to express ready for the games and then packing and unpacking.

I laugh as I look back at it. I remember my Teammate Gill having to help as he vomited and completely pooed through his clothes at take off. I have so many special memories from that time. We experienced so much in Louis' first eight months of life. He has been with me to tour with Wales in America, stayed with me the whole of the Lacrosse World Cup in Canada, and has come to Paris to meet me as I completed the gruelling London to Paris Bike Ride.

Louis can't remember any of it, nor will he remember being passed from stranger to stranger, travelling thousands of miles to trainings, competitions and he doesn't remember me being away from him. So, lesson learnt here. Don't not do things when you have a small baby because you worry that your child will grow up not quite right or angry with you.

In fact, Louis will now go to people easily. We can leave him with people he may not know very well and he is confident, he always feels safe and secure and knows he is loved. When you ask him if Mummy should play lacrosse or stop, his answer is always 'Mummy play!'.

If I ask him why, he will say because he gets Nanny time or Daddy time and that he likes Mummy and her friends winning. So you see, following your hobbies or career can work in your favour.

Ok, so after that exhausting first year of being a mum, I realised that just working in the gyms wouldn't give me the life balance I wanted as a mother. I still wanted to work but the stress of having Clubs that relied on staff made me want to look into finding another way to fulfill what we needed.

By March 2013 I felt like things had gone a bit stagnant. Previously I had achieved something every year. In 2004 I graduated as a Sports Scholar from Maryland, travelled the World and coached lacrosse in Australia.

In 2005 in Annapolis during the World Cup I made the All World Team, and spent the summer working Sports Camps and travelling. In 2006 I completed my NQT. In 2007 I opened gym number one and was Assistant Coach at the Lacrosse U19 World Cup. In 2008 I opened gym number two. In 2009 during the World Cup in Prague I again made the All World Team. In 2011 I qualified as a Zumba instructor. In 2012 I became a mum and gained more fitness qualifications.

As you can see, I was in the habit of always wanting to achieve something new each year. Link that with being a mum and having the guilt of not seeing my son because of work and training; I took up an opportunity to be a Network Marketer so that I could spend more time at home.

I did extremely well at the start, building a team and great customer base, earning over £2000 a month from that part time business. But over time, for one reason or another, I fell out of love with it. I loved the products and I could see that the business model really did work. But something kept telling me that this business 'wasn't for me'. I wanted something I was passionate about and so I found myself looking for something else.

Now fast forward to November 2015, six months after baby number two arrived. I had one of those 'Laura' moments, when something comes into my mind and I just 'do it.' I had retired from International Lacrosse in 2013 the day after my fourth World Cup with the aim of simply being a mum and working in the gyms.

Anyway, I picked up the phone and called the Welsh Lacrosse Coach and said I would like to come back to the team. That was it. I had to prepare this postpartum 33 year old body to be able to compete at an International standard again. But how the hell was I going to do it? I had a six month old and a newly three year old.

I had a partner who worked irregular hours and I also wanted to contribute more to the household bills etc. So, I simply started to make my own workout videos. I had to find ways to fit in exercise; I would not use 'no time' as an excuse, even though I was super busy helping run six businesses and run our household!

I faced every obstacle a mum could face and often failed at overcoming them all, so once again I had to keep working until I found solutions.

Things such as childcare; I was lucky to have help with childcare but I used it up for work and playing Welsh Lacrosse . This meant I would feel too guilty giving the kids away again just to keep fit. So, I had to find a way to workout either in the home, outside with my kids in tow, or when they didn't need me, which (regardless of the time and how tired I felt) was at night when they were asleep, or early morning before they woke up. I also wanted an exercise class that I could take Toby to. I actually found a good one but I missed the workouts as I spent the time feeding or trying to keep him in the buggy and would leave feeling annoyed I hadn't worked out.

I looked at home workouts. With the kids home, Dad away and the baby needing to be fed, being at home was a common occurrence. So home became my main location for workouts. Videos on YouTube were great but you either needed equipment, or workouts were too long or didn't describe what the outcome of the video was. I ended up spending hours finding one workout that would be suitable. I quickly realised that I needed to copy a workout that was made by a person that knew what stage my body was at and adjust that to my current fitness level, especially as I was a new mum. And there was no person better than me to do that!

Time was a major issue for me. A lot of online fitness videos were out there, but none catered for the time I had. They were either 20-40 minutes long, too intense or too easy. I worked out that twelve minutes was my ideal time; I could work really hard during that period and still have time to get my other jobs done.

I felt guilty all the time; guilty for not playing with the kids, guilty for not cooking their food from scratch, guilty for going to work. But I learnt that I also felt guilty if I was tired and snappy. I knew that if I exercised for 2-12 minutes I would feel happier and more energetic almost instantly which meant I would be a happier and more playful mum towards my boys.

Motivation and Support: I had no mum friends who wanted to keep fit and as I was so busy I didn't get time to take the boys to baby/toddler groups. I yearned for an exercise program that covered everything at once - exercise that allowed mums to workout, allowed time for children to play, allowed mums to bond during and post-class and get to socialise and make friends over a cuppa after class.

People would constantly comment on how much energy I had, or ask how did I keep so fit? Friends would often ask for advice. I found myself naturally wanting to help, and before I knew it I was starting my first solo business on line at www.fitmuma.uk. My mission was, and still is, to show busy mums different ways to keep fit physically and mentally without feeling guilty.

This business started out of nowhere. I remember searching for name ideas and asking my Facebook friends which of my ideas they liked. I found a logo, set up a Facebook group and

I shared it with friends. That was the birth of the six week Summer Home Workout Program and it was a huge success, so I kept the idea and adapted it.

Then I thought 'sod it', I am going to start some classes. I knew in my head what would work for women as I had worked it out whilst running our gyms. Women needed a one-stop place to work out. Somewhere that could provide them with an exercise class, a place to get measurements, set goals, have a food plan, socialise, and also make it an experience for their child too.

With all that on offer there would be no need to go to a fitness class and then pay more to go to a slimming class. I also knew that going to one exercise class a week would not be enough. That is why I combine the online workout programme with the classes and personal training sessions I do. They get accountability by seeing the instructor and friends at a class, and also get work to do at home.

It was and still is a great programme because it solves many of the problems that mums face. Don't they always tell you to have a successful business product which needs to be a solution to a problem? Well I had found the solution. Mums have no childcare to worry about. We provide nanny helpers within the class so the children can come and exercise with them. The videos also allow them to workout at home with the children.

Mums have no time: our weekly online Busy Mums Home Workout Academy videos are twelve minutes long. This was a magic number to me in my training for a world cup. It was short enough so that I would still be able to do the house chores, and also short enough that I could motivate myself to do it. The dishes could wait 12 minutes, right? But 12 minutes is also long enough to get my heart rate up if necessary.

Guilt: the children come and have fun at the classes too. You don't need to walk through the door at work and hand baby over again. You bring them to class or you do the home workout with them. We teach you mental coping techniques to help you to understand that your kids NEED you to look after yourself.

No money: our mums don't need a gym or any equipment.

Exercising safely: there are so many so called 'postnatal courses' out there, but many don't pre-screen you and simply give you exercises that are going to cause more harm than good. I learnt that the hard way. So I trained and qualified with who I believe to be the most in-depth training provider on women's pelvic health, Holistic Core Restore.

Being self-employed has been and still is a rollercoaster. You have great days and then you have tough days. There are days when the outside world may perceive you as winning, and some days when they may perceive you as losing.

You see, there is a trait I have and it's a damn good one to have. I never fail. I may have a project or task or business that may not be giving the results I wanted, but that doesn't mean I have failed. To me failing is giving up and I never give up.

The way you deal with so-called 'failing' is a make or break in your success in life. Some see 'failure' as not reaching a target or desired outcome, but to me 'failure' means that I have not learnt from the experience.

What I also don't do is 'blame.' I can't bear blaming someone or something for a failure. If something you are in overall charge of has not worked out, when it comes down to it, it is simply your fault. The sooner you understand this as a business person, sports person, or person in general, your life will become more successful. Hold yourself accountable.

As we are talking about 'perceived' failure I want to say *"don't ever base a decision on fearing people will think you are a failure"*.

Something that hugely stands out in my memory is the closure of the first gym that we opened. We should have closed it sooner but kept it going because of the incredible community we had built. In truth I was also scared of what people would think. Back then I didn't want people to think we had failed. I'm fine telling you now that at the time people were horrible to us about the closure:

I had people ignoring me in the street, people coming up to me and telling me 'rumours' that had got to them about the closure which were completely fabricated. But what I learnt was that it *doesn't really matter what people think*. The truth is that if I really had wanted to put my heart and soul into that club, I could have made it work and it would still be running successfully today.

Instead I connected to my core values and the most important role was and still is being a mum. Continuing to run two gyms from such a distance as we were doing meant that we weren't having time with our sons. When we were home with them we were continuously worrying about what work needed doing; it was draining on our family time and we needed to put ourselves first for once and the right decision was to close that club.

As I write this, I think about my times in the gyms and working as a network marketer. I think about my times as a boss, the good and the bad. I learnt so much from those initial eight years; owning those two franchised clubs helped make me the person I am today.

I have learnt that communication is vital and you should never just ASSUME anything. You need to be clear with your thoughts, visions and tasks. You need to remember that other people not only learn in different ways, but also see things differently. Explain what you need and ask them to clarify their understanding; questions are good for this.

I have learnt that you should be clear on your expectations from the start for with staff and clients alike, as this builds trust, it's the same for promises. Try not to over promise or under-deliver as people will lose respect for you.

You need to create a community that feels part of your tribe. Give people ownership and responsibilities to help make them feel worthy and important. You know you have created a good tribe when they stand by you and are your voice.

The best bosses are the ones that lead by example and know their staff. If you work in the business you inspire but when you don't work in the business staff can start to hold grudges and see you more as the enemy which leads to less efficient working.

The same can be said about obstacles and challenges. There are two kinds of people. Firstly, the ones who hide from challenges and like to blame poor results on other people or events. These are the ones that give up as soon as obstacles arise, or as soon as someone tells them something negative about what they are doing.

Secondly, there are people that thrive on challenges and perceived 'failed' events. I have had challenges at home and in life that most people would not bounce back from and I am proud that I have pushed on regardless.

Before I start getting upset or feeling down about an incident, I will tell myself straight away *"this has happened for a reason"*.

It may be to make me stronger or to teach me something, or to even keep me from making a mistake that I might regret.

I am exactly the same when a challenge is set for me. Whether someone has told me I can't do something or that something is going to be difficult, I will want to prove him or her wrong.

In 2017 at the Lacrosse Home International Tournament between Wales, England and Scotland (it was three months before my fifth World Cup), I found myself with less playing time than I was used to. I'd had a difficult time with ankle injuries and was slow getting back to full form.

I felt that I had sacrificed so much to play; not only did it cost me thousands of pounds to play but I had severe 'mummy guilt' because of the time I was going to be away from my children during the upcoming World Cup and World Games. I had been picked to play for Wales at the World Cup from 8-22nd July and then for Great Britain at the World Games in Poland from 22nd-30th July. So, I was going to be away from my two sons for twenty-two plus days. I did not want to be away from my sons just to watch the games from the sidelines.

I had three choices. To get angry at my coaches for not playing me (but it wasn't their fault, it was mine as I wasn't performing), to quit Lacrosse or to SHOW THEM. I knew what I was capable of, I just had to believe I could get to the standard I needed to be at so I could get back on that field.

I thank my absolute lucky stars for finding an incredible Physiotherapist and friend in Sean Connelly; he spent three solid months working with me to rehab my ankles and get my fitness and confidence back up to scratch. I went on to get not only the time on the fields that I wanted, but was also honoured to receive a Most Valuable Player award. Without Sean's help I know I wouldn't have done it.

Now I know that is sport, but it is the same in business. Don't let people dictate what you do. If you are told it's just a dream to want to run a business, then turn up and SHOW THEM that you can do it. Secondly, seek out the help and tools from people who could help you.

Whilst Sean was my mentor in the sports world, in August 2017 I turned to Female Success Network for my business guidance. Thankfully they saw the potential in me immediately and working with them has been an absolute joy. I honestly believe that my business would have stagnated but for their involvement and guidance over the last year.

Since I joined the amazing ladies within FSN and the Mastermind group I have won Working Mum of the Year, been shortlisted for South Wales Personal Trainer, Fitness Class and Fitness Entrepreneur of the Year. I have gone from running face-to-face classes to a monthly online membership and full day 'Retreats', as well as providing personal training for women.

I am about to start Year Two of the Mentorship by adding three more businesses to my portfolio. One is a business focused on Women's Pelvic Health; it is scary how many women think 'leaking' is normal or don't know how to check if they have diastase recti! I will be networking with local health professionals with a view to becoming the local provider of education and exercise on pelvic function.

I am really excited about a new business involving girls and sport. Sport offers so much more than just physical activity; it can help equip you for life and my sole aim is to inspire girls to take up sport for life.

I will be offering a platform and raising awareness of female athletes to inspire girls to aim for top level sport, looking for the 'athletes of the future' and helping them to get scholarships overseas. I am looking forward to working with a friend from FSN (www.alisongoodwin.co.uk) on these exciting businesses.

As I said before, a business idea needs to be based on your passion; can you tell that sport is mine?

I've been fortunate enough to be surrounded by some incredible athletes and trainers who taught me some valuable lessons which I have brought from the sports field to the business world.

The most memorable thing for me came from our Sports Psychologist during my time on the famous Maryland Women's Lacrosse programme on a scholarship. I remember sitting in a room within the Sports Complex surrounded by some of the top players and coaches within the sport.

I remember, hearing the words *"take it moment by moment, step by step"*. In sports' terms that mean you do not think about the outcome of the game; if you do you become distracted from the task at hand.

Let me give you an example; in a game of sport, if a ball is coming your way, you just need to focus on catching the ball and then what your best move with the ball will be. You should only think and focus your attention on what that one thing is, what you need to do in that one moment to move towards your desired goal. If you relate that to business, you simply need to focus on doing one thing at a time but do it, no procrastination; you need to treat it with the respect it deserves so that you focus on the 'now'.

In sport you learn repetition and visualisation and this can be a huge benefit in business. I'm going to admit that I like to watch videos of lacrosse moves. I will then close my eyes and picture myself doing a particular move over and over again, and lo and behold I will then find myself doing it exactly the same in games and matches. I do this mental visualization before important meetings, retreats and talks and it never fails me. It makes me feel more confident as I have already played everything in my head.

As a teenager playing at International Level in two Sports from the age of 14 years, I was taught 'practice, practice and practice' until you could do the skill with your eyes closed, until that skill became part of your make-up and until you could do that skill habitually. I believe that I succeed because I will only take the 'non comfort zone' option. In sport I will practice the skill I know I am not good at, and likewise in business I will only say yes to a task that scares me; after all that's how we learn.

One of the best habits I have is exercising. You are most probably thinking 'how does this help you be successful in work and business?' Well, in my eyes exercise is the answer to everything. Think back to a time when you had a good workout. Think about how you felt? I am guessing you felt less stressed, energised, proud, motivated, and you had clarity.

Now think back to a time when you felt stressed, tired, moody, grumpy and you couldn't think straight or come up with ideas. I bet your half hour job took two hours, or maybe you've just had to read this line ten times before it went into your head? Now tell me if I am wrong but, am I right in thinking you hadn't been exercising or getting any fresh air or eating well?

Exercise makes you feel BETTER and that in turn makes you happier and more confident; you not only deal with situations better, but you are more productive. It is no coincidence that exercise stimulates your brain and you're therefore more creative with improved memory recall; it also helps with confidence. A confident person will attract more positive people, it's that simple.

My 'productivity' secret therefore must be exercise and self-care. Even with incredible planning to create time to work, if my mind is not awake and motivated then no 'good' work gets done. I always have workouts that I can do in the office or when I'm out and about which can be fitted into my daily routine. I also work optimally when I have eaten well (balanced, unprocessed meals that don't give me sugar peaks), when I'm adequately hydrated, have plenty of fresh air, sleep well and of course when I have exercised.

I firmly believe you should surround yourself with like-minded people and for the past couple of years I've been working in elite sport with women who share the same passions and belief systems as me. Without question, when I surround myself with my teammates I work harder and am more motivated. This applies to business as well.

All told I have been self-employed since the age of 26 years, but it has been lonely. It's hard for employed friends to understand self-employed life or understand the struggles that go with it. It often feels that people think because I am self-employed I am cash-rich but like any business or job there are financial struggles; of having to balance life demands, or having to deal with difficult and rude clients and staff; the difficulty of never being able to switch off. To keep going, I knew I needed to surround myself with people who wanted to learn and who wanted to work on their business. Thankfully that is when I came across Female Success Network.

The best thing that has come from being part of a group, is being surrounded by like-minded people. People that are driven and people that have great core values and people who want you to succeed.

I have attended many events, training sessions and network meetings over the years through the work I have done. These have included the times I owned a couple of franchises with Curves Ladies Fitness Centers, sessions with a multi-level marketing company I worked with, and finally events within the fitness industry.

They all seemed to center around 'ego' places where women have wanted to outshine others regardless of how they act in the process; where women have formed cliques and not included others; where people act and speak as if they want you to do well, but don't really want you to do well at all because they fear that you may outshine them.

The group of women at FSN is different; there is no competition, everyone wants you to succeed. They treat your business as if it were their own. They aren't afraid to tell the world about you and often set you up with opportunities that have no benefit to them. They do not judge; your wins are their wins and your losses are theirs too.

My last bit of advice is typically FSN and that is having the 'JUST DO IT' attitude. The worst feeling in the world is regret. If you have an idea, or a hobby, or want to speak to someone then please just do it! What do you have to lose? Absolutely nothing!

So please, go. Go and do whatever it is that you want. Get the ball rolling and then get in touch and let me know how it went.

Sending love, gratitude and positive energy your way

Laura

x

(and a big shout out and massive 'thank you' to my family for always loving me and making it possible for me to follow my sporting and business loves.)

Laura Rhian Warren

Laura is an inspiring International sports loving, energetic entrepreneur, multiple business owner and mother of two beautiful boys Louis and Toby. She has a passion for showing other women the value exercise can have across all areas their life.

Laura shows that motherhood nor age should be seen as an obstacle.

She believes that every woman can follow her dreams regardless of life's hurdles. She believes that exercise can be the answer to almost every problem anyone faces, and therefore she aims to get as many people involved as possible! Laura demonstrates that even the busiest of people can be the healthiest versions of themselves.

Laura has vast experience and knowledge of everything exercise and wellness related, for everyone from the unfit to the elite.

She graduated as a Sports Scholar from the University of Maryland with a degree in Kinesiological Sciences, before moving on to complete a PGCE and NQT in PE Teaching. Laura has many fitness qualifications ranging from a Level 3 Personal trainer to female fitness as a Holistic Core Restore Coach.

Laura has over 14 years' experience of working in female fitness industry through Personal Training and having owned 2 Ladies Fitness Centres and now a new gym www.Fitin30.life with Business Partner Sharon.

She is the founder of fitmuma.uk, inspiring mums to take care of themselves physically, mentally and guilt free.
Laura shows mums the 'I can attitude' and teaches that 'taking care of themselves is part of taking care of the family.'

Laura has represented Wales, as both a Coach and a player in Lacrosse and Football. Reaching the highest level possible competing as a Female Athlete, she has played in a U19 World Cup as well as five further Major World Cups. Laura has been named on the "All World Team" on two consecutive occasions and has won numerous MVP's.

She was a fully paid Sports Scholar on the University of Maryland Women's Lacrosse Team where she won an ACC Championship and reached the Semi-Finals of the prestigious NCAA Tournament. Most recently, Laura was part of lacrosse history by representing Great Britain at the 2017 World Games, assisting the sport in moving towards competing at the Olympics.

Laura is passionate about showing girls that sport and exercise can enhance their future through the skills and habits they will gain from participation. She has run her own sports camps and coached lacrosse in Australia and America as well as the UK. Her passion for sport, exercise and wellness is undeniable and unwavering. She inspires the 'unfit', 'exercise hater' by providing help through personal training, classes, workshops, retreats and online presence.

She supports women to regain their confidence and pelvic floor, abdominal and overall fitness following delivery or many other traumas. She encourages and inspires the elite sportswomen in her peer group through her leadership and motivation.

Laura's drive, passion, energy, determination, entrepreneurial flare teamed with her 'Just do' attitude has seen her recently pick up numerous awards. Laura won the 'Pitman Working Mum of the Year 2018' and was recently shortlisted for the South Wales Personal Trainer of the Year, Fitness Entrepreneur of the Year and the Class of the Year.

Laura won numerous awards on Training Camps while With Curves and won the Shining Star Club Award and "Smile' Club of the Year.

Laura has collaborated with numerous fitness professionals to share her work via podcasts and often shares her thoughts and insights with the likes of the BBC.

Websites
www.fitmuma.uk
www.Laura-warren.comlaura
www.Laurawarrenlacrosse.com
www.fitin30.life

Instagram fitmuma.uk
facebook https://www.facebook.com/Laurarhianwarren
https://www.facebook.com/fitmuma.uk/

Email: fitmuma.uk@gmail.com
Phone: 07725554957

Leigh Howes

Never Stop Growing – My Journey
The phone rang. I paused for a second and my heart missed a beat. A little voice in my head doubted me. A louder voice didn't. I answered the phone.

'Hello, is that Leigh?"

"Yes, it is, is that Steven?"

"Hi Leigh, yes, Steven here. Are you free to talk?"

"Yes, of course" I replied with both excitement and trepidation.

"Thank you so much for attending the final interview process yesterday. We all really enjoyed meeting you. Whilst you don't have as much experience as some of the other candidates we met, we saw so much potential in you that we would love to offer you the job."

1998 was the year my career really truly commenced: the moment that I turned the corner on my own potential. When I stepped outside of the four walls of my comfort zone. The doubting voice: off you go now. Leigh has just arrived in the room.

My curiosity for business and earning money started when I was very young.

I started riding horses at the age of 7 and from the age of around 9, I was at the yard tending to mine and the riding school horses every day that I could. I was eager from a young age to earn my own money. As a small framed girl, when I asked the owner of the yard if I could start working there, he was concerned that I couldn't lift the wheelbarrow, so instead, I did everything else I could, from collecting rubbish to cleaning tack and picking the courgettes he had growing in a nearby field. When I proved that my work ethic was typically stronger than others of my age, he gave me the chance to work as a groom. By the age of 14 I was not only running the yard at a weekend, I was leading hacks of large numbers and teaching both children and adults to ride. There literally was no stopping me. I had a massive passion and hunger for horses, for teaching and for earning money.

My curiosity for business continued into school when it came to choosing my subject options. I was always an average student, fortunate to be placed into the upper band but always middle of the class. Never stood out for underperforming or overachieving. That was until option choosing time.

"Take History or Geography as one of your options" was the advice they kept telling me. "It is important for your future" they said. Truth be told, I had zero interest in either of them, neither did I understand them.

So, I did what I have done my whole life. I didn't conform. I challenged the status quo. Whilst many of my friends took up History or Geography, I didn't. I chose Business Studies and Information Studies. Some said, "you only take these options when you are not bright enough to choose the others." Maybe so. Who cared? I didn't for sure.

I literally loved those classes. When some of the others were messing about, I was completely in the zone, soaking up everything that I could learn and implement.

It was no surprise that I continued to be average in all of my subjects but excelled in these. Leaving with the highest accolade I could get in my GCSEs – two A's. The foundations for my future were very much set.

I continued with my non-conforming attitude thereon. Whilst many friends went off to university. I didn't. I went to college. Again I got some stick for this. However, I simply didn't care.

I studied Business Studies and also secretarial qualifications. The latter didn't float my boat quite as much but came with the territory of the course I was taking.

I continued to do well and when I finished, took a grass roots job locally, working as a Clerical Assistant earning just £6k a year. 2 years later, I got a job locally as a PA. 2 years after this, I got a job as an Office Manager in a local Recruitment Company, specialising in Sales Recruitment within the Textiles and Housewares industry.

It was then that one of the Directors there noticed my potential and told me so. He said that he could see me working in what was then Personnel. The very thought of it scared me as I had a massive fear of public speaking. I believed that I wouldn't be able to do a role in Personnel without confronting this.

However, I researched this industry and soon realised that maybe he was right. It played to my strengths. I loved people, I was good at building relationships, I loved training. So, I enrolled on a foundation course – CPP (Certificate in Personnel Practice) and I loved it.

One day during an assessment, we were working as a team giving a training presentation. One of the ladies in my team was speaking and completely lost her way. She needed help and I surprised myself by stepping in. Not only did I help a fellow teammate, but I improvised and confronted my fear of public speaking all in one hit. BOOM. I had taken yet another step outside of the comfort zone.

A job was advertised in a magazine that we had in our offices. A recruitment Officer for Iceland; the well known frozen supermarket chain. It required experience, it required a number of skills and it also required courage to even think I could do it. The experience I didn't really have. The skills, I had started to believe I had. The courage. I was continuing to work on that.

They say a ship is safe in the harbour but isn't where it is meant to be. I applied the same principle and sent in an application. The interview process was terrifying and really full on. You would expect it to be when you were responsible for recruiting all of the Appliance Sales Managers in all of the Iceland Stores across both the UK and Ireland. Makes me smile that I was courageous (and mad enough) to go for it.

"Thank you so much for attending the final interview process yesterday. We all really enjoyed meeting you. Whilst you don't have as much experience as some of the other candidates we met, we saw so much potential in you, that we would love to offer you the job."

1998: The year my career started.

My career then went from strength to strength. I felt so blessed, however I recognised that you create your own luck. You certainly don't move forward by standing still. I was hungry, I was driven, I challenged the status quo and I had started to recognise my worth.

I received numerous promotions, studied and achieved my CIPD accreditation (at university – yep, did it in my own way) and at my highest level was Heading up HR for the Head Office of KFC (another well known brand within Yum Restaurants Int.) in Surrey.

2006: The year the new chapter in my life commenced. I became a parent for the first time to Henry, our eldest son who is now 9 years old.

What a mixture of emotions. His little face looking up at me, the thrill of becoming a Mummy and the realisation that you can love another person so very much. In contrast, the vast confidence that you lose in yourself and your ability to do your job in the process, alongside the worry of how you will juggle it all. I didn't see that bit coming at all.

Work changed then. Even at a hugely supportive company, I felt they treated me differently. In fairness, I was different. I wasn't able to hang on until stupid o'clock to finish work in the office. I had to think about someone else, my priorities had changed.

I also wanted to reduce my working week and this meant the role I was doing before, I couldn't go back to.

2010: Oh how this was hard. Stepping sideways, giving up my own office and sitting outside it. Making way for a very good friend of mine to fill my shoes. It was a difficult time.

I know I am not alone struggling with this part. The returning Mum who had a high flying career before and now finds herself lost. Without the confidence she once had, having to make so many sacrifices that just didn't exist before; this is not uncommon and it isn't an easy one to work through. I truly believe that for Companies to retain the knowledge from incredible, talented women, they need to recognise this and offer really strong support and guidance to help them through the process.

2011: A new opportunity within our sister brand, Pizza Hut and time for me to work closer to home, step back into my genius zone and make a difference, whilst heading up HR within their delivery team in Borehamwood. This was an awesome move for me, working with a great team on some really exciting projects, making way for a much happier Leigh. A Leigh who stepped back up and started to make a real difference again.

It was in 2011 that a good friend introduced me to a business opportunity. A chance for me to create an extra income alongside my job. This opportunity was working alongside a company and their Network Marketing Model. A model that I was not familiar with and it gave me my first exposure to being self-employed, as well as teaching me about sales, marketing and business development. There was a mixed response to my decision to get involved. Today, I still partner with this same company and don't see this ever changing. I wouldn't be where I am without this experience and the vast lessons, both good and not so good, along the way.

2012: The start of yet another chapter in my life. Redundancy whilst 5 months pregnant with my youngest son, Charlie, who is now 6 years old. It came as no great surprise to many of us that Yum Restaurants were looking to sell off the UK Pizza Hut Brand, but still, the timing wasn't great.

Moreover, this was definitely the kick I needed to get me where I am today. I do believe that things can happen for a reason and I believe for some, not all, that redundancy can sometimes be what we need to find the courage to make a change. This was definitely my situation. This is when my journey of true self-employment began.

February 2012: 5 months pregnant with my foot in a cast (as I had fallen down the stairs and broke my 5th metatarsal).

I looked for work, it wasn't that I immediately had the courage to go it alone. However, whilst my experience was of much interest to many companies, none of them were willing to let me work part time. It was full time or no time.

Consequently, I decided to give the freelance world a try. I had no idea of what I would do, however I knew I possessed skills that could help others, alongside a big network, a hunger and a passion to succeed. Having gained a little bit of experience of running a small business from the partnership with my network marketing company, I was ready to get started.
I haven't told many this but if I am honest, I was carrying a chunk of resentment. I resented being made redundant (despite what I now know was a blessing). I resented how I felt when I returned after my maternity leave. I resented how becoming a parent had impacted my career and how, at times,

I felt like a failure both at work and as a Mum.

I had and still do, have a point to prove to myself; that you can earn an income, work the hours you choose and be the parent that you choose to be. That is probably still a major driving force for me. It is what gets me through the dark days and drives me to stay self-employed. To be there for my boys and to prove that you do not have to be employed to achieve the success you had before you became a parent.

My mission today is to help businesses find ways to work smarter, to get creative with their model, so they can get flexibility and freedom to value their time and do the things that make them happy without compromising their income. My other big passion and mission will become clearer as this chapter reads on.

Tapping into my network, arranging coffees and letting people I trusted know I was available to support them, was the first best thing I could have done. Within one week of leaving employment, I landed my first 'freelance' gig working with a wonderful Coach who had Pizza Express as one of her clients.

Off I went to Islington, to facilitate a session with a group of their senior leaders. The look on the HR Directors face when I walked into the room was a picture. She was semi prepared, but still – a stand in arrives with a large tummy and a cast. What on earth was she to think?

However, I won't lie - my first dip in the water was terrifying. It is different when you have been employed and are delivering sessions like this within your own company and team. This was me representing a fellow coach and never having worked freelance before. What if they didn't like how I worked?

However, I had prepped. I was ready. I played to my strengths of building the relationship with the client and the guys in the room quickly. By doing this, I got them on side, was able to get the best out of them and help them achieve their objective by the time the meeting ended. To this day, I still have a recommendation on my LinkedIn profile from Amanda, who was the HR Director at the time.

Following this, I worked a good few months with another colleague who runs a very successful Headhunting Executive Firm. Again, nerve-wracking, as I had a great deal of recruiting experience but always client side, not as a consultant. But I did it. I made a difference, I made placements and I learnt a great deal.

What I didn't do, which I now know is imperative when you are starting out, was get clear on my vision/purpose. I have literally spent too many years moving from one thing to the next, part of it led by the need to generate an income, but partly because I just didn't know what it was that I wanted to do or who I wanted to help.

If I was starting my business again, I would still want to do a little bit of the dabbling (I liken this to living in a house for a bit before knocking down walls and making changes; you get to see the bits that work and the bits that don't.) However, if I had of gotten clearer earlier about my purpose and who I was looking to help, I could have stopped myself losing precious time and money. I have learnt that you must get clear early on as to who your ideal client is, the problem you help them to solve and then build your brand and your marketing message to support this. How can someone refer business your way or find you in a google search if YOU don't even know what problem it is you solve?

It took me 4 years to really get to grips with who I really wanted to help. It is only now that I am brave enough to niche and be clear on who I am talking to. Crazy really as I have helped others get clear on their message and their client but failed to do it for myself. If only I knew then, what I know now.

So between 2012 – 2014, I was an Associate for a Coaching and Management Development Company and an Associate Headhunter for an Exec. Recruiting Firm. I also helped large and small organisations with all things HR. I mainly enjoyed it, I learnt stacks and I got to be at home for both of my boys as they started to grow.

However, the cash flow situation had always been a stumbling block for me. Marketing yourself as a small business owner is, I believe one of the hardest areas to overcome and with this comes the panic over your cash flow. Working on your money mind-set is imperative early on in your journey to help remove any money blocks you may be carrying. Ultimately, this panic was what led me to a paradigm shift in late 2014.

I part shared a horse who was and is still, very dear to my heart. I had loaned her from a very good friend for 15 years. When that friend informed me that she would be moving away and asked if would like to take on more responsibility of her (more time and cost).

I had no choice, but to walk away. Not only that but I made the decision to take a break from horses altogether. I had very little time or money to take on the responsibility on my own. 33 years of horses coming to a stop. I really didn't anticipate the emotional impact this would have on me.

Early December 2014, I had just one month left with my horse. I had a very stupid accident whilst out on her, leaving me unable to move on the floor, needing an ambulance for the first time in my life. Fortunately, my back was not broken but the ligaments badly damaged and riding was out of the question for the remainder of the year.

2 weeks later, our youngest son Charlie, who was 2 at the time, was rushed by ambulance to hospital and diagnosed with pneumonia. The most horrendous week followed as he was so poorly. Me, with my damaged back laying in a bed by the side of him, willing him to be better and come home, whilst my Husband tried to keep life as normal as possible at home for Henry. It was a very difficult and emotional time.

During this time, I was working on a high-profile recruitment campaign for a major client. A Client who would most definitely not have put me under pressure to work when Charlie was so sick. However, I needed the money, I had no option but to fill this role despite how poorly Charlie was. So there I was, by his bedside, trying to hold it together, liaising with both client and candidate so that I could get the placement done, get my commission and help pay for Christmas.

Charlie did get better thankfully. We are to this day very grateful to the QE2 hospital and the team there. He was a very poorly boy and we didn't know what the outcome would be. Today, he is here and well, and we are extremely grateful.

Albeit, this event changed me. It changed my outlook and my mission once more. I wanted to ensure that I never had to be in this position again. Most who are self-employed need to be physically working to create their income. I wanted to change this for me. I wanted to create a passive income. One that could be generated, despite my need to be somewhere else more important at any given time.

So, in 2015, I decided to change my focus and priority. I stopped building my 'freelance' business and instead started to focus my energies on the network marketing business that I had got involved in back in 2011. It was hard work but I built it up.

I developed a decent monthly income; a fair sized team and qualified for a number of incentives that the company was running. I could literally run the business wherever I wanted. During school holidays, I could hang out with the boys but still be working around them and be earning an income too. I was developing a real bug for helping others realise their true potential, as well as a love for a passive and lifestyle income. I felt like I was starting to achieve my new mission.

However, over time and after a considerable amount of hard work, I started to feel like something was missing. I couldn't put my finger on it – until I attended an online programme with a fantastic Coach called Will Perry. Alongside other Network Marketing Leaders, he coached us through our challenges and unintentionally, working with him and the group made me realise what had been staring me in the face all along. What I loved to do and where my strengths lay.

It was a light bulb moment for me. I was great at getting people to open up, to face their own challenges, to help them work through and create a plan for what it is they really want to achieve. I loved the coaching, consulting', advising and training element of my work.

I had done this throughout my entire HR career, right up to board level. I had qualified in many areas and one was in Performance Management, I had studied and become certified in CBT, I had always had an interest in what makes people tick, how they behave, what constitutes good performance. This was the part of my work that truly made my heart sing, that didn't actually feel like work. I just needed to figure out who I wanted to help with their personal development. Yet again, the niche issue arose.

I also realised that despite my love and fondness for the Network Marketing Company (which I am still with today and support both my customers and my team completely), it wasn't giving me all that I needed at that time. The beauty of this industry and the company is that it continues to pay me a small passive income and I can pick it up again and build at any time I chose.

Right now, I am focused elsewhere, but it remains there for me to pick up at a later stage in my life. I remain to this day, so very grateful for the many lessons I have learnt working with this incredible company and industry. I am a massive advocate of multiple income streams and this is one of the ways that Business Owners and individuals can develop a passive/residual income.

Then. Crash! Bang! Wallop! A series of Shit Bombs struck.

In January 2015, I gave back Ruby to her owner and sharer. My heart broke a little that day and still hasn't completely healed itself.

In February 2015, my Nan suffered a major stroke and went from being able bodied to needing full time care in a home. We were so very close, and my heart broke a little more. Sadly, in August 2015, my Nan passed away. More heartbreak.

In February 2016, my remaining Nan passed away in front of me. This little heart of mine which was now a little fragile, lost yet another chunk. Whilst she had reached the ripe old age of 95.; it didn't stop the hurt that I felt losing her. It was like a giant void was left where both my Nans had been. How do you fill that?

In March 2016, my wonderful Father in Law was told he had terminal cancer and had 8-10 months to live. I was with him at the appointment when they told him. I was truly starting to feel a little battered and bruised. But I kept going and kept the mask on. Finally, in February 2017, my Father in Law passed away quietly, without medication and in his own bed. This is what kept us all strong, knowing that he left us with the dignity he deserved.

Then the final shit bomb. On 31 March 2017 my world imploded in a way I could never have imagined when I was diagnosed with an aggressive form of Breast Cancer. You couldn't make this shit up. Even writing it, I can see how the preceding trauma and grief could have potentially led me to this point.

I was one of the lucky ones because I trusted my instinct and caught it early. 18 months on and I am so grateful to be here and clear of it. I have gained and grown in so many ways. I am obviously a damn sight stronger than I thought and ever gave myself credit for.

Perspective has taught me a great deal – not least to put myself first again. To realise that I am no good to anyone broken and that my health is more important than any success I may be striving for. Additionally, it has highlighted to me what I enjoy and who I want to spend my very precious time with. It has therefore pushed me into being super clear on what work I want to do, who I am here to help and ultimately, my purpose.

Today I can say with confidence that I help small businesses work smarter, to help them get the skills they need to grow the business they love. Why? Because I want others in business to learn from my mistakes, to avoid the pot holes that I fell into.

To prove that it is possible to design a business that we choose, that gives us freedom to have a life and to put ourselves first. Alongside this, I am on a massive mission to help women appreciate themselves, value their time, see themselves as a priority again and avoid burnout. I don't know if I was in burn out mode when my diagnosis appeared.

I do know that I wasn't in a great place, that I might have appeared it on the surface but underneath and inside I was covering up stress that I don't even think I knew I was suffering from. They say great things can come from adversity and I am living proof of that.

I am not completely finished on my journey of recovery and I know that healing myself mentally and physically will take time. However, I am a better, stronger person that stands here today, and I know that I have an important message to share so that others can learn from some of the mess that I found myself in.

So, in summary from me to you:

Go grab the opportunity, don't over think it. Time is ticking every single day and when it goes, you don't get it back. Please use my perspective to help you find the courage you need to be the person you have the potential to be.

Be clear on your goals. Write them down. Set the sat nav. It will save you wasting time and fuel driving about lost. Once you know where you are heading, you can then map out clearly the journey you need to take to get there and who you want to be travelling along with you on the way.

Value your time and your worth. I continue to be on a mission to prove that you can work flexibly and still be successful. Phil Jones, one of my mentors, taught me a fantastic formula to help me value myself and my time and ensure I charge the amount that I am worth. Start with the end in mind of what you would like your income to be in either turnover/profit, then figure out the number of hours and weeks you want to work, then you have a simple sum that helps you understand what you should be charging by the hour/day to achieve your financial goals. Without this, you run the risk of working excessive hours to get the income you need, which for most of us goes against why we started out in the first place.

Get focused. I am a serial magpie. I love anything shiny and I have a head full of ideas. My challenge is in the execution because I have a terrible habit of starting projects and not always finishing them. This is led a little by my lack of focus and also a little of my limiting beliefs (a whole other book right there). I don't believe it is about managing my time more effectively. I know for me, it is about managing my focus. When I am clear on what I need to do, have completed my forward planning (I will write out at the start of the week what my 5 big goals are and plan in the action I need to take to fulfil these), have removed distractions (notifications off, Wi-Fi off, earplugs in), set the timer and planned in regular breaks, I am so much more amazing. It is why I work well under time pressure because I do not get distracted. Try it, I promise you will achieve more.

Establish a routine. The other area for me is creating lasting habits through my routines. This, alongside my focus is what maximises my productivity and also keeps me sane. Juggling and running a business can be testing, a routine will help you become more consistent and create new positive habits. Include within this, time for yourself. Time to switch off. You are not a machine. You are a Human Being, NOT a Human Doing. Remember that.

Lastly. Inner Circles. If you are a sole trader, when it is financially viable – join one and/or get a mentor/coach to lean in on. I run Your Inner Circle; a mastermind of 8 female business owners who work together with me to work through their problems, support each other, cheerlead each other, brainstorm ideas, lean on each other and cry together when times get tough. Running one of these is amazing. BUT - investing in ME and finding my own inner circle of support has been critical to my progress. Working on your own can be lonely. Having a sounding board in a safe space can really make the world of difference to the confidence you discover in yourself. Alone you can go fast, together you can go so much further.

It is one of the reasons why joining the Female Success Network Mastermind was perfect timing for me and just what I needed. I nervously joined when I was mid-way through a gruesome treatment plan. Despite being online, it is like I have gained a whole new family. Sisters I never had. They lift me when I am down, cheerlead me when I achieve and give me a swift kick up the arse when I need it.

I joined them at a difficult time and I have felt so loved and supported by them all, but particularly Abi and Sarah, who make me believe that I can achieve anything I put my mind to.

The icing on the cake was on 31 March 2018, one year on from my diagnosis when I received a picture in my branding colours from them both, with the most beautiful card and words saying:

Always remember you are BRAVER than you believe
STRONGER than you seem
SMARTER than you think and twice as
BEAUTIFUL as you'd ever imagined

In the card, they told me that from now on, this date would be one to celebrate, not one to feel sad about.

I am where I am today for so many reasons. I have achieved so much that I am proud of and am on a mission to make a difference out of the adversity I have faced and the obstacles I have overcome.

However, I have not got here alone. I have got here with love and support from my husband, my boys, my parents and extended family, my friends (new and old) and so many amazing strong and supportive women in my life, not least my unstoppable soul sisters within the Female Success Mastermind.

I am grateful every day. I am learning every day. I am on a mission every day. I am a survivor.

Thank you for reading my story. You can follow more of me over at www.leighhowes.com which has links to my social channels too.

About Leigh Howes

Leigh Howes started her career in recruitment before spending more than a decade in a very successful corporate HR career for high profile brands such as KFC, Pizza Hut and Iceland.

In 2012, she faced redundancy and like many career women, questioned the suitability of companies who wanted to employ her, but at the detriment of her career or family. Her choice – step back her career or go full time. Never one to conform, she challenged the status quo and it was then that her entrepreneurial journey started.

Throughout, she was unashamedly a work horse. Hungry, keen to learn and achieve. Leaving the office late and burning the midnight oil was pretty standard practice.

In 2017, after a series of personal challenges, she got dealt a further blow, when she was diagnosed with Breast Cancer.

It was the realisation that many other things were in fact unimportant that gave her massive perspective and forced her to look inwards. She stepped off of her own hamster wheel, dug really deep to find ways to cope and in turn made some big changes in how she designed her own business to enable her to live a life that put her needs first.

These lessons are now what she teaches to others; that wellbeing and happiness are a critical enhancer to both performance and success.

Today, Leigh is an advocate of running a business on your terms, that fits into your design. Her Find your Flourishing (™) Programme enables her to partner with busy entrepreneurs and executives and pull apart the jigsaw of business or life and put it back together in a way that fits and brings a smile to your face.

She is also the founder and driving force behind Your Space (™) and Your Inner Circle (™). An online members area and training academy where she sources and works alongside a 'Talent Board' of entrepreneurs; who share their skills with small businesses to help them grow and a Mastermind for Females in Business who meet monthly, both on and offline, to get the support, empowerment and cheerleading that they need to grow and scale their businesses.

Her latest passion project sees her collaborating to form a day retreat for busy woman needing to pause, reconnect and reset. A venture born out of her own experience and learning that slowing down, really can help us to speed up.

Combining her experience, knowledge and personal adversity, Leigh is on a mission to help us all put ourselves first by valuing our time and creating a business and life that we design and truly love.

www.leighhowes.com
hello@leighhowes.com

Linda Mawle

Finding my spark again!

I can remember vividly the day that I decided what I wanted to do with my life when I was a 'grown up'. Running my own business certainly wasn't part of the plan! I was just 15, really only a child myself and was spending the summer with my older sister and her family. My new nephew Jack had recently been diagnosed as having cerebral palsy and we as a family were trying to understand and come to terms with all that this entailed.

I guess emotions were running high. On this particular day that I recall so well, his physiotherapist had come to the house to work with him for a while. I don't remember much about the specifics of what she did, but I remember that I just sat through the whole session and watched her get to work.

Jack himself was not at all impressed at all with the physiotherapy he had to do but I was transfixed. This person was going to help us. She was going to give us hope, structure and practical things to work on to help Jack be the best version of himself that he could be.

I know now with hindsight that this was a very simplistic view of a physiotherapist's role but for me, from that moment on, I just knew. Knew without any doubt that being a physiotherapist and specifically working with children with cerebral palsy was exactly what I wanted and needed to do with my life.

I can honestly say that there has never been any change to this conviction in the past 25 years since this point. I am now 40 years old and whilst many things have changed for me over the years I am just as totally convinced today as I was as that 15-year-old girl that being a specialist paediatric physiotherapist, working with families and children with cerebral palsy was and is, exactly what and who I am supposed to be.

To me, being the best physiotherapist I can be, was and still is a very personal thing. It was never about the 'job' or the business. I owe it to all the amazing children that struggle daily as my nephew does, to the best physiotherapist for them that I can be.

My journey from that day forward was not always an easy one. However, I qualified, got my first job and slowly but consistently worked my way to becoming the specialised paediatric neurology physiotherapist I wanted to be. I can honestly say that running my own business was not in any way part of my plan for the majority of this time.

I did not come from a family of business men and women. My dad taught me very well that working hard and achieving the best that we could in life was important but everyone I knew had a traditional job. I was not exposed to business ideas and entrepreneurial ideals and really had zero desire to enter the business world at all.

Until a few years ago I did not desire to have anything other than a job that I loved and enough health to do this job until I was ready to retire. I was not looking at any other options. If someone had suggested to me that in a few years I would be running my own business full time I would have laughed at the suggestion.

So what changed? In 2009 I had my third child. I was finding it increasingly hard to juggle the demands of working in a job where I felt emotionally linked to turn up every day and be my best self for the clients that I loved, and also being able to be the best mom that I could be to my three children that I loved even more.

I felt that I was being pulled in too many directions and could feel that my internal stress levels were increasing week by week. Financially as a family we weren't in a position where I could give up my job for a while and so I decided that I needed to explore other options. I was in my early thirties, faced many working years ahead of me and could not face the possibility of being so stressed for the rest of my working life. However, not doing physiotherapy was not really an option for me! It was too personal a career choice.

I decided at this time to take on a couple of private clients, dip my toe in the water of having my own private practice and see how it felt. I was very loyal to the NHS and was not ready to fully walk away and for me approaching it this way felt like a safe option. I could have a taste of running my own business without needing to really become a proper business woman. Make a small change whilst not properly making any major life changes.

I'm generally not a risk taker in life. I'm Mrs 'laid back' and usually like to stay firmly within the safe zone in all areas. I do however like to be in control and struggle to be in situations where I feel out of my depth and unsure of what I am doing. I always considered myself as good at my job and was not at this time as a young mom ready to feel like taking on too much of a new challenge.

Leaving the NHS when my family were so young and dependent on me and the reality of running my own business full time would have placed me so far out of my depth I felt that I would have sunk.

So, I started seeing my few private clients and quickly began to love this new element to my physiotherapy career. I loved having the freedom to explore and test the limits of my physiotherapy skills without some of the pressures and limitations of working within a large organisation.

I felt some of the stress lift simply because I had reignited my initial passion for my career again….and there I stayed!

Rather than recognising all the amazing possibilities that my private practice could offer me and running with the opportunity to control my own life with my own business, I spent the next 7 years staying within my NHS role and seeing a few private clients in the spare hours and days off that I had.

The problem was I still had no idea how to be a business woman. I felt very loyal to the NHS team I was part of and the NHS in general. For some people this may seem strange, but it was all I had ever wanted to do and so walking away was always going to be an incredibly hard decision for me.

Over the next few years I kept the status quo but I could gradually feel the stress and discontent starting to creep back into my life. My enjoyment of my employment was mixed, there were parts of the job that I still loved and lit me up inside and parts that I was struggling to adjust to. I began to dream of the day when I could leave and run my private practice full time.

The spark of excitement had been ignited within me. But when to make the jump? I was once again afraid. Afraid of the 'what if's?' What if I was a failure? What if I couldn't be a successful business woman? What if it changed me and made me into someone I didn't want to be? What if I wasn't good enough to stand out amongst the competition?

So, I waited and waited and then waited some more! All the time plotting in the background and waiting for my moment to really go for it.

A few more years passed and then in 2015 I unfortunately experienced the sudden and tragic loss of someone close to me. It shook me to my core. Made me look at how blessed I was in life and how things could suddenly change in a heartbeat and turn life totally upside down. It was as if a switch was turned on inside of me again.

Just like it was when I was that 15-year-old young girl realising what her path was in life. I didn't want to wait any longer, I wasn't prepared to go on feeling stressed all the time. I knew without any doubt that I was ready to make a change, ready to make a leap of faith into the unknown and leave the security of the job I had been in for 15 years and step out on my own to be the physiotherapist that I needed to be.

I knew that I needed to be my own boss and do things the way I felt they needed to be done. For people who have run multiple businesses and been around businesses all their life this probably sounds totally ridiculous and dramatic but for me it was a massive decision. But FINALLY one that I was prepared to make.

I left the NHS toward the end of 2016.

The responsibility of making a success of my private practice was now up to me and me alone. However, after all the years of procrastinating to get to this point the amazing thing was that I was no longer afraid. I finally felt that I had done what I was supposed to be doing. In my gut I felt that it was the right thing for me, for my family and for the children that I so desperately wanted to help. I got to work.

I had one mission for that first year in full time business, to get back my love and passion for my career. It had been lost for a little while, but I knew that it was still there inside of me and so The Children's Physiotherapy Practice was established.

During the next 12 months I met some amazing families. Got to work with the most special young clients and found my love for physiotherapy again. Things were going well! Stress levels had returned to the normal level of a busy working mom and I was emotionally in a much happier place. I knew that I was a good physio (always striving to be a great one!) but what I was beginning to realise was that I actually knew very little about running a business.

My business model at the time was a fairly simple one and so I was able to muddle along with the business tasks, doing the basics and focusing fully on the actual client contact element of my life.

However, a nagging doubt began to creep back in. Could I sustain this business for as long as I need to? What will I do if I need to grow? How can I improve the business flow and get some structure in place? The actual answer was that I had no idea! I began to realise that at some point I would need some business help and advice, but I had no idea to whom to turn to for this. I started to keep one eye open for business learning opportunities.

I have no idea how I stumbled across Female Success Network and in particular the mastermind group. I had not previously known Abigail or Sarah and had no other contacts within the group. But I thank my lucky stars that somehow, I found them or they found me!

I knew fairly quickly that the mastermind environment was where I needed to be. I needed a strategy, business basics and a plan for ensuring both initial growth and then sustainability for the Physiotherapy Practice.

There was no way I wanted to go back to a job now that I had experienced the freedom of working fully for myself. I was sure that Abi and Sarah and the mastermind environment were the right people, in the right place at the right time. I was in!

I've never really been heavily motivated by money. Don't get me wrong I have no issue with earning a little more! Three growing children come with plenty of expenses and I'm not one to turn down the chance of a nice family holiday somewhere hot! But money is not my main driver in life.

One of my deep centred concerns with running my own business was that this part of me would need to change. I had seen glimpse of greed amongst other business owners with a culture of thinking of profit before people. This was someone I knew I did not want to become. I discussed this from the outset with Abi and Sarah and felt immediately reassured that I was in safe hands.

My business goal by this time was to earn a comfortable living, have a structure that allowed me to remain stress free and able to focus fully on the needs of the clients and most importantly have the time and energy to be the best possible mom to my three gorgeous children and wife to Darrell.

I have to be totally honest and admit that that final aim is still a work in progress.

I think time boundaries are one of the biggest challenges I face with being my own boss. Time organisation is something that I struggle with and I find it very difficult to switch off. Difficult to turn off the notifications, emails and to do lists and focus fully on my family. I feel that I need to be available to my client families at all times but of course this is an expectation I have set for myself, I know that the families themselves don't expect this of me.

It comes from a good place of wanting to support and be there for my clients, but I am well aware that I need to try harder to set more boundaries around my family time. I think that if I was to give advice to someone starting out with a new business it would be to decide from the outset what hours of work are going to be, what an average week needs to look like and ensure that rest, family time and health need are fully scheduled and prioritised.

I've forgiven myself as getting momentum in a new business takes some effort but going forward into the next 12 months rest, health and family needs to be a bigger priority for me. I know that my client and business in general will benefit too as it means I will continue to be able to show up as the best version of myself and be of greater service to them also. Win Win!

I think the best piece of business advice I have received in the past 12 months was just a very simple one, to simply believe in myself and trust my instincts. I know me best! I know my business, I love my clients and I only have their best interests at heart.

Surround this with some simple but smart business structure and planning and I'm on the right path. If I could pass on my version of this advice I would say look forward with confidence and focus on yourself.

I've struggled with comparison over the years but I'm learning to just 'do me' and stop looking left, right and backwards to see what everyone else is doing. If I focus on me and my business I will attract the clients who I can best help.

I must trust in this way of thinking as this is the only sure way to ensure I stay authentic and aligned with my goals. It's so easy to look at others and be dragged off course via fear of failure or missing out.

I'm learning that if I'm happy with my efforts at the end of each day then I will never be failing at all. I do however wish that I had gotten started sooner and I guess that's another piece of advice I would give to others. If you are not happy with something in life, then work hard and do what you need to do to change it.

I am so much less stressed than I was a few years ago and I had the power to change that much sooner than I did. I've learnt through this journey that following your heart tends to lead to the right destinations.

My year within the mastermind has taught me so much more than I expected it would. I wanted straight forward business advice and I got this by the bucket full. The monthly strategy calls have been challenging but in a good way. I've been pushed to move my business forwards with accountability and clear expectations.

I now have a plan, structure to my back office, a gorgeous website built by me (with a fair bit of help!) and most importantly a calmness that I'm in control, and where I need to be now and I know where I need to be in the future.

However, what the mastermind group gave me more was something that I didn't expect and something that I didn't even know I was looking for. It has given me such a close relationship with the most amazing group of business women and I thank my lucky stars every day that they are in my life. All different businesses and all totally different personalities, but all supporting each other in our business and personal life to be the very best version of ourselves we can be. The support I have felt in this adventure has been priceless.

What Female success network have created is special. As I already said I was very fearful of becoming money driven and hard hearted in business. What I have discovered is the total opposite. Abi and Sarah have shown first hand through their own business structure that it is totally possible to run a successful business and make money whilst remaining totally true to your core beliefs and values. They have helped show me it is possible to provide an individualised and client specific service.

The FSN mastermind provided this and it has helped me see that I can provide this too for my clients. I will be forever grateful to all of my mastermind sisters and especially Abi and Sarah for the safe space they created for me to grow into the business woman I wanted to be. I'm a totally different person to the unsure physio who stepped up and asked for business help 12 months ago.

So where am I now? The Children's Physiotherapy Practice is going from strength to strength.

After my own family, it's my love and passion in life. I truly love being a physio again and I am now blessed to be able to focus all of my time and efforts on treating the children with severe disabilities that I care so much about.

It's what I want to do with the rest of my working life and I feel very privileged every day to be able to do it. I am so proud of myself for taking the leap and taking control of my own life to make it work best for me and my family.
I cannot imagine working for a large organisation again, where I am not in control of the type of input I want to give to families.

I travel to see children all around the midlands, Staffordshire and Shropshire both in their own homes and schools. I am able to see them frequently and so make rapid progress with their goals and treatment.

The structure of the business is growing and I now have a small team working alongside me to increase The Practice's availability and treatment options. My latest investment of time and money has been to become a MAE's practitioner. A specialist approach for the treatment of children with cerebral palsy.

It has transformed my understanding and taken my skills to a whole new level. I am now even more exited for the future and what I can offer my clients in terms of therapy to safeguard their future progression.

I feel my greatest strength has always been to put myself in the place of the child and their family and try my hardest to see things from their perspective. I'm proud of the focus this gives to my treatment sessions.

I still don't think I'm the greatest business owner that I could possibly be. First and foremost, I'm a physiotherapist and this will always be my main focus of development. However, via FSN I am now proud to call myself a business woman too and I'm learning to not be ashamed of my achievements.

I've learnt some key business skills that will hopefully safeguard my business' future and allow me to continue to be self-employed and live the best life I can create for me and my family. I know I've also made friends for life!

I love being a physiotherapist and I love running 'The Children's Physiotherapy Practice'. I hope that I can continue to do both and make a difference for many children and their families for many years to come.

With grateful thanks to Abi, Sarah and my mastermind friends. I couldn't have done it without you!

About Linda Mawle

Linda is a highly specialised neurodevelopmental paediatric physiotherapist from Staffordshire, UK. She is the owner and lead physiotherapist of The Children's Physiotherapy practice and has a heartfelt passion and desire to provide children with complex disabilities or developmental concerns with prompt, high quality, individualised assessment and treatment options.

Linda qualified with a BSc in Physiotherapy from the University of The West of England in 1999 and, following a short period of generalised experience, began to specialise in her paediatric career in 2001. She has worked continually within paediatric physiotherapy since this time and has now 17 years of experience in this field.

The length of this experience, both in private practice and within the NHS environment, has enabled the building of a broad and specialist skill base as well as developing the unique flexibility required to work successfully with a wide variety of children and their families.

Linda established herself as a self-employed independent paediatric physiotherapist in 2009. She specialises and has a particular passion for the management and treatment of complex neurological conditions within the paediatric community. Her caseload primarily including Cerebral Palsy, Acquired Brain Injury, post SDR surgery rehab and spinal cord injury.

This management involves providing ongoing active therapy, liaising with the wider team including solicitor and case manager involvement, report writing and advising on specialist equipment and orthotics.

Linda prides herself on her ability to recognise and adjust to individual client and family requirements to ensure successful therapy provision is achieved.

Linda is registered with the Health Professions Council (HPC), is a member of the Chartered Society of Physiotherapy (MCSP) and the Association of Paediatric Chartered Physiotherapists (APCP) and has recently qualified as a MAES practitioner. The Children's Physiotherapy Practice primarily covers Staffordshire, The Midlands, Shropshire and Worcestershire but all enquires are welcome.

Outside of her working life Linda is a wife to Darrell and mom to three amazing children who are her drive and reason for being. She feels totally blessed to be able to balance being a mom and a business woman and work with special children who deserve the best life possible.

CONTACT

EMAIL – linda@tcpp.co.uk
WEBSITE – www.thechildrensphysiotherapypractice.co.uk
FACEBOOK – The Children's Physiotherapy Practice

Lindsey Fairhurst

Be That Girl

Wednesday 10th May 2017: 38-degree heat and 60mph driving along the famous Sheikh Zayed Road, a seven-lane bustling motorway. I have tears streaming down my cheeks, feeling as though I am hyperventilating. No, I am hyperventilating. I just want to get home as fast as possible and hide from the world. Get back to my marina apartment, my "safe haven" and dive into my bed. People who have known me for a fair amount of time will know this is not the Lindsey they know! I had been feeling like this for a few months.

To set the scene a little, I live in Dubai; it has beautiful weather and it's a beautiful country. I am able, fit and healthy. I have great friends and an amazing husband. I have a promising full-time job as a Personal Assistant within a global company and I have security. However, I was unhappy inside; I felt miserable and - worst of all - I didn't know why.

In fact, the thought went through my mind that if I just bump the car, they will take me to the hospital and I can hide from the world. I will not have to do anything or speak to anyone! How selfish when I look back, to have such negative thoughts, but I felt like I didn't know how to get out from under the dull cloud.

Ironically, as I began writing this chapter it is the 16th May 2018, twelve months on from that time. I feel that I have grown massively as an individual since then. This was a time in my life where I felt trapped by discontent.

Nothing seemed to make me shine or give me the 'Lindsey sparkle' that I was known for. It was no one's fault; my husband, Kev, (also my best friend) was so supportive. He reached a point where he didn't know what else to do to try to make me happy.

My Dubai friends, and family in the UK were supportive; mum and dad even flew out a few months prior to support Kev and check I was ok. I felt lifted and stronger when they were here, but after they left I seemed to slope back into what I can only describe as a state of depression. I still don't know if it was or wasn't.

Either way, I didn't want to admit it at the time. I could not see the wood from the trees as they say.
On reflection, I felt this darkness surfacing a few months earlier, in January 2017. I had been to the UK for a few weeks holiday and had landed back in Dubai, as I stepped out of the airport I had no sense of excitement. I really didn't want to be back.

I just felt like turning around and getting back on the plane and go home to the UK. I felt sorry for my husband having to put up with my negative attitude and - dare I say - lack of appreciation for what I had. I didn't want to be *that girl* but I felt stuck.

Our move to Dubai in 2015 was one of biggest challenges we had faced as a couple and an extremely stressful time. The process started in March, and we sold my car and all the house contents in June. We moved out of our home in the July, with Kev leaving in August.

We lived apart for over 3 months and I finally moved in November. We had sold most of our life, packed the rest into 8 suitcases, moved to a desert and set off on a new adventure. All security we had was in the past and life as we knew it was no longer.

I networked within my then-company and transferred roles from the UK to the Middle East Office. I had been with Johnson & Johnson for 5 and a half years and I loved my job. I progressed from being Personal Assistant to a General Manager and senior leaders, to supporting a Managing Director within the Middle East and his direct reports.

So, along with the new home, culture, lack of network and friends was a new job. Everything was new, fresh, and challenging.

On reflection, 2016 was an amazing year; we lived well, made a new network of friends, arranged yacht parties and started Kev's business. We lived in one of the most iconic buildings in Dubai marina. We were swept up in the glitz and glam of the Dubai life. It was fast, furious and I was taking in as much as I could. We felt like we were living the dream or a constant holiday.

During 2016 I traveled to and from the UK three times. I didn't realise it at the time, but I was struggling to let go of our past and accept our new life. After researching, it seems many people in the expat life feel this way, so it's not uncommon. I just didn't realise it or see it coming, and it was having a huge impact on me internally.

As 2017 kicked in, the reality of Dubai life and being an expat kicked in: I wasn't truly settled. I was beginning to feel mentally torn between being in Dubai - living with my husband as a wife should do - and then feeling sick to the pit of my stomach that I no longer lived in the UK, on the doorstep of my parents, sister, family, and friends.

I started to think what if something happens, what if something happens to nan or my parents?

I will miss our nieces and nephews growing up! I felt so confused and I missed the familiarity of UK life. For the first time in my life, negativity and doubt set in. I let it set in and nothing seemed to remove this feeling.

I was starting to resent our move, adding pressure to my marriage. I felt like I was failing at work. In fact, I was failing at work because I was unhappy and unmotivated. I was not being the girl they saw at the interview; I was not being the best version of me, the Rockstar PA. At the time, I was unknowingly confined by the 9-5 world,' I didn't want to be that girl. I wanted my sparkle and shine back.

As I said in my opening line, I was not in a good place and things were about to take another turn. In May 2017, I was called into a meeting and delivered the news I was being made redundant. 'Thank you for 7 years of service'... I was not expecting that. So, after 7 years with a company that I had worked extremely hard for, it was time to close the chapter.

Even though I felt sad, part of me was relieved. Ever the optimist, I could use this as an opportunity to move onto something else, something that would lift me up, a new challenge, a place I could shine. How wrong was I!?

I started to look for a new role, with interviews straight away. I didn't stop to have a break, or really think about what I really wanted to do. I didn't think about what was going to light me up, what I am truly passionate about.

Many people who feel in situations like this stick at jobs they are not happy in for years. I was not going to be one of those people, regardless of the high salaries on offer. I wanted out. I needed time and space to work out what I wanted to do.

I am not money motivated. I love nice things and you will always see me with a designer bag and a glass of fizz! As I had climbed the corporate ladder to become a senior personal assistant and business executive, it was never just about the money. I really wanted to make a difference in someone's life. I thrived on being part of a team as it is what made me tick.

So, after the mammoth task of emigrating in 2015, followed by a fast and fun filled life during 2016, it's fair to say 2017 was not my best year. The first five months were upsetting and miserable, I was made redundant, moved house and felt in limbo. With all that before October, it's fair to say that I was at a low point! Something had to change, and I realised that it was down to me and my mindset.

On reflection, I had come from my comfortable safe life in Blackpool, where I was surrounded by family and friends and felt as though I had been dropped into an alien world. A displaced girl with no one around her except a husband who had his own career challenges to pursue. Everything around me was new.

Who do I ask for help? Who should I trust? How do I meet people? For the first time in my life, I felt that life was beating me. I lost who I was. When I looked in the mirror, I didn't see Lindsey; I saw a stranger, a lost, girl. After 18 months in Dubai and countless new challenges, I decided enough was enough. This is sink or swim. I was now hell-bent on bringing back Lindsey.

I played to my strengths: 16 years of PA experience, being incredibly organised and a mastery of planning. I started to think about what I truly want for the next few years. I hadn't had a plan for a few years as we were just going with the flow of the Dubai expat life.

This takes me back to what I mentioned before in that we were not accepting our new life, and that life means commitments, stability, routine and responsibility.

I started to accept that it was ok that our life had changed. We had to grow as a couple and with this we would experience some growing pains along the way. From this, I chose to draw on the wisdom of my dad.

When I was little, I used to suffer with bad growing pains in my legs. I'm not sure why as I only ended up at 5ft 1! My dad used to make me a hot water bottle to ease my leg pain. He would say growing pains are good because you're changing, becoming stronger and learning lessons. Throughout life nothing is certain; the older you get the more challenges arise, but in life you always need to be growing in some way.

I started to think how I can grow and learn from the last years career experiences. I thought about what I loved doing for work and how I am truly passionate about being a personal assistant, doing, serving, providing and being super active. A P.A's work is far from just making cups of tea, answering calls and filing your nails. I think that the role is often severely underestimated.

You must have a certain skillset: the ability to think quick, adapt to change within seconds and the ability to make decisions that impact leaders within global organisations. You must anticipate, plan and organise, all whilst assessing and analysing risk. You must be able to show up and step up. You become part of the leadership and senior management team. It's a pivotal role, and chances are that you are privy to more information than the senior management team because you are the right-hand girl (or guy) to the leader; you are offered unparalleled access into the world of that person completely. You're empowered by the leader you work for and, in return, you empower other people.

Throughout my career, I am proud to say I have supported, Managing Directors, General Manager, Quality Manager, HR Group, COO, CEO, Vice Presidents, Country Manager, Marketing Director. Meanwhile, smack bang in the middle of my PA career, I was also a wedding planner for two years, adding a huge amount of responsibility and co-ordination to my daily life.

I created a business support team and trained staff, lead multiple charity initiatives and spent 4 years as site ambassador for Corporate Social Responsibility division at my last company in the UK. I have a qualification in leadership and management, though I never went to university besides that and I am proud to say I am mainly self-taught by working hard and courses. More recently, I have reached a new high which is a pinnacle point in my career: supporting a President, CFO and CEO within a global organization in the Middle East.

Since mid-2017 I have worked a lot on my mindset. My mantra has become 'collaboration over competition', especially since entering the business world. Someone is always going to be doing a similar thing to you.

You must be your own kind of beautiful. Believe in yourself.   Be your best self.   Believe in your brand.

When I was 16 and facing some typical teenage drama, my Mum shared with me a very odd statement. I recall it was delivered in a stern tone. "Lindsey, you need to learn to love yourself or no other sod will!"

I didn't initially interpret these words as one could; I had to become extremely vain and self-conscious about my every look, even though I tend to glance in every mirror I pass by - a running joke with my girlfriends. Instead, I took these words in that I had to grow in confidence. I had to learn to be stronger and more respectful of myself.

If I had self-respect, then other people would respect me similarly, both men and women. I became confident in myself. Yes, some women may have longer legs than me - not hard considering my height! Some women have more beautiful hair or eyes, drive better cars or may have things I wanted. However, it's normal to have times where you compare yourself to others. I learned quickly to accept that I am who I am and I will become what I work to become.

Over the years, as I grew and went through the normal highs and lows of life's growing pains, advice from my parents served me well. Yes, there were silly mistakes; we all make them and - more importantly - we learn by them. I am respectful of others, and at any opportunity would lift another person up, not tear them down. Life's too short for all that crap.

As I look back, I applied this to my corporate career as well as my personal growth. Year on year I raised my game, stepped up, accepted new challenges, responsibilities and found mentors in those around me to support my development.

Because I am an ambitious and love a challenge, I had started a business in 2014 within the network marketing industry. At the time, we lived in the UK and this was a great way for me to have a side business as well as a full- time job. The beauty of network marketing lies in how flexible and low cost to set up it is, as well as the learning and personal development you gain. Furthermore, you can work from anywhere if you have WIFI and a can- do attitude. When we moved to Dubai, my business came with me and was easy to run online.

I had been hearing a lot about a lady called Abigail Horne. She was extremely successful and ambitious in the network marketing Industry. As you do, I decided to follow her on social media. Abi had a few businesses and I loved her energy for life, people and success.

I noticed she had a website created and it was amazing, extremely professional, vibrant and totally on brand. I looked up the lady who created the website and made an enquiry: Sarah Stone, expert in photography, websites and digital styling. Within a few days I connected and contracted Sarah to create my website. I started to write content and draft out the type of layout I wanted.

At the time, the site was to reflect my network marketing business. Sarah and I had no way of knowing what the site would become in the future.

I invested in myself, I invested in Sarah, and I invested in her process to create the website. Straight away we clicked. The website was fun and took a good few months as I wrote all the content myself. One thing I want to mention is that, within minutes of speaking to Sarah, I knew she was the one to work with. I have learnt in the last few years that you don't always have to work with or please everyone. You are not going to be everyone's cup of tea and it is important to find the right fit for you whether that be business or personal.

August 2016, during one of my many trips back to the UK, Sarah and I spent a fab day together shooting for my new website. As I look back now at my decision to follow Abigail, which led me to see her website, to connecting with Sarah, to choosing her to create my website and brand, I can't help but smile. That has turned into so much more and had such an impact on my life. Here's why….

I stayed in touch with Sarah and over time she shared with me that she was starting a new business with Abigail! To my excitement, not one but two awesome power women were creating a new business platform for aspiring female entrepreneurs.

This news came to me at a time where I really needed it. I felt like this was my answer, a new project to focus on, something to help me get rid of the grey cloud that was over me. Was it a possibility to create a business of my own, something for the future? Something that will give me a different purpose, inspire other women, create a legacy? A business that will pay me for each hour I work and allow me to work from the UK or Dubai?

The girls launched Female Success Network in August 2017, I joined the 12- month mastermind program. This program was designed to support women to set up business, offering them guidance, ideas, structure, routine, and an online uplifting environment. In the beginning, I had no idea for a business, I was unsure what I had to give or offer, and my self-esteem was low after the ups and downs of the last twelve months. However, I was prepared to dig deep. I was prepared to learn.

In the first week of the Facebook mastermind group, we were asked to introduce ourselves. The group was closed and private. I set about doing a livestream as did 23 other women.

During my livestream I broke down. I opened up to complete strangers; it was like a cry for help. I needed support in some form and just opening up made me feel better. It was a turning point for me: being honest with myself, admitting out loud that I wasn't happy about my career situation and that I needed to do something about it.

Admitting that I needed to change and work towards creating a role that fulfilled me signalled the start of my turn-around.

I had invested in the 12-month program and I was prepared to get the most out of it. During the first four weeks, we were asked to brainstorm ideas for businesses.

The concept for my business came from a 5-hour session where I used post-it notes and A4 pages to do an accurately-termed 'brain dump'. Also, I spent time looking over my CV and dissecting it, breaking it down into what I loved about my career, what I would like to do again and what was I passionate about. What I didn't like doing and wasn't passionate about.

Along with my one-to-one strategy sessions with Sarah and Abi, they supported me and agreed that it was a fantastic idea to use my sixteen years experience as a PA and step into the virtual world. The Virtual Assistant was born.

My mission from the beginning was to research, learn, highlight and note all about virtual assistants. I had planning, organisation and time management skills from my career. I now needed to mix that up with new systems, how to manage clients, new processes, learn how to find clients, how to price my services, booking, on-boarding clients and top tips for working more efficiently. That side was a complete new world for me.

I spent a few months on research, planning and network. One of the main things I found easy was deciding on my niche. After a little work and research, I chose to support females in business, specifically women who felt overworked, overwhelmed and needed to outsource tasks to enable them to focus on other areas of their business. It was as simple as that.

I wanted to create a brand, so I worked on my marketing, made relevant changes to update my website and planned a launch date for January 2018. Whilst researching and learning new areas of business, it became a little overwhelming at times.

I used a seven steps method coached by Sarah and Abi. Every week planning was key. Each Sunday, I would choose my seven tasks that I would focus on for that week. They would be focused around financial gain, how to move the business forward or areas of personal development.

I became so focused on what I needed to achieve I was not looking left and right at other people. I was using my seven steps as a guide, working out the time each step would take me and building it into my week so it is achievable. To stop the overwhelming feeling, breaking it down made it easier.

Having 100 small tasks to complete sounds crazy, but if you do seven a week for fourteen weeks it is significantly more manageable. It's just a case of listing what you need to do and time-lining this into to your 14-week plan. Reviewing at the end of the week was important. It provided a form of accountability that pushed me forward and drove my intrinsic motivation. I was personally responsible for delivering each week.

Even though my goal was to create and grow a business as a Virtual Assistant, I had to focus on other areas of my life to help me get there. It meant being aware. I started reducing decisions by planning ahead more often: food prep, journey prep, clothes prep.

These were all little things that had fallen out of habit over time. I can admit that I had let bad habits and negative mindset kick in. I wanted to stop being the old me and wanted to be a new me. I had to form new habits. I knew this would not happen overnight but each day I changed one thing, which was something I learned from a book called 'The Compound Effect'

I listened to motivational speakers and I trained myself to think differently. I decided that I wasn't going to continue like this, and my mindset changed. I changed!

Gradually, my confidence increased, my network grew and - most importantly - my smile returned. I woke one morning realising 'I'm back' and I have never looked back since. Since those dark days, everything has improved in my personal and work life. I learned that my future is determined by me and only me. No longer will I make excuses when I can make solutions.

In order to "Be that Girl", I visualised the girl with a stronger mindset and a career that lit me up, the girl who was back on her game and had the 'Lindsey Sparkle'. I had to focus and work to become the girl I wanted to be, which involved making changes.

I ask myself daily, if what I am doing is contributing towards me being "that girl". If the answer is no, I realign my focus, put the sugar foods back on the shelf, stop scrolling and focus on a task, get off my ass and hit my 10k steps for the day. Less TV, more grind to move me forward with the virtual assistant business. It is all up to me.

Along with my seven steps per week, I created a tracking chart. I would track my exercise, eating, water intake, morning routine and evening routine. This is still not perfect, but it is better than it was and I am continuing.

In September, I will be launching a 30-day group tracking challenge. This is for anyone. Whether you want to create a new habit to walk 10k steps a day, or drink 2 litres of water, or have a full list of twenty things you want to change, I will be with you! You can "Be That Girl". You can download a free copy of the tracking sheets from my website.

Starting as a virtual assistant is a new business venture. Even if you are just wanting a few hours here and there, you still need to have a plan and understand the basics. You still need to be professional and have the correct documentation, routine, systems, processes and advice.

Also, your skillset and services need to be on point and shout "hire me" to any potential clients. If you want to read a little more about this, you can find our Virtual Assistant online community group on Facebook. It offers lots of free support, advice, videos and tips.

My main piece of advice for anyone starting out in the virtual assistant world would be to follow a plan and have guidance. If you are looking to become a full-time VA, it will certainly give you that flexible lifestyle. You choose your hours and your rates, you choose who you want to work with, services you offer and create a business plan. Work out your income requirements.

My advice is not to leave your job until you are ready and financially stable in the VA world. I was fortunate to have Female Success Network to support me and guide me. I had invested financially in this and as clients started to come, my investment paid off.

I know how hard it is. When I entered the VA world to start my research, it was at a time I had decided not to be in full-time employment. I had no income and lacked the security of a full-time job. As I live in the UAE, I would be classed as self-employed, so I had no healthcare cover, no visa and I had no set process to follow to become a VA.

However, I did have the support of my husband (which helped me financially), an abundance of enthusiasm, my coaches, a plan we created and my twenty five cheerleaders from the mastermind group. With all of this present, away I went and threw myself in at the deep end.

I had no pre-made breadcrumb trail or stepping stones to follow, which is why I am currently creating them for other women to follow. I am extremely excited about the VA blueprint and process.

I know it will be a fantastic solution for women who want to start up as a virtual assistant but don't know how. It will help women who want to work from home, get paid for each hour worked and have a flexible working pattern.

'The first steps to Virtual Assistant' is an E learning course that that will be launched this month and is made up of seven modules which are broken down into a selection of videos, presentations, downloadable and readable content. It covers the following topics: Goals & Dreams, The Planning Stages, Onboarding Process, Booking Clients, Systems & File Management, Managing Clients, Time Management & Batch Content. It is great guidance and support for those just starting out.

I have had guidance and support from Abi & Sarah and our monthly one-to- one sessions have been invaluable. I have always been loaded with lots of questions. They both supported me in creating and setting up the Virtual Assistant brand, including launching, finding clients, adapting my website to reflect the new business, showing me the way, providing the tools, training, guidance and giving me a kick up the backside on days I felt like giving up!

During my 12-month mastermind program Experience, I feel I have been on a huge personal development journey. I have met 25 amazing ladies who have also set up and developed businesses. It has been an emotional journey for us all. We have helped each other, become a tribe with a vibe, an online family and virtual go-to support group.

We have developed friendships, given each other endless support and had an online supercharged, powerhouse environment to tap into 24/7! I am truly grateful for them all.

I would like to take this opportunity to thank Sarah & Abi for this book. They are two women who have given me so much throughout the last 12 months, and this book is just one of them. I feel blessed to be able to share my story with other women. My Virtual Assistant brand has been brought to life by having the right people around the table.

I chose to make changes and it has paid off. Through my new network, I have launched and connected with clients. I have also been asked to feature in this book which is a dream! I have put myself forward to speak at a TEDx event later in the year.

The Virtual Assistant brand was scribbled on a million post-it notes in October last year. We have recently expanded the team and I expect to grow again in the next 12 months. I am extremely excited to show and continue to inspire other women to do more and be more. I was born to give and bring happiness to those in my life.

I invested in myself, I invested in Sarah and Abi, I invested in the Female Success Network Brand and they have not once let me down. If anything, they exceeded my expectation with the constant giving and support. I have learnt more in the last 8 months than I have in the last few years.

That - combined with my sixteen years PA experience - and I can't wait until next month, when the Virtual Assistant Training Academy will be opening. We will have our 12-week Rockstar VA blueprint program going live.

So much has happened in the last twelve months. Once I changed my mindset, created a vision of the girl I wanted to be and started to work towards that, everything started to change for the better. I wanted to change, learn, grow. So I did.

Now it's time to share with others the methods, blueprint and processes to do the same, including how they can start a new career and business, become part of our Virtual Assistant organisation, build a new network, change current circumstances, change their mindset and become a better version of themselves.

I want to help them think about the person they want to become, take the steps to get there and ...

Be. That. Girl.

About Lindsey Fairhurst

Lindsey Fairhurst is a Virtual Assistant, supporting Female Entrepreneurs and a Virtual Assistant mentor.

Originally from Lancashire in the United Kingdom, she now lives in Dubai with her husband. Loving the fast-paced life, she is a highly motivated and committed individual who strives for success, not just for herself but those around her.

Lindsey has over 16 years' experience as a Personal Assistant and business support executive. Throughout her career she spent 6 years in Ibiza, 9 years in the UK and currently works from Dubai.

With certifications in Leadership and Management, Executive PA, organization and planning she has turned her passions into a career.

She is the founder of The Virtual Assistant brand which includes a wide range of services and outsourcing options for clients. The online training academy for aspiring VA's and accountability courses for women in the online business world who are looking to raise their game and take business to the next level.

Launching Autumn 2018 will be The Virtual Assistant Blueprint course. Using her 16 years' experience, personal learnings, strategies and business blueprint this 12-week program will enable Lindsey to support women to move into the world of online administration as Virtual Assistants.

Her ambition is to help women grow and take that step into self-employment. To show them step by step how they can use their administration skill set, passions, experience and allow them to develop and further their careers in a way that works for them and their lifestyle.

A vibrant, passionate and enthusiastic girl who specializes in empowering women to become a better version of themselves and taking the steps forward to create a life that fulfills and serves them.

CONTACT:

Email **Lindsey@lindseyfairhurst.com**

Website **www.lindseyfairhurst.com**

Facebook **https://www.facebook.com/thevirtualassistant9/**

Linktree **https://linktree/thevirtual_assistant**

Instagram **https://www.instagram.com/thevirtual_assistant/**

Lisa Dolman

My first experience of work was at the age of fourteen. I remember asking my Dad for more pocket money and his response was "Of course you can, but you work for it!" So off I went to work in his business every Sunday.

I have great memories of those days working with my Dad. His work ethic rubbed off on me at a very early age and the first lesson I learnt that you had to work for what you wanted. It also taught me the value of money and this is something I am determined to teach my daughters too.

My Father has been an entrepreneur all of his working life and has recently celebrated fifty years in business. I have always been very proud of his achievements. He is definitely my biggest inspiration.

At sixteen I left school and joined the family business alongside my Dad and Brother. I wasn't particularly academic and I didn't try hard enough at school but I knew early on that I was very driven to do my own thing so school didn't really fit in with that. Further education was not an option for me and to be honest I didn't find school an enjoyable process. I was painfully shy so it was a no brainer that I would leave as soon as I could. I wanted to be in the world of work.

After a few years of working for my Dad I decided to spread my wings and applied for a job as a cashier in a bank. This was my first taste of the "corporate" world and I owe a lot to the training I received in those early days with the bank. I quickly realised there were progression opportunities and received promotions. However, at the age of twenty I started to question whether this was the career for me. I still wasn't the most confident and although I had grown so much since being there, I started to feel that it just wasn't the right path for me. The industry at that time was extremely sales driven. I had huge targets and I felt the pressure. I was starting to consider what my career options were within the industry but I knew that the further up the ladder I climbed the more intense the pressure would become and in all honesty, it just didn't light me up!

I spent my last days at the bank dreaming of being self employed even though I didn't know what I wanted to do! I would talk to my colleagues about my goals and dreams and they were amazingly supportive. Great friendships were made in this job!

I discussed my feelings with my Dad over one Sunday lunch. At this point I was really miserable in my job and considering going back to work for him. My pride didn't want me to do that as I am all about moving forward but I needed to do something.

That Sunday was the first day of my future. I didn't know it at that point but one passing comment was to shape the next eleven years of my life. "Why don't you open a Bridal Shop?" Dad said.

I used to walk past a beautiful boutique on my way home from school and would often draw wedding dresses as a child. As a young teenager my parents had actually explored the idea of opening a Bridal Boutique. It was my Mums dream and was something they came close to doing but sadly it didn't materialise.

I started to research business start ups and the bridal industry, getting a feel for the designers I liked. I definitely had the bit between my teeth and got to work drawing my ideas and cutting outfits out of the Next directory catalogue of what I would wear in my future business. It may sound crazy but its only now that I look back and realise the role my visualisation had in the start up of the business. My recent personal development and study of the law of attraction has proven that unknowingly I was bringing this business to life without realising it at that stage.

After researching the industry for a few months it soon became apparent that there were quite a few boutiques near to where I lived and all of my favourite designers were stocked in the area. This was a bit of a blow as each designer carried an exclusivity area of 10 miles or more so I was going to have to look a bit further afield for the perfect area.

Having had no luck, one day I typed "businesses for sale" into a search engine and clicked on the top result. I selected the industry and sector I wanted this business to be in, not really expecting to find much. A few listings came up in Birmingham but there was only one that caught my eye. This listing had no photo and minimal information unlike all of the other businesses advertised which all had their company name and shop front pictured. However words like "Well Established" and Affluent Area" caught my eye and before I knew it I had registered my details and applied for more information.

A day or so later an email came through with the particulars of sale attached.
Lesley's Bridalwear, set in a 19th Century Old Chapel, established for twenty seven years and it stocked two of my favourite designers!
This was it!

When I showed Dad he was just as intrigued as me and one Wednesday evening we found ourselves driving over to Solihull for a meeting with the owner. As we pulled up outside I was bubbling with excitement. Based on the busy Warwick Road in Olton, The Old Chapel is set alone amongst trees and near a railway bridge. I remember being taken aback by its beauty and thinking what a perfect venue for a bridal boutique! I was sold before I walked through the beautiful arched chapel door but with a gentle reminder from Dad to be 'cool' I quickly composed myself and we went inside.

Needless to say when we stepped into the building we were both in awe of the sea of wedding dresses, the sparkles, the beams and character of the business. I could see myself there. This was my business. The one that I had imagined!

The following day we looked at the figures and finance options. It was a pretty big investment for a twenty-one year old to consider but I had Dad's full support and I didn't feel at all worried about it, just excited.

We met with a bank manager who sent me off to do a business plan. Funding options on an existing business which had a proven reputation and history were more forthcoming than I expect a start up would have been. Taking over a business as opposed to starting from scratch had its benefits in that respect, and because was already established it meant that I secured the labels I desperately wanted to represent.

Six months later, on the 1st October 2008, during the deepest recession since the second world war and at the age of just twenty one, we exchanged contracts and Lisa's Bridalwear was open.

We sat in the solicitor's office and I remember my Dad looking at me and asking "Are you sure you want to do this Lise? Business is hard sometimes and I don't want you to have the worries that I have had!"

"Yes Dad 100%" I replied.

It was a Wednesday at around 4pm when we exchanged and I remember coming out and saying to him "What do I do now?"

His response was "Don't you have a business to run? Get over there and meet your employees".

The Chapel was open until 9pm so off I went. I walked in and I felt far removed from my comfort zone. I felt so intimidated and out of my depth.

Until this point I had not met the staff. I had never managed people before and I was worried at how I might be received. This was the first time that my age really bothered me.

At that time the bridal industry was run by mostly older ladies. The former owner was retiring and my inherited team members were older than me so straight away I felt quite self conscious being a boss to ladies in a different age group. This age barrier was a huge test of character . Thankfully they were extremely welcoming and took me under their wings. I learnt a lot from them and I am grateful to them for taking care of me in those early days. However as time went on I took great lessons from this first 'management experience'.

Relationships in business are so so important. You need to be able to trust and communicate well with your team. I am very fortunate to have a great relationship with my workforce but in those early days I did find my age – or perhaps my insecurity around my age - a barrier and this became more and more noticeable until I started to feel like an employee in my own business.

This was entirely my fault as I had almost become too close to them so the line between boss and friendship had been crossed. They now appeared more of a 'mother figure' to me. It became quite difficult to be the boss and I started to lose confidence. Sometimes people would assume that the ladies who worked for me were the owners of the business and I would happily hide behind that. This was to avoid comments such as "Oh wow you are young to run a business like this, how have you done it?"

I used to hate the curiosity on people's faces and the questions so I happily started to sit back a bit and allow the other team members to take the lead. Not wanting to stand up and admit that yes I have started a business at such a young age and to be proud of who I was. It was a vulnerability and perhaps naivety that I couldn't have helped at that time.

A huge lesson for me and one which I have learned first hand, is not to get too close on a personal level with your team, as relationships do break down sometimes and that is hard when effectively you are still someone's employer, even though you may not have a personal relationship anymore.

I am thankful to have a good working relationship with my team today, however there is a line and I now know not to cross it.

On the contrary, being so young in an industry which tends to be dominated by older women has had its benefits and I do owe a lot of my success to being a similar age to the average bride to be. As I have got older and started to become the face of my business I have discovered how to use this to my advantage.

At thirty-one and a recent bride myself I can now relate to brides on a different level and in a way that perhaps some cannot. This, along with my knowledge of social media and incorporating platforms such as Pinterest into our consultations, offers a bride a lot more than just shopping for the dress.

It is much more of a bespoke experience when you visit Lisa Rose Bridal and my ability to think outside of the box and stay on top of market trends , as well as at the forefront of social influences, has ensured my business did not succumb to the recession and is going strong today.

With the negativity that surrounded my age and my battles to be taken seriously in the industry it has lead to a lot of self limiting beliefs and my confidence was rocked further around the time I had my first daughter. In the 12 months leading up to her birth I had hit a real low.

A very special lady, my seamstress, passed away in early 2013 after a short illness. It was a huge shock. She was loved by all who knew her and I think about her often. Her presence is all around at the Old Chapel and I take great comfort in knowing that she played a huge part in the first 4 years of my business life.

Faced with losing my seamstress, a crucial member of the team at the height of summer, and amidst the grief, I was in a sink or swim situation. I had found it hard to find a seamstress at such short notice and this special lady taught me to do the alterations so that I could undertake the work myself. I had never sewed a button until this point – it was a huge growth period for me and I owe her so much. So much, that my first daughter's name Eleanor was inspired by her. I went on to seamstress for two summers.

Now they say not to get so busy working in your business that you forget to work on your business. For those two summers I was a mess. I was overworked, I was disorganised, I was stressed, I had welcomed my first child into the chaos and my business suffered immeasurably. Cash flow was exhausted, I was exhausted and I wasn't sure if I could continue. I was a mum now, could I really be a mum and run a business?

Overheads were draining the business as I had to bring in extra help to cover my maternity leave and I honestly thought it was time to call it a day. I recall lying wide awake night after night looking for jobs as I was ready to throw in the towel.

Then, in February 2014 a freak accident changed everything! In a storm an enormous tree fell into the Chapel... Literally into the chapel! Eleanor, my eldest daughter was 3 months old at the time and I just thought 'right, that's enough, I'm out'. Half of my stock was destroyed and I lost the entire contents of my sewing room. The place was water damaged and needed a lot of work to get us back up and running. I honestly thought this was the day the doors would close for good.

Little did I know at the time that that accident was to turn my business around. I was given an opportunity to start again! I invested into new designers, I employed a new bridal consultant, developed a new website and I completely re-branded the business. Lisa Rose Bridal was born in the October of 2014! A fresh and modern new look inside and out which I feel was better connected with me. I had an exciting fire in my belly to make this business successful.. for everyone!

So, there I was with a one year old daughter going through a huge re-brand and trying to balance business with being a mum! It was and still is a huge juggling act. It isn't easy and I never ever feel like I am nailing the work/life balance. I now have two beautiful daughters, we welcomed Olivia in the September of 2015 which resulted in more time away from the business for me. This time we were moving in the right direction and I was able to take time away from my business to enjoy my second daughter. The team did a great job in my absence.

One thing for sure though, is 'mum guilt' never goes away. Every single day I have a tennis match in my head over whether I should be working or spending more time with the kids. It's so hard to switch off sometimes as I am passionate about my work and I do want to be a successful business woman and role model for my girls so they can be proud of me. I want them to see my work ethic and instil that into them as my Father did for me. Yet at the same time I don't want to miss a moment of my girls growing up.

It is a constant battle but no matter how many times the doubt creeps in and I don't think I can cope, I always do, Its just what we mums do... cope!! I wouldn't change a thing!

Over the last two years I have been on a huge personal journey too which has been difficult. I now understand how much of an impact your mind and mental well being have on your focus, your energy and ultimately your success – in all areas of your life, including business!

I have always had a very negative outlook on life. The glass is half empty kind of outlook.
'Expect the worst and you can only be pleasantly surprised' was my favourite quote! It was a defence mechanism I used to protect my feelings. Little did I know how much this outlook was actually shaping my life.

The turning point came back in 2016 shortly after I got married. Though I was on cloud nine having just married my lovely husband Phil, a wedding photographer (keeping it in the family!), I was battling so much hurt and upset in the months that followed. While on the outside the business was doing well, inside I was struggling.

My relationships began to break down with several people around me which I found incredibly difficult. It was a huge test of character for me both professionally and personally. I felt like I was close to break down.

In a quest to understand how and why this huge change in my life had happened I started on a path of personal development. I was desperate to find some peace and stop self sabotaging. I was turning all of my hurt and upset back on myself and I was desperately unhappy. One thing I found out the hard way, is that no matter what anyone says or thinks about you, nobody can hurt you as much as you can hurt yourself! The mind is a powerful thing.

Even though the business was doing OK, inside I was falling apart and I knew at that moment that I needed to do immeasurable work on myself, otherwise things were going to go downhill and I risked losing everything.

I began listening to audio books. The first one being The Secret by Rhonda Byrne. My Husband had been trying to get me to read this book since 2010 but I had such a fixed mindset that I thought it was a load of nonsense. I had given it a go a couple of times and shoved the book back in the bedside drawer but when I downloaded it to my phone it really captivated me. I would say this book has been an influential part in changing my mindset from a fixed mindset to one of growth.

I started to use the information I was learning about the law of attraction to understand why certain life events had taken place. Although uncomfortable to come to terms with, I now realise that we attract everything through our energy and our vibration. Standing back and taking ownership has been a huge area of growth for me and a great healing process.

This personal development journey led me to Female Success Network in 2017.
My lovely friend Laura Moss and now 'business bestie' who also features in this book tagged me in a post on social media one Sunday afternoon. "Join this free Pop Up Group for female entrepreneurs".
Now open to new opportunities and ready to step out of my own way I decided to go for it.

That pop up group was six weeks of heaven for me! Everything I had been reading about was being shown to me in this group! It was six weeks of personal development, business advice, friendship and of course two angels in the form of Sarah and Abigail!!

Did I attract this? Of course I did, my mind was opening and I was ready.

I was hooked and shortly after I signed up with Female Success Network to take me into the next chapter of business.

Being in business can be lonely. I have never had a 'business bestie' until now. I have never been one for networking events or groups. In fact I would run the opposite way!! I am quite a solitary creature I suppose but being in The Female Success Network has broadened my mind so much and as my first year with them comes to an end I am so grateful to be surrounded by so many inspiring and strong female entrepreneurs. A tribe of women who have my back and I theirs. To Sarah and Abi I am forever grateful to you for creating this!

So what is next for me?

The future is bright and business is doing well. I am continuing my personal development as to be honest I am kind of addicted to it! Investing in yourself is an investment you will never lose on!

Ten years in business is an achievement I am immensely proud of and I feel that I am now ready to move into the next phase. I am going from bridal consultant to business consultant and I am so excited to be opening the doors to my business and sharing exactly how I do things. I have learnt so much from my years in this industry and I would argue that this has been the most testing decade for bridal retailers and many other wedding businesses. There have been external threats I have had to overcome too, from the rise in brides choosing to buy online from China over a boutique, and the opening of huge outlets selling gowns at a fraction of the price less than two miles from my business. Not to mention the recession!

I have so much insight and knowledge to share with fellow retailers and start ups. It is so important that small businesses stick together and help each other to grow, particularly in an industry as niche as mine.

My first ten years in business have been a rollercoaster to say the least. Many highs and many lows. It isn't easy, but it is rewarding and I am ready to inspire a new generation of retailers in creating a profitable and sustainable business in the industry that I know and love.

I would like to thank my husband Phil, and my daughters, Eleanor and Olivia for their love and support as I embark on the next chapter of my career. You are my WHY!

This chapter is dedicated to my role model, my inspiration and my biggest supporter, my father Roy!

And in loving memory of Elvezia.

About Lisa Dolman

Lisa Dolman is a Bridal Industry entrepreneur and the owner of Lisa Rose Bridal in Solihull. She started her business at the age of twenty one and is now celebrating ten years in business.

Lisa comes from a family of entrepreneurs and knew from an early age that she too would enter the world of business.

She has grown to be one of the most well known and leading high end bridal boutiques in the West Midlands and has created an niche bridal experience that is unrivalled in the area. However this has not been without its trials and tribulations.

Being so young and inexperienced Lisa had a lot to learn and risked losing everything on several occasions. She started her business at the height of the recession in 2008 and some may say the odds were stacked against her.

However her business has grown through these testing times as well as with her family and she is now a mum of two beautiful girls aged 4 and 2.

Juggling business and parenthood hasn't been without its challenges either but Lisa's drive and determination to be a successful entrepreneur is the reason she is still thriving in business today.

To celebrate her success and the ten year anniversary of Lisa Rose Bridal, Lisa is compiling all of her knowledge and launching a Consultancy arm to her business with the aim of inspiring fellow retailers, as well as a new generation of boutique retailers starting out in their dream of creating a profitable and sustainable bridal business.

Contact :

Email : lisa@lisadolman.com
Website: www.lisadolman.com

Lorna Park

"Give me the child for the first seven years and I will give you the man"
Jesuit Maxim

Cold sweats came over me. Really, is this true? This is not what I had planned. Have I really produced a man that will suffer from stress, have no confidence, get bullied, give up at the slightest hurdle and is so terrified of making a mistake he would rather not even try?

I had come across this quote during a desperate search for help in understanding why my nine-year-old son was in such a mess and it set me into a tail spin.

"I've failed him," I thought. What was meant to be my biggest success had turned into my biggest failure and now, it was too late to change things…

I had always wanted to be a mother for as long as I could remember. I loved kids, I adored my nephews and I genuinely thought I would be a natural. When we found out we were pregnant we were over the moon.

The love we had for this unborn bundle was palpable. I genuinely couldn't wait for the day to come when he or she would arrive. I felt great being pregnant, in fact I was full of energy and was definitely in that "glowing" bracket that people talk about. Everyone was so excited for us and we were on cloud nine.

At this point in my life I had a managerial role in a company that took care of vulnerable and elderly people within the community. The responsibility was huge, and for me, it was the most stressful job imaginable. I was lucky, I had the most fantastic team that worked alongside me in the branch and the most dedicated and professional care staff out in the field.

We were proud of our achievements, we were fulfilling our contracts, the level of care provided was high and our inspection grades were fantastic.

However, at a time when I should have been taking care of myself, I found myself taking care of everyone else, I was working up to a hundred hours a week and now suffering from stress and fatigue.

With all the pressures from work, I was really starting to suffer and on reaching 6 months pregnant, I just couldn't cope with the stress anymore, and I burst into tears in front of all my staff.

They were worried about me and my health, they packed my bag, made me a doctor's appointment, and told me to go home.

My blood pressure was through the roof and the doctor immediately signed me off work and told me to rest, but unfortunately, that didn't make any of it less stressful. I didn't want to leave my staff, neither could I afford to be off work and be on sick pay.

I was in a complete state, it was then that I began to feel really poorly. I couldn't see properly, and my legs were giving way under me. The doctor was called and found my blood pressure to be dangerously high. I was developing Preeclampsia, a dangerous condition that could affect my baby's organs.

My symptoms continued to escalate so it was decided the best course of action would be to induce me. I thought this was a great idea, as by this point I just wanted my baby to come, but sadly this also turned into a bit of a nightmare.

After 48 hours of labour with nothing really moving forward, suddenly the room was filled with doctors and before I knew it we were being rushed into theatre for an emergency section. The baby's heart rate was dropping fast, and they needed to act quickly.

It was terrifying, but in no time my little boy was here.

I was barely aware of what happened, although if I shut my eyes, 11 years on, I can still see the image of him being held up over the screen for that second before being taken out of the room to be checked. His little squished up face and body is permanently imprinted in my memory, as is the rush of love I felt for him. The 11th of January 2007 was the happiest day of my life.

I was a mummy and I was going to be the best mummy out there. OK it hadn't been the best start for us all, but he was healthy and that was what mattered. I couldn't wait to get him home.

I suppose I had thought, that once he was here, all the stress would be gone, and I could have the joyous experience I had dreamt of. But when he was unable to latch on properly, I found myself stuck in hospital, attached to a breast pump trying to feed my baby who was starving and no chance of getting him home unless he put on weight. I tried everything. I was sore, my breasts were cracked and bleeding, and I couldn't stop crying. Like really couldn't stop crying…

We started to top him up with formula and after a week he put on enough weight to get us home under the care of the district nurses. It was great to be home, but feeding was still an issue and every time he fed I would sit and cry with the pain. After about 6 weeks my husband had had enough and gave him a bottle. He couldn't face watching me go through the trauma any longer.

Looking back the poor little thing was picking up on my anxiety about feeding him. My stress, was stressing him out. He also had colic; as I cried, so did he. It became a vicious cycle for us both.

And then, another stress, my husband received the news that the company he worked for had gone under and he was now redundant. A printer by trade meant another job was not on the horizon, as traditional printing was being squeezed by the digital market and was becoming a tougher and tougher business to be in. I can't imagine what was going through his mind at the time, with a new son to care for.

I was trying my best to stay upbeat, while the truth is I was crushed inside. I felt like a complete failure. I couldn't give birth to my son myself and now I couldn't feed him either, what kind of mother was I?

It was slowly becoming apparent that I was a mother who clearly had post-natal depression. Luckily for me I had an amazing network around me, especially my sister who whose daily visits got me through the darkest times. Eventually the sun came out, my spirits lifted, and my health improved. Once the colic was gone, my wee one was actually the happiest thing around, always smiling, loving cuddles, he just melted my heart.

There was just one issue. We were skint. With me on maternity and my husband looking for a job, things were really tight.

So, 6 months after my son's birth, the decision to return to work was kind of made for me, we needed the money, and hopefully this would also help to alleviate some of the stress and pressure on my husband too.

On returning to work, I also received a back payment for the time I had been off sick during my pregnancy. This had been paid at statutory rates originally, however I questioned this decision and they had now paid me the difference which was a huge relief.

Going back to work was stressful, but I managed to find some hidden strength in me that I hadn't had before. I went on to open another branch for the company in a new area which within a year was the most successful branch in the country in both profit and inspection grades.

It did make me sad though that I was missing out on time with my lovely boy. He was now in full time care as my husband had found another job, and I missed him terribly. What a start to his young life, surrounded by anxiety and stress and now we could throw guilt into the mix for good measure.

Sadly, more anxiety and stress for the poor thing wasn't far away, as at age two he started to show signs of having something wrong with his bowel. I really struggled to cope with watching him running around in circles screaming and crying in pain and becoming terrified of going to the toilet.

The process of discovering the problem, was intrusive and lengthy and meant years on medication for him. I hated seeing him so stressed out, but he always bounced back. He seemed very resilient, a confident happy little thing.

When redundancy number two came along, my husband found it really hard, but at least this time I was in full time work. Even though I was desperate for change and longed to do a job that meant I could spend time with my son, I was too scared to leave. Although my husband found work reasonably quickly, there was no guarantee it would last. My job was our security.

Also, we had just found out that I was pregnant again... After 5 years our little boy, was going to be a big brother and he was so excited. He was desperate for a little brother or sister.

I was healthy and happy, and work, although still stressful, was under control. Given my previous, traumatic experience, it was decided that a planned section would be best and would help keep my stress levels to a minimum.

On January the 13th our second son entered the world and our family was complete. This time was going to be so different. Everything had gone to plan, he latched on straight away and seemed like a wee natural. I felt calm and in control, until...

Just a few hours after his birth I heard a funny noise coming from the crib beside me. I was still numb from the section and couldn't really reach and to my horror my son had started to choke and was turning blue. I screamed as loud as I could to get help and just managed to grab a tiny bit of his blanket and tip him onto his side. It was a nightmare. Here I was back to square one, a nervous wreck again!

The hospital staff were amazing and looked after him all through the night. Evidently choking can be quite common with babies that are sectioned as the mucus doesn't get squeezed out during delivery. When they brought him back in the morning he was fine and hungry. I was delighted that he seemed to be great at feeding. I was so happy that I was going to get this experience with one of my boys, and all was good until day three, when he choked again.

After that he just started shaking his head and refusing to latch on. I was devastated. I remember my husband coming in to visit, to find my screen round the bed and a couple of doctors with me. I was inconsolable as my son had lost a dramatic amount of weight overnight.

I remember seeing a look of fear on his face as he thought something was terribly wrong. "I can't feed him," I spluttered through the tears. "Get her a bottle please," he replied, "she is not going through this again." He was right, I just needed someone else to make the decision.

So home we went and although I didn't have post-natal depression this time, I wasn't the calm and collected mother nature I had hoped to be.

And then, when my son was just three weeks old, my husband was made redundant for a third time. It felt like history repeating itself, but it proved to be the beginning of a better future. Just as things felt like they couldn't get much worse, an opportunity presented itself which seemed to be the answer to all our problems.

The owner of our local village Post Office had recently died, and the Post Office was now up for sale. My husband and I had no real business background, but it seemed like such divine timing. It would give him a full-time job and it meant that I could leave all the stress behind and actually be able to have time with my two boys. It wasn't really like us, but we jumped at the chance, got a business mortgage, put in all our savings and were lucky enough to have amazing family that helped us get up and running.

We loved it. We transformed the old run-down shop into a gorgeous village Post Office and gift shop and for the next two years it was fantastic. We worked really hard, but it was worth it.

Being self-employed was definitely the way forward for us. We were devastated after two years, when the Post Office came to us and told us they were changing their contracts and that we could either leave the network or go down the "modernization" route, which would mean that the way they paid us would change and we would lose a considerable amount of money.

We had no choice but to stay, as we had put everything we had into growing the gift shop, but once again we were back to struggling financially.

I felt like screaming, what was it about us, what had we done to deserve 3 redundancies in 5 years, and now this? The thought that I would have to go back to work in a similar environment as I had before just about killed me.

I remember making a definite decision about how I was going to handle yet another bad situation; I could either fall apart or decide that things were going to get better. I knew that we didn't deserve this, and it was up to us to go out there and take our future on a different path. I put it out there to the universe, that I needed something new, something different. And of course, the universe answered.

Just at that moment, I was introduced to Forever Living Products, a network marketing company. Joining the company meant that I would be able to work flexibly and still be there for the boys. It would give us the extra cash we needed to keep the Post Office going as we continued to grow the gift shop side of our business.

The one thing I hadn't banked on was, that through this new business I was going to meet the people that would go on to completely change our lives forever.

Anyone who understands network marketing will know that an important part of it is self-development. I had never come across this before in my previous working life, so it was a new concept to me. But there was no doubt that in Forever Living, we were actively encouraged to develop ourselves.

The motto was definitely, "If you want to grow your business, you have to grow yourself." We were recommended books to read, trainings to watch and encouraged to soak up everything we learnt. The more I learnt the more confident I became, and there is no doubt, "learning is earning."

However, the more I learned about myself, the more I learned about others too. And in particular, I started to really see my elder son's insecurities coming out. For instance, he was really good at Judo, he showed a natural talent for it and was doing really well, but decided, after getting beaten in one tournament to just give it up, out of the blue.

He had always worked hard in school but he seemed to have stopped trying. And as for reading, we just couldn't get him to pick up a book at all. What was more worrying was that he would get really stressed out if we encouraged him or tried to read with him.

He'd never thought of himself as a great reader, more of a maths brain, but this was extreme. He just seemed to lack any sort of internal motivation to do anything. He kept saying he was rubbish at things and appeared to be worried about everything.

He was overreacting to everything and his behaviour started to deteriorate. I felt awful. I felt it was all my fault. Had I not bonded with him properly? Look at all the stress he been surrounded with. But it was when I heard him crying himself to sleep at night, that I knew there was something more.

Finally, he admitted that he was getting bullied by a boy in school.

I was so shocked; my son had always been a really popular boy and was actually a bit of a leader within his group. Being bullied was not something I had ever thought would happen to him. It had been going on for ages now and it was beginning to really break him down.

He'd lost his confidence and was really struggling with everything. It also transpired, that at the very beginning of the new school year, his new teacher had decided to do a reading test with the class. Because he already doubted his reading ability, he had got really stressed out at the thought of it, and understandably hadn't done very well.

Due to the results of the test the teacher had dropped him down two reading groups from the one he had previously been in, and he had decided not to tell us. I must admit that I felt a bit lost with it all.

But the school were great, and very supportive, and he was starting with a brand new teacher in the new term so I hoped that things would improve. I also started to look for ways that I could help him, when I came across the Jesuit Maxim.

"Give me the child for the first seven years and I will give you the man"

Was it too late? My son was nine now. What on earth could I do to help him?

Just as I was searching for answers, a book landed on my doorstep. My lovely mentor Anna Terry had recommended it within our group to help with our business and I, just like with all the other books she had recommended, had ordered it that day.

The book was called "Mindset" by Dr Carol Dweck

I literally couldn't believe what I was reading. There on the pages set out as clear as day, was my son, his behaviour in detail, his attitude to life, his lack of persistence, resilience, confidence, his negative self-talk, his stress and worries, his decisions, but what I couldn't get over was that it wasn't just him I was seeing it was ME. Me as a child of a similar age, me growing into adulthood with all the same insecurities, me giving up on things, my fear of failure, my lack of persistence.

Now I hadn't grown up with the same stresses and issues in my early years as my son had. My mother is one of the most calm, realistic, pragmatic, deeply loving people I know. Our bond is really strong.

The only thing I could think of was that my sister was highly academic, and I was very artistic, and I believed that academia held more merit in my household. This of course wasn't the case, my mother was a music teacher after all, but I believed it at the time.

My husband was also right there on the pages. His personality written there in black and white. The pages we were all on, were the ones describing someone with a fixed mindset and all the personality traits that can go along with it. And there dancing along the pages, happily loving life was my little five-year-old, with his growth mindset still intact for all to see.

It completely blew my mind. I had never even heard of a fixed or growth mindset before!

A Fixed Mindset is when you believe that you just have a certain amount of intelligence or ability. For example, you might think you are good at English and bad at Maths or only have a talent for sports and not anything else and no matter how hard to work, your level of intelligence or ability will stay the same. Whereas a Growth Mindset is the understanding that you can develop your abilities and intelligence. It is the belief that you can get smarter, and that effort makes you stronger.

Now if you'd asked me, I would have said that I had a pretty open mind, more of a growth mindset than fixed, but actually most of us after the age of about 7 or 8 tend to move towards a fixed mindset and outside influences play a massive part in that. The way we are praised, the way we are taught in school etc.

Now I understood the Jesuit quote and where it had come from.

Help was at hand though, as the book explained that a growth mindset can always be developed, and although it would take practice, especially for us adults, it could be done. I started to immerse myself in learning on the subject.

I also took a course given by an incredible lady called Nyic Pidgeon, a Positive Psychologist who taught me about how the brain works and how we can bring more happiness and joy into our lives, (her work is heavily influenced by Dr Dweck.) I started to see how praise played a massive part in how our mindset is developed.

For example, me feeling that my sister was academic and I was artistic, is a perfect case in hand. We came from a loving home where praise was given a lot. I was praised for being good at singing and she was praised for her academic achievements.

I was a good singer, but when I came up against others that were better than me, in true fixed mindset style, rather than work on my craft and develop my skills so I could improve, I just believed they were better. I lost my confidence in my own abilities and eventually gave up. I realised that the way we had praised our son for his Judo was exactly the same. We praised him for his natural talent and he believed he was good, so when it got tough he lost his confidence in his ability and eventually gave up.

We decided to start praising effort and hard work instead, showing the boys that this was our top priority. Instead of asking how their day was, we asked them what they had worked hardest on.

We encouraged them to make mistakes and learn from them. The language we used started to change. The dinner time discussions we had were different.

We started to discuss things like intrinsic motivation, the law of attraction, how the brain works, feelings and emotions, goal setting; all the things I was learning about growth mindset and positive psychology. I was particularly amazed at how well my elder son engaged with the discussions and was able to understand some pretty difficult subjects.

Amazingly, the results were immediate. His confidence started to grow, he started to see that the more he read the better he got at it. The more effort he put into his football, the more his ability grew. He began to practise his guitar without being told to, he started to become engaged in school again, he was more resilient and certainly more persistent.

It was life changing for all of us, and as if the planets had aligned in our favour, his new teacher knew all about growth mindset too. I'll never forget when we walked into her classroom for the parents' open evening, to be faced with a full wall dedicated to growth mindset. It was wonderful.

I became an avid reader and learner, which is something I never thought I would be. I started to use guided journals as a way to develop and document my learning, and as it was helping me, I started to look for something similar that could help my son develop his understanding too.

I desperately wanted to find something that he could have for himself, that challenged him, taught him all the things I was learning, but in a fun engaging way. Something that would encourage him to write down his thoughts and feelings as he worked through the information.

Basically, some kind of growth mindset/positive psychology journal. The only one I could find was American and geared to much younger children. It didn't cover anything like the subjects that I was looking for, so I decided to try and write one myself.

My Great Big Positive Life journal was born.

It started off as just a small booklet, but my son loved it, and enjoyed the different activities as well as all the reading that was involved. Once it was complete he asked for some more and that's when I knew we were on to something. If this could make such a difference to him I was sure there were loads of other kids out there who could benefit from something like this too.

I did some research, chatted to other parents, and the feedback was amazing. Many parents were facing the same obstacles as us and were really concerned about the lack of confidence, resilience and persistence their kids seemed to have.

They were also worried about how their kids could thrive in a world where real life was being distorted so much by the online and social media reality they were starting to find themselves in.

I knew that along with my husband, I could come up with something really good. My passion for the subject and his experience and contacts in the design and printing trade made a winning combination.

The more we discussed it the more passionate we became about actually doing it properly and turning it into an actual business. One problem, we had no idea how we could bring something like this to the marketplace.

The businesses we were currently running had clear systems that we just tapped into, but starting from scratch was a completely different ball game altogether.

Once again, the Universe came to my rescue, and just as we were working out the possibilities of starting another business, and not getting very far, Female Success Network was launched. Knowing the two incredible women behind it I knew that signing up to the Unstoppable Mastermind was a no brainer. And so it has proved to be. Like some kind of magic fairy dust, every time I have lost direction, faced a challenge, doubted myself, they have been there, to get me back on track, stay on mission with their insane business knowledge and kind hearts.

This journey hasn't been easy for me. The writing of the journal alone has been the hardest thing I have ever done. The whole process has challenged me more than I ever could have imagined. But the sense of fulfilment and knowing deep down the difference this could make to so many kids, has driven me to make it the best it could possibly be, whilst Abi and Sarah have driven me to be the best that I can possibly be.

There is no doubt that Female Success Network Mastermind is special. Your "vibe definitely attracts your tribe." And just as Abi and Sarah are the most supportive, honest, open, talented

pair of women I have met, the rest of the women within the Mastermind have proven to be the same.
It honestly feels like a privilege to be surrounded by such incredible, creative, energetic, loving, diverse, passionate, human beings, and their support has been invaluable.
Female Success Network is led with truth and heart which I feel is quite unique. Abi and Sarah have opened themselves up to us, and as a result we have been able to watch them step into their own shining light, with them not just telling us, but actually showing us, how to do the same.

My Great Big Positive Life just wouldn't be the same without them. xx

Lorna Park

Lorna Park is a mum on a mission. Creator and co-founder of My Great Big Positive Life, she is passionate about helping children develop a deeper understanding of their own Mind, Body and Souls using the principles of Growth Mindset, Positive Psychology and Mindfulness.

Worried about the increasingly stressful, noisy world our children are living in, whether it be from the endless succession of testing them from a very early age, the rise of social media and the constant comparison that comes with it, or the never-ending need to be entertained, Lorna feels that sadly, not only are the days of having a carefree childhood gone, but that children are not able to switch off in order to create a clear and calm space in which to grow.

Through her own personal study into the recent developments of Neuroscience, and inspired by the work of Positive Psychologists and Authors such as Dr. Carol Dweck, Niyc Pidgeon, and Arianna Huffington, she truly believes that once we understand how our brains work and develop, we are able unlock the key to our own future happiness and success.

Inspired by the changes in her son Charlie (11), and seeing first hand the impact working on Growth Mindset, Positive Psychology and Mindfulness has had on his own self belief, resilience, persistence, stress levels and over all health, but disappointed in the resources available to him, she has created the "My Great Big Positive Life Journal", for children, so they can empower themselves with the techniques and knowledge that will allow them grow into strong, powerful, unique individuals, comfortable with who they are and able to live their own great big positive life.

The first of it's kind in the UK, My Great Big Positive Life Journal "Superstar" Edition (for ages 9+) guides it's owner through each of the principles using different methods such as reading, creative writing, activities and exercises. Encouraging personal engagement, the journal is a place to develop positive daily habits, a place for self reflection, a place to set individual goals and measure outcomes, and offers space such dream space and genius space to encourage imagination.

Covering a wide range of topics such as "Making Friends With Failure" "How to Rewire Your Brain" "Just Breathe" "Mindfulness Matters" "Random Acts of Kindness" "Dream Big" "Attitudes of Gratitude" "Choose Happy" " The Power of Yet" "You Ain't Nothing But A Goal Digger" "Stay True To Who You Are" and many more, the emphasises is on the child to develop their own individual journal of joy, at their own pace and create something special and unique to them.

Lorna is now devoted to spreading the My Great Big Positive Life message far and wide and alongside her journals, is creating a special place for parents to come together so they can go on a great big positive life journey of their own, she is also very excited to announce that work on My Great Big Positive Life Journal "Little Stars" Edition, for children aged 5-8 is already underway.

CONTACT:

Email: mygreatbigpositivelife@gmail.com

Website: mygreatbigpositivelife.co.uk

Facebook: www.facebook.com/mygreatbigpositivelife

Instagram: www.instagram.com/mygreatbigpositivelife

Natalie Tilsley

I cowered as another piece of crockery came hurling towards where I was hiding under the sofa. My father was sitting above me, I could see the swell of his weight as I hid underneath it. He had his arms outstretched across the back and he was laughing. My mum was not laughing, she was the one who was hurling expletives and whatever she could lay her hands on.

I was around 4 maybe 5 and shortly after I remember just my mum, myself and my brother moving into a new home without him.

This early memory clearly impacted on me, the feeling of not being good enough for my father, not being important enough that a school sports day, or parents evening was one he could attend.

This feeling stayed with me for most of my childhood and if I'm truly honest is something that causes a sadness to this day that as a parent myself, not having a desire to be a part of a child's life in any capacity is one I simply cannot comprehend.

Although my biological father wasn't around to guide me through childhood and into my teenage years, I did have my pops, my dad and a real top guy mum married when I was 7.

On more than one occasion I did use the excuse that as my father wasn't around I could do as I pleased (this is one I did throw at pops many times, sorry). As a consequence I didn't always heed the advice mum and pops gave me and was a bit of a rebel at school.

It was the summer of 1985 when the white envelope fell onto the doormat, a moment everyone during their life will experience, results day.

Instantly the phone rings and it's my bestie Becs, I opened my letter and squealed 9 passes... "are you sure?" she said, what do you mean am I sure? of course a few B's, a D and the rest are C's, not bad considering we never revised and we were in the top groups at school. We had better things to do than study! Like clubbing on our fake ID's, I mean come on who hasn't?!

As it turned out I was holding the results sheet the wrong way up and the C's were actually U's. UNGRADED. Becs results were not much better hence she queried my initial joy. She did go on to pass all her subjects, attend Uni and more and has achieved incredible success as one of Australia's top eco designers and founder of her own clothing and lifestyle brand www.tluxe.com !

Clearly my time behind the fag shed smoking and skiving off school was not the smartest way to spend my time at school.

Now I had to re-set my compass and work out how to explain to my parents I wouldn't be taking my place up at Loughborough and embarking on my dream to travel the world using the 7 different languages, I had spent the past 5 years supposedly studying. Now I had to get onto a YTS course, not quite what I had planned and quite a wake up call.

You see I have always had plans, mum said if I wanted something I had to work for it, so I would plan. I mapped out a reward chart as a younger child showing how much my parents would pay me for jobs I would do. 2 pence for this and 5 pence for that and so on, all adding up to the amount I wanted to have each week. I'm not sure how long this lasted but I'm pretty sure that whilst my parents encouraged this early entrepreneurial spirit, their wallets may not.

I recognised early on that you needed to have a plan and I would write down ideas to make money. Some never came to fruition, some were shockingly bad ideas, some were sheer fun and some were absolutely not within the law but hey I was a kid and you have to push the boundaries. Don't you?!

I have always been fiercely independent, inquisitive and one who always looked out for ways to earn extra pocket money. From paper rounds, babysitting, evening work after school in a factory pressing jumpers and even becoming a perfumier!

As a child did you ever crush flower petals into water to make your own 'perfume'? The joy of making up little bottles of this fragranced water and smelling the sweet aroma of fresh flowers, well this was one of my early ventures into making some extra pocket money.

Together with my cousin Jo Jo we would go out in the morning armed with our 'kit", which consisted of some bottles and a bucket of water and we would happily go along to people's gardens 'use' their lush flowers and sit quite literally on the pavement outside of their homes making our potions. Quite oblivious to the fact we had picked away at someone's lovely flowers for our own purpose. To cap it all we then went and knocked on their door and sold them our fresh handmade flowery perfume, most actually bought it albeit a few did send us off packing!

Having attended 13 schools growing up as my pops was in the RAF I could either be a wallflower or enjoy my childhood and make friends, so that's exactly what I did, networking and making connections wherever I went, some schools I even went to twice. I have great memories of freedom as a child and being able to go out all day and cause mischief, I simply viewed it as having fun.

My journey into the working world after leaving school made me realise how easy being a kid really was, no financial worries, freedom and being able to just innocently go through life without much of a care in the world, it was a real eye opener and having flunked my exams, my options were limited.

Starting out in a hairdressers I thought this would be a great job, an older cousin Jane was a hairdresser and she always seemed so cool to me - well this job didn't last long. So I joined a YTS Scheme, earning a whopping £25 a week + £2.50 for bus fares, I had the grand sum of £27.50 all to myself.

Mum said I should save a third, pay board a third and the rest was mine, well I didn't pay board and I didn't save. Poor old pops would drive me into town for nights out (as I had missed the bus and was running late aka wanting to save money on the bus fare) having to listen to my TDK90 tapes of 80's music playing Cyndi Lauper 'Girls just wanna have fun'.

Financial lesson not being learned here, saving / investing your money at an early age will stand you in good stead later in life. Sadly, for me I didn't learn a valuable lesson, fortunately though my hubby is good with money!

I am a sponge for learning new skills and taking in information and knowledge so despite my shortcomings at school, it was a swift learning curve and one which I grasped at every opportunity. Subsequently I have gained a range of qualifications from A level's, to Accounting, Training, Credit Management and also have a post graduate from Nottingham Trent University in Business Management and a plethora of various courses in between.

I truly believe in education, whether that is through the system or through self-development. I spend a great deal of my time in the car commuting from the Midlands where I live to the East Coast of Lincolnshire where my Businesses are located. I will listen through the audible app at least 2-3 books a month if not more. Educating yourself and absorbing knowledge is in my opinion a great asset which will take you through life and its rollercoaster journey.

I cannot write a chapter of a book without mentioning my babies, who are my world, my reason for existing, my life and the reason why I have been a serial entrepreneur. Admittedly a small part is my own drive and need to succeed and be the best I can be but my babies come before everything.

My children literally are my productivity secret, my powerful weapon, my armour and who without knowing are the reason I exist day by day. Quick breather as I'm sat in a cafe in a market town writing this and tears are streaming down my face as I think of the sheer undiluted love I have for Jamie and Sian. I must also include my adorable Hugo, our Chocolate Labrador who I am unashamedly obsessed with.

I was 17 when on the 19 September 1986 when my little soldier came into this world (he will grimace at this term of endearment but hey Mum's have that privilege!) to say it was a huge milestone where my compass was seriously re-set is an understatement. My life was to change and take a direction and I thought of myself as a mature grown up, so this should be a breeze, however I was just a child myself trying to wear the big boots of an adult and now a mother.

It was challenging, I made mistakes, but boy did I learn so much in a short period of time. I wasn't a stay at home mum and I guess my failure in achieving the exam results at school spurred me on to prove to myself I was capable and that I could still achieve, so as soon as I could I went out to work for a firm of Solicitors. Jamie was looked after during the day by his Nanny, my mother in law adored this role and having a family support network was vital to me as my parents has recently emigrated to Spain.

Becoming a mum at such a young age is something I do not regret. Jamie has grown up to be seriously cool, respectful, likeable, genuine and great fun to be around. He attended Uni carved out his career as a Quantity Surveyor specialising in large scale projects and is truly content doing what he loves. He has built his own dream life many thousands of miles away in Australia with his girlfriend of 10 years Chloe. She is the ying to his yang and as a mother I could not wish for a more suited partner for him to spend the rest of his life with, Chloe is quite simply blinking awesome.

6 years passed before my Princess Sian, this bundle of independent joy bounced into my life on the 10th November 1992. I wasn't actually sure if Jamie would remain an only child but I guess it's all about timing when the time is right good things will come to you.

Life has been entertaining with Sian and the great beauty of having my babies is seeing them come into their own, both are so different. Sian is feisty, has a strong will and is an absolute grafter. Not only funny, quick witted and generous she's also untidy like her brother was at home, what kids aren't !

Sian knew early on what she wanted to do with her career and she is now a highly respected Veterinary Nurse working out of hours responding to emergency cases. She has always had a passion for animals and this has been a huge bond between us. As I slowed down my career in her teenage years we were able to share a love of horses which I introduced her to at 4 years old.

As a parent I see my role as one who is there is to nurture, guide and encourage my babies so that they pursue every dream possible.

I have always been a great planner throughout my working life and this has led me to a system called PLAN DO REVIEW. A piece of advice I would give to anyone starting out in a business venture would be to not to under-estimate the value in not only mapping out your plan of action but to implement it without procrastination. It enables you re-set your compass, re-evaluate where you are at versus where you want to be. Assess if you need to change the co-ordinates, implement a different strategy, stop an action and start doing something different. If you do not take this element seriously you won't see a clear picture of the vision you created when you first had your business idea.

During the summer of 1996 whilst finalising my Institute of Credit Management exams I went along to my first ever assessment centre for a job role, something I had never experienced before. A full day of interviews, tests, presentations, role play and group exercises.

Thankfully my tutor at the ICM gave me great advice about being prepared, structured and doing research into the Company, its mission statement and its values and prepared me on what to expect from the day. It held me in good stead as I got the job and its where I met Matt. I wasn't love at first sight or anything corny like that we were both married at the time and not looking for 'love'. However, I was aware my marriage was deteriorating, which was solely down to me, I just did not work at it and sadly it came to an end in early 1997.

As a department we socialised a lot and I guess spending so much time in each other's company Matt just grew on me. He is funny, professional and was an unexpected distraction following the demise of my marriage. Matt is my rock and not only has a wonderful relationship with Jamie and Sian but also has to put up with my ideas, my relaxed attitude to life against his organised one and is the constant cog in my wheel. I do not tell him often enough how much his love and support means to me. So tell your loved ones you care, do not hold in your emotions, share them and enjoy a good work/life balance too. This is important.

I had become another statistic, from being a teenage mum, a teenage bride, to now a single mum at just 29. I was consciously aware of the example I was setting my kids and this played on me, so it was time to re-set my compass yet again and pull my boots up and get focused on being the best Mum I could be

Again being the mum at home wasn't an option for me.

I chose to change career paths in 2003 following time away from work due to a knee operation, I felt that the time had come to move on, I was not comfortable with recent Management changes and made a decision to walk away from a stable secure well-paid job.

Although at the time I was leading a team of B2B Telesales people and had moved through the divisions of this company beginning in our Investment support unit. I was well networked within the organisation, I was diligent and respected in my role, and in the position I held I had Profit and Loss accountability and my team had recently delivered £3 million profit, achieving a 6% profit growth against a company average of 2.5%. I was proud of this fact and thoroughly enjoyed working here.

The company had funded my post-graduate in Business Management at Nottingham Trent University and supported developing my leadership skills. Having this further education at a higher level opened my eyes to the importance of broadening your skillset and I am grateful for being given that opportunity.

Experiencing the recent changes on a day to day basis and knowing that it was not a situation I was comfortable with was the push I needed to make my foray into property developing and being my own first real true boss. Equally probably not the best of timings to walk away from my career as Matt had proposed and we were getting married at the end of 2003.

I asked hubby what he believes are the habits that make me successful and carefree and why I simply don't worry about income. His response was simply it is my can-do attitude, I am always very clear on the route I wish to take and where I wish to go to. I am tenacious and cope well under pressure.

Being adaptable, having a willingness to simply get on with it whatever obstacles are in my way and staying true to my core values are part of the reason I am successful. These qualities together with Matt's ability to just let me be myself and go with the flow are habits we form at an early age and have just nurtured as we grow into ourselves.

Whilst I was putting my organisational and project management skills to good use in renovating properties I was approached by a former colleague to support the growth of his Pub Management Company. An all-encompassing operational role, I was fortunate enough to receive a good benefits package and one which also provided a great degree of flexibility in my working hours.

This enabled me to be the mum who could be at school gates in the morning and afternoons and still work in the corporate world with a regular income, all whilst still developing properties.

Following a back operation in late spring of 2012 exacerbated by what can only be described as a cocky lack of judgement by me whilst exercising Sian's horse Apollo, our cheeky piebald (that's a story for another day). I ended up with a serious back operation and 4 months off work.

This time off gave me the opportunity to again re-set my compass and evaluate what direction my life was going in. I was bored, bored of being reliant still on a paid job, a job which although was flexible and I had pretty much carte blanche on holidays, was still one which someone else controlled. The decision was made for me, I was offered redundancy and not for the first time in my working life.

Fate has a way of finding you at a time when you most need it and that is exactly what happened next. Hugo came into my life. He is a 4-legged obsession of mine, my adorable Chocolate Labrador who I am unashamedly besotted with and totally completes our family unit. He is THE most attentive, loving, full of character fur baby you could have and totally rocks my world. I had filled my nest again.

At the same time, I was approached about a business opportunity in Network Marketing, one I had turned down some 10 years prior. This time I took a closer look and found it ticked the boxes I needed. Time, flexibility, making your own decisions, working your own hours, taking holidays when you wanted, earning whatever you wanted.

Does it sound too good to be true? Most things are unless you are prepared to work for them and I was prepared to work.

I began expanding my network and growing my business within the Health & Wellness sector working under the umbrella of what I still arguably believe to be one of the best NWM Companies around. I built this around a Strategic Consultancy Business that I had also recently started which supported SME's on all aspects of licensing and business structures.

This opportunity opened my eyes in so many ways. The friends and family who didn't support you as it wasn't a traditional business, the repetitive strains of hearing 'oh is that a pyramid scheme" (which are illegal by the way) and fellow business owners becoming embroiled in a blame culture which was not entirely pleasant at times.

However quite simply put to sustain and grow your own business you need to be accountable only to yourself. This was a downside and resilience in abundance was needed during the tough times. The upside was I had a great mentor, who is recognised as one of the top leaders in the world, I gained new skills and knowledge and I finally discovered what the mind can achieve if you work on it. The best bit? The incredible friendships formed.

I will add here that the friends I have had for years are a particular group of girlies who have always been a constant in my life and for that I cherish their friendship, their laughs and the millions of Whatsapp messages a day. I know with absolute certainty that they will always have my back and frankly could not give a flying toss whatever it was I did.

If you have friends like this, hold them close and never let go. Especially my cousin Jo Jo and Diane who are both a beacon in my world.

This business saw my income provide more than that of my corporate pay, it has taken me to many destinations around the world staying in some breathtaking locations, all paid for by the Company as a reward for the promotions I have achieved simply for growing my business and reaching out and helping others do the same.

One of the greatest outcomes of my involvement with NWM (Network Marketing) was meeting Lyndsey Bishell.

NWM is incredibly sociable and after being introduced to one another we quickly forged a friendship and linked our expanding teams together, sharing our knowledge and delivering training sessions along with another lush chick Sam Webb we became a strong united force.

Sam has since re-discovered her passion for beauty and has a salon called Re-Skulpt Clinic in Bristol offering remarkable cosmetic results, if you are in the area, go check her out she is a darling.

Whilst I am no longer working on this business I am still provided with a residual income through the international networks I created and continue to use the products.

Following some cyber challenges and seeing Lyndsey suffer horrendously over a long period of time, I began to lose confidence in my own ability and a passion for a venture which had seen me flourish over the preceding 5 years diminished. So, I took on some project work which was due to last for 3 months but creeped into 19 months! This was flexible and again enabled me to re-evaluate what I wanted to do next. Should I re-establish my Strategic Consultancy and support SME's utilising the additional skills I had gained? I was at a crossroads...

Through social media I came across a newly formed group for female entrepreneurs called the Female Success Network headed by Abigail Horne whom I knew from my NWM days and Sarah Stone who I knew had a respected background creating Visual Designs in photography and websites.

I had a look around the group and watched a live feed in which a lady called Jo Gilbert was sharing about the importance of Business Planning, I could so relate to this woman and felt a pull to find out more. Following a discovery call with Abigail it was clear that this was a move from NWM and more focused on supporting women just like me develop a business idea and have the support in all areas to see it evolve.

Exactly what I needed, as I had an idea bubbling away, it wasn't exciting me, but it was an idea. Little did I know it wasn't this idea that was to become my business but something I had considered previously but rejected due to my back injury.

I remember saying to Sarah 'I'm not sure it could work?" Sarah's typical response was "why not, look at how you could make it work". I shared these thoughts with Lyndsey whilst enjoying a cheeky drink in our PJ's one evening, she said there was a massive demand for this type of business in the area. A bottle or 2 later we had the framework outlined for a Cleaning Company based in the East Lindsey District of Lincolnshire, almost 3 hours from where I lived.

It also happened to be where my parents lived and where I had recently bought 2 holiday lets on the coast, there was a demand for good quality accommodation in the area. I didn't actually plan on buying I was only meant to be helping my parents with their holiday rental but as you may be aware by now I can be decisive and impulsive.

They are 2 static caravans, which I rent out to holiday makers and I absolutely love them, they are flourishing under the brand name of Seaside Escapes. If you want to see them I'd be thrilled if you headed on over to our Facebook group and become part of our community.

Being a part of a mastermind group within FSN provided me with access to women from all walks of life all in the same position as me, setting up a new business venture or establishing an existing one.

Abigail encouraged myself and Lyndsey to have our brand Trademarked once we had found a suitable name (all credit for that goes to Lyndsey's husband Adam – thanks maud!), this demonstrated commitment to our brand, the business and the longevity of its future.

Using the advice we were being given through our strategy calls, we were able to identify what was important to us in creating a brand that would be identifiable, what our values were, our goals and our mission. Fortunately, we both are so connected we have similar likes and dislikes. So, after much playing with Pinterest our brand image was created and with the guidance of Sarah, I'm immensely proud of the fact that Lyndsey created our website with no prior experience.

That one night with glasses in our hands where the bare bones of our business were formed then became 4 months of solid planning. We analysed our competitors and what would make us stand out from the crowd, how we could be different and what we could do to attract the right customer. 'Plan Do Review' came into action once again.

We established route to markets and what areas we wanted to focus on, what type of service we wanted to provide and who we wanted to work with. Finding the right key people to work with was the most important thing to us. We knew that having a team of like-minded, enthusiastic and hardworking people around us would ensure we had a strong reputation for delivering a professional service with personalised results.

Coast to Country Cleaners Ltd® has been in operation since February 2018 and in a few short months we have seen it grow from strength to strength with 22 employees and growing.

We have 5 key areas of Service we provide;

Coastal, commercial, domestic, wellness and bespoke cleaning with a diverse range of clients. In the short time we've been operating we've secured key contracts with the local council, top holiday resorts in the area, stately homes, local businesses and individuals such as Ann who just needs a helping hand whilst her mobility is restricted and loves a good chat too! We cater for everybody and offer a personalised service unlike anybody else on the market and I'm proud to fly that flag.

Whilst 18-hour days are not uncommon I would not change it for a second. We have created through the guidance and support of FSN a business which we are so proud of, clients who we are grateful to and who we are proud to be partnered with, a team surrounding us who are simply blinking awesome and we know the foundations we have created will continue to grow. So, if you are ever in doubt or are pondering a decision simply re-set your compass and see where it takes you.

Success is there for anybody who is prepared to take the first step and to work hard for it just look at me. I was a mum at 17, I left school with no qualifications, I had a failed marriage and 2 young children. I had a choice just as we all have a choice, let the road ahead carve out its own path for me or create my own.

I chose to re-set my compass and I am totally committed to enjoying every moment, with one crystal clear focus, to be the mum my babies are proud of.

With love

    Nat x

About Natalie Tilsley

Natalie Tilsley is co founder of Coast to Country Cleaners® which is blazing a trail in the provision of a Professional Cleaning Service to a diverse range of clients throughout the East Lindsey District of Lincolnshire. Also owner of Seaside Escapes which specialises in traditional coastal holiday homes that provide a home from home break for all the family.

Becoming a mum in her teenage years and the challenges this presented left Natalie with a burning desire to prove to herself and others that obstacles can be overcome and regardless of the start you have in life you can make a difference.

Her mission is to not only be the inspiration to her now grown up children, who have been the driving force behind her quest for financial stability and to show them that you can be who you want to be, also her desire to empower others from all walks of life who may have felt simply not good enough.

That feeling of not being valued for who you are is one many can resonate with and Natalie shows that you CAN be who you want to be and you can create your own path. You just have to re-set your own compass.

A member of the Nottingham Trent Alumni where she completed her Post-graduate in Business Management she has vast experience in supporting SME's and individual business owners across many sectors. She is a highly regarded professional whose reach has enabled her to build international collaborations.

This experience coupled with her can do attitude and an unrelenting pursuit in creating an environment where the hand picked team who share the same vision, deliver a customer experience at the highest level, where standards will not be compromised is a testament to the tenacity and integrity which represent Natalie's core values.

When not commuting between her home in Warwickshire and her businesses on the Lincolnshire coast she loves nothing more than spending time with her now grown up children Jamie and Sian and her very supportive (long suffering!) husband Matt, not forgetting her beloved chocolate Labrador Hugo.

Natalie loves to connect with others and can be reached at:

natalie@coasttocountrycleaners.com
www.coasttocountrycleaners.com
https://www.linkedin.com/in/natalietilsley/
https://www.facebook.com/natalie.tilsley
https://www.facebook.com/groups/1413049098762994/
https://www.pinterest.co.uk/natalietilsley/

Nichola Sproson

Have you ever sat back, taken a look at your life and thought... "Wowzers, I created all of that!!!" If you haven't yet, or are not in a place to yet, don't worry! Up until two years ago I hadn't either..

Like most people, I did not understand that every decision you make, every thought that you have, every gut feeling you ignore determines the reality that you live and, it can change in an instant...if you just allow yourself to open your heart and let it!

Let me take you back to 2015. At nearly 34 years of age I looked like I had it made! On paper my life was great! I was on Maternity leave with my second son Finley. I had a 6 year career as a Police Constable, and my fiance John was an engineer in the oil industry.

With two 2 beautiful boys (Harrison then 3 years old and Finley just 1 year) our own 3 bedroom house in a lovely quiet location in Dover, Kent and we had just had our wedding day, a weekend long celebration on the top of a cliff in Ilfracombe, Devon with all of our closest friends and family...just perfect! Or so it should have been!!

The fact was I was so wrapped up in the reality that I thought I should be living through the judgements of society and others; I failed to see that I had settled into a life that was not mine and that I was not happy living. I was miserable, full of anxiety and I felt trapped. I didn't think I deserved or was worth a life that was better.

Feeling stuck I carried on doing the only thing I knew how to do, push my feelings aside and playing out the role I had given myself, anxiety getting stronger with every push.

During this time my main focus was my career as I was due to return to work after 14 months off on Maternity. If I am really honest with myself now, I have always wanted to help people, but the only reason I became a Police Constable was a last attempt at a good, strong, solid career with a good pension at the end of it like society led me believe I needed to have.

Let's face it if you are going to work doing the same job risking your own safety for others for 35 years of your life, you need a decent pension at least!

I was 27 years of age when I joined the Police force. I thought that this was it, I was in it for the long haul and there didn't seem like any other option for me, no going back…this was as good as it was going to get! What a crazy mindset to have, I honestly did not think that I would be able to retrain or pursue an alternative career…it was now too late.

Being a Copper had its ups and downs and the "JOB", well it changes you as a person, it did me any way. You put walls up, get hardened to the things that you see and deal with without even realising you have…you have to, it is part of the job, it becomes the 'norm' and I was ok with that.

Life changes, most of the friends I had fell away and my behaviour changed, with a constant reminder that I was now a pillar of society there to uphold the law 24/7. I never quite got used to that especially since I had been quite the party girl before, but that's a different story. Ha!

To be honest I was pretty lucky and I had a great team of officers around me, all the Inspectors, Sergeants and colleagues I had within the Police all had a strong bond together and the laughs we had to get us through those long shifts makes you a family unit, I will be forever grateful to the support I had from every officer I ever had the pleasure of working with.

On reflection I was a good PC. I did my job and I did it well, but I never felt like I was an officer. It just was not me and I did not enjoy it. I much preferred to sit with the victims of crime and take statements than actually be out there and I don't actually like confrontation, seems so funny looking back that was my actual job for 7 years.

After having my first son Harrison, my whole perception of the Job changed again. I now had a little human being who depended on me, needed ME! Before I didnt think about the dangers of the job but they started to become more and more prevalent.

As a Police Constable you face many situations that you would never normally be in, in real life. You detach yourself from the reality of what is going on and if you do not deal with it mentally, it can bite you in the ass! This is what happened to me and was the start of my anxiety!

In 2014 I was in the report writing room at the station heavily pregnant with my 2nd child Finley. Some of my team were out assisting the Mental Health Team on a routine job. All of a sudden the radios in the office went crazy with shouts that there was a knife and officers injured. Every available officer upped and left the office...except me!

I sat, hands on a moving stomach, listening to the radio not knowing the extent of the situation and wondering...what if that happened to me!... Luckily even though some officers received stab wounds there were no major injuries and every officer that returned dealt with the situation with the usual banter...excitement over...next job.

Soon after that I went onto maternity leave forgetting about the incident, or so I thought.

Finley was born and all of a sudden life got crazy. With working in the oil industry, John was away...A LOT and I found myself trying to cope with having a 2 year old and a newborn on my own for the majority of the time.

I was up to my neck in night feeds, day feeds, housework, nappies, baby puke (Finley did like to be sick) potty training and Harrison would not leave his brother alone, which meant I had to have one of the boys with me at all times. They could not be together out of my sight.

At this point in my life I had no knowledge about how the Universe works, the Law of Attraction, Angels, Divine Timing or Synchronicity. Now I know that I was majorly out of alignment with myself and my life's purpose, and was about to get my butt kicked into gear by the Universe!

Something magic happened and my life began to change, events began to unfold before me and I was ready to listen. Don't get me wrong it gets messier before it gets better but sometimes it all has to come crashing down before you can build yourself back up.

My younger sister Sarah joined a Network Marketing Company. I had absolutely no interest in the business at all but wanted to support her and help her anyway I could.

Over the next few months I watched and to my amazement she started to do things out of her comfort zone and looked like she was having fun. I met Sarah's upline 'Abigail Horne' and watched her story unfold with keen interest...I could do that! I had eight months left before I had to return to work and could build the business up when the boys were asleep giving me something to do in the evenings when John was away and I was just sat in front of the TV wasting away.

With excitement in my belly, New Year 2015 I started my own Network Marketing business...I had found the solution to all of my problems and was determined. All I could think of was if I could make enough money John could come home to work locally. I just wanted my family together.

It was Abigail Horne who first introduced me to The Secret Law of Attraction, and the idea that everything you think about you become. This made perfect sense to me and was the first time I started to think about everything as energy. How had I never come across this before? My mind started to open up and I started to see the possibilities I had available to me, and I was willing to work for them.

The business took over! Every waking minute I would be watching or making training videos, networking or mentoring my small team of twenty. All I could focus on was getting higher up so I could get John home and not go back to the Police Force.

This was about to drastically backfire;
I was all over social media showing people how happy I was and how great I was doing but inside I was a mess.
Everything was going in slow motion, I stopped going to visit my friends and hardly left the house.

By running my business I was fuelling my stress and anxiety, having mood swings and crying at the drop of a hat. When John was home I made little or no time for us as a family and I became frustrated and angry that he could not support me. But, how could he support me, I was obsessed and so closed off to what was going on around me that I retreated further inside myself.

By the time I was due to go back to work I was at breaking point. I was tired, stressed and the anxiety had well and truly kicked in. Even though my relationship with John was at an all time low, and believe me we have had a few, I longed for him to work closer to home to be a family. But the thought of going back to work as a Police Officer, put me into overdrive. I was in the prison of my own mind and I didnt know how to get out.

Finally I made the decision to go to the Doctor where I was asked if I wanted antidepressants or counselling. I chose both, I needed them.

I returned to work as a Police Officer. Both my Inspector and Sergeant could not have supported me more in trying to integrate me back to work, easing me in very slowly and gently. I went back to the station on light duties, which for me meant working in the office and in civilian clothing (normal clothes).

A month or so passed and it was decided that I would go into work still on light duties but in uniform so I could become accustomed to wearing it again. Unfortunately for me some wires were crossed and I was assigned a job out of the station straight away.

This instantly triggered major anxiety for me and on the way to my locker to pick up my airwaves I had my first ever panic attack. I dashed to the ladies locker room where I broke down crying, hardly able to breathe just pacing up and down. It was so scary. I had left my mobile phone up in the report writing room which was three floors up...I had to get upstairs.

Not wanting to bump into anyone I took the stairs instead of the lift. I saw my friend who asked "Are you okay?" This little sentence felt like the worst thing ever, I was not okay. Not being able to talk about it I dashed into the next toilets where I continued to pace up and down trying to catch my breath, with tears streaming down my face freaking out everytime I caught a glimpse of myself in uniform in the mirror.

A colleague came into the toilets and saw what an absolute state I was in and went and spoke to my Sergeant who came into me and calmed me down enough for me to be come out of the toilets. It was then the embarrassment of the whole ordeal kicked in. I was utterly mortified and felt so so stupid.

We went to the canteen as I could not face going back into the office in fear of having another attack in front of my colleagues. It was decided that I was in not fit state to continue my shift and I left to go home. I didn't know it then but I never returned to do another shift as a Police Constable ever again.

Around the same time my relationship with John broke down and we separated. I was now a single mum to two young boys, no career and a mortgage to pay. How had it come to this? Everything I had been fighting for rightly or wrongly, I had lost. The split with John was not an easy one and lead to over a year of arguing and animosity between us.

Totally broken I continued with my counseling and ended up having 11 sessions instead of the original 8. If I had not had those sessions I don't think I would of had the strength to continue and know that deep down the relationship breakdown was for the best , for me, John and the boys, although it did not seem like it at the time.

Believe it or not at this point my Network Marketing business was at its strongest and I was just about to hit my next promotion. But with the weight of the cost of what I had lost I just could not turn up for my business, I had burnt out. In the darkness of that time Abigail Horne was my pillar of light. From the moment I met her she had seen something in me, a strength that I could not see. She believed in me when I did not believe in myself, and this was all I needed to know that I could do anything I put my mind to when the time was right. But now was not that time.

I did not know who I was? I did not like the person who stood in front of me, I did not recognise myself in the mirror. I had no self confidence, no self belief, no self worth. Who was Nichola Sproson? I did not know. I had played the role for so long that I had completely shut down and lost myself along the way...I was numb and hated myself for what I had become and have never felt so alone.

I had shut myself off from most of my friends and living in Dover, Kent, away from all of my family I had a very small support system. Not being able to pay the bills or put food on the table, I started to get myself into thousands of pounds worth of debt with my Dad.

I went into denial and into autopilot mode with the boys and although I retreated further into myself with despair, they were my focus my only joy in life. I had to get through this, I had to pull myself together for them. The question was "How?"

Time for a bit of Divine Intervention! I began to get thoughts pop into my head that I needed to have a card reading, something I had not done for a long time. I would not have said I was spiritual but I believed there was something bigger and I was open to receiving guidance in any form.

People started to randomly give me business cards of tarot readers, and I would see adverts in various places for different clairvoyants and mediums but none felt right. The message "Write a facebook post asking for local card readers" kept coming to me and I kept ignoring it. After a couple of weeks a friend wrote the exact message I was being told to write as her status. In the comments two mutual friends recommended the same person a lady I had become connected with months before as I had approached her about my Network Marketing business.

The penny dropped. Her name was Tina Pavlou The Angel Lady. I don't know how I had totally missed this, I loved her positive energy and just thought she was a little crazy and super eccentric. I had no idea what an Angel Lady was or did, I just knew she was the one I needed to see and booked a reading for the following week.

After the reading I was blown away, I had never experienced anything like it in my life. She knew things she could not have known and was so spot on it freaked me out a bit, in a good way. At the end of the reading she looked me in the eye and said "It's so nice to meet a true sister" and gave me the biggest hug you could imagine. Neither of us knew just how true those words were or the sistership that was about to unfold.

My spiritual Journey of transformation and self healing had well and truly begun!

A couple of days after my reading my life began to explode, as well as my head. Ha! Tina messaged me asking me if i needed some healing as I had just popped into her head. With no idea what "healing" entailed I just said yes and got into my car to drive to Ramsgate.

On the way my Mum called to say that my sister Sarah had been rushed into hospital with internal bleeding after a hernia operation. I mentioned this to Tina on arrival an she casually said "Oh that's why you are here so we can send distance healing to your sister" I must admit I thought WTF but went along with it. Tina got me to lie down on the bed of her treatment room and she put on some meditation music.

I could not tell you what happened as I was gone within seconds, flat out asleep. When the healing session finished, I came to and Tina said she had sent healing to my sister and that the Angels were with us. 'Erm ok if you say so', was my first thought but at the same time I had a knowing that this was truth.

As soon as I stepped my foot out of the door I received a text from my mum to say that Sarah had just come out of surgery, she was in recovery and fine. What the hell had just happened and what the heck was that healing we just received...I hadn't even asked!!!

Turns out that the Healing modality was called Usui Reiki and about to change my life forever. Reiki is a phrase the Japanese use for "Universal Life Force Energy". The practitioner channels this Universal Life Force Energy in a hands on healing in either a treatment of self care or for a treatment of others. This energy raises your vibration clears your energy blocks, and enhances health across your physical, mental, emotional and spiritual well being.

I knew this was what I was meant to do and signed up to learn Usui Reiki level 1&2 straight away, with Tina who is a Reiki Master Teacher. I did the day long courses back to back over a weekend in May 2016. Reiki 1 on the Saturday and Reiki 2 on the Sunday. This is not usual practice as there is a 21 day detoxing period after, but Tina felt this was the right path for me and I trusted her judgement. I trusted her from the moment I met her.

After this weekend my life exploded into change, I was not the same person I was before. I started to become very aware of the fact that everything happens for a reason, and that there is a higher power guiding, assisting and helping us if you only ask for it. The first thing that happened was I got myself a Job and the synchronicity around it astounded me and confirmed what I had begun to open up to. My neighbour tagged me in an advert on social media for an Admin position in an Estate Agents.

It was perfect for me, 9:30am-1:30pm Monday to Friday which would allow me to do all the pick up and drop offs of the school run, and I had weekends off so I did not have to worry about childcare for the boys.

Now this is the mindblowing part. Not only was it my perfect job for the time, it was Tina who had posted the Advert and was herself working in the Estate Agents during the day. I had no idea she had another job! You just couldn't make this shit up.

Over the next five months up until Tina left the Estate Agents to pursue her career in the Metaphysical full time, I worked alongside her everyday sucking up the knowledge like a sponge during the working day, and at weekends assisting her teaching Usui Reiki classes, becoming a Usui Reiki Master myself in October 2016.

I was working hard on healing myself, having Reiki swaps weekly to raise my vibration and keep my energy clear. The higher my vibration got the more day to day life got easier to deal with, I came off the antidepressants and my anxiety vanished.

To my surprise I noticed that I started to eat less and less meat, I just did not want it in my body anymore. I had been a big meat eater all of my life and I mean a big meat eater, I was a blue steak kinda girl, but by the time I had completed my Reiki Masters I was Vegetarian. I was not expecting that but apparently it is pretty common for meat eaters to become veggie/vegan the more your vibration rises and the more conscious you become.

Now this might all read as nice and fluffy but believe you me healing and working through your energy blocks, brings up your shit. The deep rooted stuff you have kept buried inside you for years, it will come out.

There is no hiding from it, but if you work through it and release it, the feeling after is just immense. This is what is commonly known as a 'Healing Crisis', as your body is going through a deep healing process. Believe you me they are not pretty, and the mood swings are pretty intense going from raging anger to a blubbering wreck on the floor in seconds. But when it's over you are like, what was that all about and you feel much lighter as your vibration raises higher and higher.

Alongside dealing with Healing Crisis I noticed that the people around me started to show their true colours. I started to recognise what friendships were healthy for me and which were toxic. Amongst those who I regarded as my closest friends there were those who turned out to be people I could not trust and as much as it hurt like hell, and as hard as it was, I had to walk away from them and let them go, for myself. I was finally ready to step out of the victimhood, let go of the dramas of others and to put myself first.

In March 2017 I had a minor operation which needed rest and recovery time, so I went to stay at my Dads house with the boys for three weeks. Being back in my home town of Stoke-on-Trent surrounded and supported by my family I felt a shift happen within me...It was time to move home.

I had been living in Dover for 13 years but now I was struggling, really feeling the weight of being a single parent. Not getting on with John I had hardly any support network to help with the boys, and although I had a network of friends whom I met with during the day at weekends, but I found myself alone most evenings once the boys had gone to bed. Our house had recently sold and I made the decision to put my needs first and move to where I would be supported and the boys would grow up surrounded by their cousins.

Nearly a year had passed since I had learnt Usui Reiki when I learnt Angelic Reiki level 1&2 with Tina, who was now also an Angelic Reiki Master Teacher.

I learnt how to channel Healing Energy from the Angelic Realms via Healing Angels, Archangels, Ascended Masters and Galactic Healers to promote powerful transformation and healing on the physical, mental and spiritual levels raising my vibration and consciousness towards Ascension. This was proper upping the game to next level healing and exactly what I needed to assist me in the move back to Stoke.

I started to work more closely with the Angels asking for guidance and telling them outloud what I needed, and you know what I got it too, never once doubting that they wouldn't deliver. I visualised a 3 bedroom house in a quiet area with just a square lawn in the back garden so it was easy to maintain. Within a week of househunting I found the house, it was the first and only house I viewed.

My next request was for a part time job, that I would enjoy doing with lovely people to work alongside. I received a voice in my head telling me to pop a status on social media asking if anyone knew of any part time work. This time I listened and this is where the synchronicity comes in again.

A friend who I met whilst working my Network Marketing business said she was recruiting and to send her a C.V. I did not knowing what the job was for but I did know it was mine. A month later after I had the interview I started my new part time job as a Customer Sales Officer in a bank whose ethics are in alignment with mine, and an amazing team who all get on so well, there really is not a bad word spoken between anyone.

It was now August 2017, just two years since I had first gone to the doctors to receive antidepressants and counselling for anxiety, completely lost in myself and now I was happy, healthy, supported and surrounded by family.

Wow...what a turn around. In the same month I became an Angelic Reiki Master Level 3&4 and an Access Consciousness Bars Practitioner which essentially dissipates the electromagnetic charge that gets locked in our brains by the thoughts feelings and emotions that we have stored over time by lightly touching 32 points on your head.

Loaded with Healing tools I knew I wanted to eventually give back and help others to heal themselves like I was doing, but I was not quite ready. One of the best pieces of advice I had ever been given was "You have to heal yourself first, before you can heal anyone else" and I did not feel healed enough in myself yet. I felt I had a long way to go and still struggled with self worth and self confidence issues. I prayed for help and it arrived in the form of Abigail Horne.

Abi had teamed up with a lady called Sarah Stone whose photography and website developing skills I had admired from afar. They were joining forces to create something called the Female Success Network, it was exactly what I had been waiting for and I just had to be a part of it. If anyone could help me, the woman who truly believed in me could. I signed up for their 12 month Mastermind programme straight away, I am a firm believer in investing in yourself.

There soon became over 20 women all with different businesses, bouncing ideas off each other and helping each other out. From the beginning it was such a safe space to be in, and each and everyone of us had each others back. Abi and Sarah never cease to amaze me with their knowledge and encouragement, truly giving, beautiful people. Even though I did not have a business we discussed ideas and I was learning and growing so much from the group.

I had been Vegetarian for a year now and I had naturally started to give up other animal related products, not drinking milk or having butter. As a New Year's resolution I decided to give myself a Year to have a plant based diet. I decided to journal my journey publicly via social media and my page Destination Vegan was born.

At the same time I started to really look at my food an Integrative Nutrition Health Coaching course came onto my radar and I began my studies with the Institute of Integrative Nutrition. This was a total curve ball but I had never felt so aligned with what I was doing and the path that was unfolding before me.

Even with all of this learning I still had work to do on healing myself. I signed up to do Tina's next courses in Theta Healing. Theta is the purest healing energy. It teaches you how to go into a Theta meditative state and prayer to clear limiting beliefs and live with positive thoughts through Creator of all that is. It is through Theta that I have cleared and removed most of my limiting beliefs, have realised my self worth, and come into balance with myself.

I had done the groundwork, and now was the time to really dig deep and face my inner demons. It is through Theta that I realised Forgiveness is the most powerful and freeing tool you have in your box, not only for others but for yourself too. If you do not forgive you can not move on and you stay stuck, it is as simple as that!

I am now a strong single woman who knows who she is and loves herself. I know what works for me, how to have balance in my life and to always trust my gut instinct. There are no negative influences in my life, instead I only have people who I can trust and build me up, with a sisterhood that is so strong it is unbreakable...together we are unstoppable.

My friendship with John is fantastic, that relationship has been healed. We can enjoy days out together with the boys, and he comes and stays with us in Stoke. He is the most amazing Father to our boys and I am so grateful to have him in our lives.

It is now August 2018, I have been on the most amazing journey of self discovery and healing which will continue. I am a published author and about to launch my own business, helping others to heal themselves.

Wowzers, I created all of that!!!

About Nichola Sproson

Who is Nichola Sproson??? This is the question that fuelled Nichola to look deep within and find out who she truly was. A healing journey of transformation, self acceptance and self love that would lead her to assist others on their own journeys of self healing.

Nichola, a mother of 2 young boys and an Holistic Healer in Stoke-on-Trent, Staffordshire, is both a Usui Reiki Master and an Angelic Reiki Master. Nichola continues to expand her knowledge and self healing quest through seeking out new modalities to add to her practice along the way, including Theta Healing technique and Access Consciousness. Although Nichola has always wanted to help others she firmly believes that "You can't help others to heal if you don't heal yourself first."

A Vegetarian for 15 months, and wanting to heal from the inside out, Nichola realised she had little to no knowledge of health and nutrition. Aligning herself with the Institute of Integrative Nutrition she began her studies. Nichola knows that everyone is different, everyone has different needs, and no one knows you better than yourself. All the answers are within.

Nichola's desire is to empower others to listen to their own bodies, work through any blocks and make small sustainable changes to heal themselves by themselves, creating balance and harmony within their life.

Contact:
Email - nicholasproson@gmail.com
Website - www.nicholasproson.co.uk
Facebook - www.facebook.com/destinationvegandiaries

Sarah Hardie

Before I became a personal and group trainer at the age of 24 I didn't have a clue what I wanted to be, other than a princess of course. I knew I wasn't made to sit at a desk, I've been there, and it was soul destroying for me. I knew I wanted to have my own business one day.

I wish I would have figured it out sooner and found my passion in health and fitness earlier so that I had more time to learn and gain skills. I'm still learning now but I do wish I had more experience and knowledge than I did before I started my own business, so I could plan and map out my ideas better.

I have been lucky enough to spend 4 magnificent and crazy years living in Australia. I had a lot of lows, from toxic relationships, addictions, anxiety, depression, loved ones laughing in my face at my ambitions, to being taken advantage of by people who I thought were my friends.

But, I have had so many more highs. I was given amazing opportunities, I travelled to Bali and Thailand, worked with one of the worlds leading fitness trends and became a manager too. I've met incredible people along the way and made lifelong friends and did things I would never have done back at home in Manchester. I transformed into a totally different person.

I found the real me. I went from being someone lacking in confidence and having no clear path, someone who sat back and let life pass them by, I settled for what I thought I deserved. The health and fitness industry changed this for me.

Australia is one of the front runners in the world we call health and fitness, and in my opinion far beyond what the UK has to offer at the moment. Australia is where I studied and had the chance to work with some of the leading names in the industry.

The world of fitness taught me self-love and self-worth. I started to believe in myself and my dreams. I had goals and aspirations and for once I could see myself achieving them. I finally knew my worth and I never ever looked back.

Starting out in the fitness industry I was so out of my comfort zone. I had been going to the gym and been active all my life, from swimming, karate, Thai boxing, horse riding and more. But my first job in the industry was as a group trainer.

Most people wouldn't think of me as a shy or quiet person, but to stand up in front of up to 50+ people and introduce myself, the class, then go on to demo and explain anywhere between 9-30 exercises. Keep in mind I had to do this 3 to 9 times a day, 6-7 days a week, was daunting for me.

My voice would crack, I would forget my words and names for the exercises or equipment, I couldn't look at anyone and to be honest I hated it.

Once I got a few classes under my belt I started to come out of my shell and I realised that this was 'my' studio and 'my' class and that all these people are here to be trained by 'me'. I quickly moved on to becoming the manager of this gym because I had grown and learnt so much.

However not all I learnt was rainbows and unicorns, from having to discipline staff, working 60+hrs a week to realising that people aren't always going to do what you ask of them, even if it is their job.

I learnt that criticism shouldn't be taken to heart and that it does and always will make you a stronger and better person. I've faced a lot of obstacles in my life, like every other person on the planet, but I found that I am a much stronger person for overcoming these obstacles and not letting them defeat me and by not backing down.

Failure is part of the learning process and learning from your mistakes is the best thing you can do in my opinion. I don't let my failures defeat me. I dust myself off and think of a solution to my problem, a way to get me further than last time so that I can keep moving forward to achieve my goals and dreams.

When I started my journey into the industry I didn't have a lot of people around me to guide me, as I was 10,555 miles away from home, my friends and family. I kind-of stumbled blindly for a while until I made some wonderful friendships with people in the industry that taught me so many lessons.

From colleagues to clients to my own coaches, mentors and employers. I still to this day keep my relationships intact because firstly they are my family from down under, but you never really know where in the world this life is going to take you and to be able to call on a friend if needed is a great thing.

My advice to anyone starting out is to learn, learn, learn and then learn some more. Knowledge is key. Experience things as much as you can so you can find your path sooner than I did. Make friends and stay true to yourself because there are a lot of people out there in this big bad world that will try to drag you down, and sometimes they may succeed. But always remember why you started and drag yourself back up.

Taking a look back on all the brilliant people I've been lucky enough to meet I have been given some great advice. My favourite one is short, simple and straight to the point. "don't ever stop".

Don't ever stop trying to achieve what your heart desires. Don't ever stop dreaming. Don't ever stop and quit because of 'this' and 'that', because in the long run the reason you became so successful will be because you never let 'this' and 'that' get in your way. Don't ever stop thinking your worth it and deserve it. Then on the flip side, don't ever stop living in the moment, cherish and hold it in your heart. Don't ever stop being humble. Don't ever stop being you!

Using this advice and all the advice I've been given along the road to drive me and inspire me to sculpt the life I want, I think the real reason its working is because I truly am a hard worker. I believe in myself, my morals and my commitment to empower women.

I don't let people tell me that I can't, because what I've found out is that those that laugh at you and your goals and tell you that you can't are the people who seem to be lacking in their own lives and I choose not to let that negativity in to my little bubble of positivity!

I also use lists, for EVERYTHING! I make lists to keep my productivity going. I find that if I know exactly what I need to do that day, I can get through it a lot easier instead of just jumping between social media, blogs, clients plans and back, I tend to get a little lost. I also get some sort of excitement when I get to tick off another job well done!

Once I decided to come home and be closer to my friends and family, I saw that I had a great opportunity to bring my knowledge of the Australian health and fitness industry back home to the UK and implement everything I know to build a successful business.

I knew I wanted to and had to empower women just like I had been empowered when I started my fitness journey. I wanted to create strong, beautiful, women who would love and treasure themselves on the inside and out no matter their shape and size.

My ambitions and desires are to educate women that you can be healthy at different sizes and you can sculpt and transform your body and enjoy the whole process.

I contacted the Female Success Network through I friend I went to high school with. She had such amazing things to say about them and was already on the road to great success herself. From the first video chat I had with Abi and Sarah I knew they were for me.

They supported my ideas and thoughts and told me what would and wouldn't work. I like honesty and it's a very difficult thing to find in the business world as there are so many companies that will tell you your idea is amazing even when it's not, just to get that pay cheque.

These ladies aren't about the money. They are about creating successful, powerful women. They give us the resources and advice to put our ideas into action and they have created such a positive and uplifting environment. Through their help and guidance The Sculpted Method was born.

About Sarah Hardie

Sarah Hardie, is the Founder of The Sculpted Method™. Her passion in life is helping the everyday woman create the greatest version of themselves there can be. Like you, Sarah has tried every fad diet and found that the weight always went back on.

Her life was always an active one from an early age and she started going to the gym at 14 however it was only after moving to Sydney, Australia that she found her hunger for fitness and gained her Cert lll & lV in Health & Fitness.

Sarah has trained with some of the world's finest fitness professionals, including WBFF Diva Fitness 2016 World Champion Hattie Boydle and WBFF Diva Fitness 35+ 2017 World Champion Alicia Gowans. Her purpose is to empower women of every shape and size to eat well and enjoy life.

Sarah Hardie

www.sarah-hardie.com

Email - info@sarah-hardie.com

Instagram – sarahjlhardie

Facebook – www.facebook.com/thesculptedmethod

Youtube – Sarah Hardie

Twitter - sarahrdie

Susan Hughes

THE ONLY WAY IS UP……..Yazz 1988
For whatever reason in life we all hit rock bottom at some point or even many points in our lives.

It doesn't matter what rock bottom means to you or anyone else, it is your interpretation and if you feel like you are there, for whatever reason, then it is very real.

Throughout my life I can list those times, as I am sure you can, it's easy to remember the bad stuff isn't it? That one thing that tipped you over the edge at that time in life. How it felt and how you never want to go back there.

Hitting rock bottom to me has been quite liberating, you might think this is a strange reaction to the 'bad stuff' but as I look back on those times I now see how hitting rock bottom only made me stronger and more determined in life.

As I type this I can hear the song by Yazz, yes I am that old. THE ONLY WAY IS UP. I remember singing and dancing to this in Nightclubs, I remember being young with the world at my feet, I remember good times, what I don't remember is consciously making those life changing decisions that have brought me to where I am today.

I am not saying that I didn't make the decisions, of course I did, what I am saying is I don't remember sitting down and consciously thinking things through, asking the question 'what if?' or any other questions, I just 'did. I didn't ever think of the consequences of my choices I was too busy living my life.

It always surprised me and still does when people say I am driven, focussed, inspiring.......... to me, to my husband and boys I am just 'me' a wife, a mum a doer.

As you get older you choose your path in life, whether consciously or in my case many times subconsciously, and you are then on that treadmill of work, mortgages, bills, children etc. etc. The treadmill that keeps you on a path that you don't always want to be on but see no way of getting off.

Don't get me wrong the majority of my life has been a very happy one, the decisions I have made on the whole have been good ones, looking back would I change anything? probably not but what I do take from looking back are the lessons I have learned.

I live my life by this one saying "Never have regrets", Why? Because regrets are in the past, they are gone, you made those decisions for whatever reason at the time, whether right or wrong you can't change them now, you can only take away the experience, the lessons learned and use that to make you a stronger, better person, to know yourself better, to deal with whatever life throws at you better.

This book has come at a great time for me as for once in my life I feel I have something to share, something to offer you as the reader, and if only one person reads this and realises that they can do or be anything they want to no matter what stage in life you are at then I am happy.

As I sit here writing this chapter I am in a good place in my life, I am 51 years old, happily married with four very tall, handsome boys, I live in a beautiful Canal Town (I always thought I was a city girl at heart), I'm studying for a diploma in Interior Design, writing this chapter for the book and about to embark upon my third self-employed business.
It still amazes me when I say that!

If you had asked me in my twenties, thirties or even mid-forties would I be a business woman, own my own business, be my own boss or even class myself as an entrepreneur, I would have laughed out loud and have been that person who said not in a million years, it wasn't my ambition, it wasn't ever on my radar.

Yet here I sit in my fifties and about to open my own shop (not just any shop but one of those shops that all my life I have loved to go in to browse but have been denied in recent years with having 4 boys), having already done two self-employed businesses that I didn't start until I was 48 and 50. I guess what I am trying to say to you is that you are never too old Never too old:

- ❖ To have a dream
- ❖ To reinvent yourself
- ❖ To try something new
- ❖ To have goals and aspirations
- ❖ To step out of your comfort zone
- ❖ To just go for it
- ❖ But most importantly of all to pick yourself up from rock bottom

In order for you to understand how I got to this point you do need to know where I came from and some of my journey along the way. So here goes, a delve into my past.

I am the youngest of six children. Two boys and four girls. Your typical working-class family, I grew up on a council estate with hard working parents, very proud parents who managed to buy outright the house I grew up in. We lived in a very busy and sociable house. We were all brought up the same, polite, respectful and with a strong work ethic. All in we were a very traditional family.

I have often heard that being the youngest of a large family makes you stronger, louder, a fighter. I guess it makes sense as you have to be all these things to be heard in a busy house. However, I was completely the opposite, I was quiet, shy, preferred adult company and conversations rather than being with my siblings, I was very different to them and have even been known to say I felt like an only child.

They probably wouldn't agree as we were all very close in age, but I always trod my own path. Lots of things have happened over the years, as I am sure it does in most families, that I am not going to delve into. That's another story, one for my brothers and sisters to tell if they ever choose to, I'm sure we would all see things from very different perspectives. But there are some events I need to highlight for you to understand me as the person you see now.

Like I said I had a very traditional upbringing, you worked hard at school, or not, in the case of some of my siblings. Me, I enjoyed school, but looking back didn't reach my full potential. It was no one's fault, it was just a different world back then.

You weren't encouraged to do well at school, in fact on numerous occasions I was told I wasn't clever enough for my chosen career, whereby now you would be guided into the right subjects and know what results you needed, that wasn't the case back then.

From the age of seven having being given a nurses dressing up costume that is what I wanted to be. Looking back now I know I could have achieved much more and probably would have had even higher aspirations for myself, but I knew no better. We didn't live in the world where you went to university or even college, school didn't encourage you and my parents had no experience of those other options.

Did I go into nursing once I left school……no, I left being one grade short to even be considered. So, I left school thinking I had no other option than to get a job. Not once did anyone say or encourage me to work a little harder, think about resitting an exam, it just wasn't the culture back then, you left school at 16 and you got a job.

So that's what I did, see what I mean about subconscious decisions, I wasn't brought up to question I just did. Did what my Mum and Dad did, did what my siblings did, did what everyone else I came into contact with did. The world is a very different place now with so many opportunities open to us. The world truly is our oyster.

I already had a Saturday job working in a food shop, but I was fortunate enough to get a temporary job in an office as a statistic clerk. It sounds as boring as it was. I used to get all my work done within an hour then had to pretend to be working for the rest of the day, so when a full-time permanent position came up in the shop I was working in I took it.

It makes me smile to think I started my working life in a shop and will now probably finish my working life in a shop, not just any shop though…………**my shop!**

This job suited me much more, it was busy, active and most of all sociable. I love being busy, loved the contact with the customers. It was this decision to work there full time that was to change the course of my life.

If I hadn't gone to work there, I wouldn't have served a girl I went to school with, I wouldn't have found out she was starting her nurse training and I wouldn't have told her that's what I had always wanted to do.

One simple conversation led to her asking me why I wasn't doing it, led to her telling I could sit an entrance exam. Not once had anyone ever suggested this to me, why would they it was prehistoric times……..heaven forbid it was pre internet times.

I had never thought to question if there was another way I could achieve my dream that I had had from the age of seven, I had just been given my first lifeline.

So, at the age of 19 rather than 17 I started my nursing career.

As I am writing this I am finding it fascinating that not once so far have I mentioned that during this time I met my first boyfriend at the age of 15, I had a mortgage at the age of 18 with him, I got married to him at the age of 20, and we had split up by the time I was 24.

See a very traditional upbringing, subconscious decisions, I never questioned, I just did, that was the path my parents and siblings had taken, it was all that I knew in life. To me now that was another life, a very different person to who I am now.

Nursing my vocation
1987, a pivotal year. I started my nurse training, it was the year I got married. Both these events were massive turning points in my life. Becoming a nurse opened my eyes up to a whole new world I knew nothing about. I was experiencing a massively different type of life to that which I knew.

Meeting inspirational people both colleagues and patients, experiencing things at a relatively young age that makes you grow up very quickly.

Being married during this time stifled me, if I had sat back then and thought about who I was I would have realised being married is not what I wanted.

Don't get me wrong I wasn't unhappy and it wasn't me that caused the marriage to end. I was too young to have settled down and be married, cliché I know. From getting married to qualifying as a Staff nurse I just grew up, that's what working in the medical profession does for you, you see and do things that puts life into perspective.

Whilst your mates are out having a beer and a laugh, you could be saving someone's life, having a conversation with a grieving relative, supporting someone who has a life-threatening illness.

My very first ward as a student was haematology, one of my very first patients was a 19 year old boy with leukaemia, he didn't make it to twenty. It puts life into perspective doesn't it?

I am not skipping over my nursing career, I did it for twenty years and was bloody good at it, I made a success of it, within 3 years I became a senior staff nurse on a busy Plastic Surgery ward, within six years a Ward Manager. I then went on to study a degree and became a Clinical Nurse Specialist in my chosen field.

I would love to bump into those teachers that told me I wasn't clever enough. It's not all about academia but about how you apply yourself. Don't ever let anyone ever hold you back. If you think you can do something and have the drive and the passion to want to do it, then do it.

On the whole I loved my nursing career, I met some amazing people along the way, I also met my second husband. It seems strange saying second husband as we have been together for 22 years and have had our four boys together, in fact my first marriage was so long ago that I don't even feel like I have been married before.

My second life

You might be mistaken in thinking that I am referring to my second marriage as being my second life but to me it is my life after nursing. I never thought I would give this up, but life has a funny way of throwing you curve balls.

My second life began with my beloved Dad dying when I was 39, with having three boys under the age of 4 and nearly losing our second son from a ruptured appendix the day after my Dad's funeral, he was only 23 months old, and then breaking my foot, all before I turned 40.

I truly was at rock bottom and something had to give, for me it was my career. There were days when I didn't want to get out of bed, days where I just couldn't stop crying, I did go back to work but I was no longer functioning as I had before.

Dare I say it, yes I had a breakdown and yes I went onto anti-depressants along with having some counselling. Too many of us don't admit when we are not coping, mental illness is very real and I have no doubt in saying it affects all of us at some point in our lives, I truly believe it's the people we believe to be strong, the copers in life that it hits the hardest because you not only have to come to terms with all the feelings that you have when suffering with depression you also can't quite believe it's happening to you because you have always been so strong and capable.

If you had asked me before I was twenty, or even thirty, did I want children, the answer was no, and here I was now almost 40 giving up my lifelong ambition of being a nurse to become a fulltime mum to three little ones and a housewife. Not the life I had seen for myself but when you meet that special someone it all just feels right at the time.

Although it was a relief to take the pressure of going to work out of the mix it wasn't always plain sailing. Adjusting to being a full time Mum was hard, it didn't come naturally to me, it highlighted to me the distance between me and my family and my true friends who lived all over the country and that whilst we had lived in our house for many years that we didn't have much of a network of friends locally.

It was a difficult time, I was still grieving the loss of my dad, coming to terms with what had happened with our son and adjusting to for want of a better phrase, losing my identity. I had been a nurse for 20 years and that had gone overnight.

Two years later we had our fourth son and life was busy, tiring, but happy. It wasn't until my youngest started school that I actually thought about who I was. I had been so busy sorting out everyone and everything else that I had totally lost who I was and what I wanted.

At the age of 46 I hadn't a clue what I wanted anymore. I threw all my focus and energy into losing the 3 stone I had put on having children but something was still missing. I felt like I was on that treadmill of life again. It was controlling me rather than me controlling it. I couldn't see a way to make things different, the option to go back into nursing was too difficult juggling 4 children.

Then along came my second lifeline. I was offered the opportunity to start my own network marketing business. I hadn't a clue what I was doing and little did I know that this was to be the beginning of an amazing journey which has led to me to the point I am at now.

This new experience brought back my drive to make something of myself, I discovered I had skills I hadn't a clue I possessed. I became great at retailing the products and loved meeting new people and the social side brought back a spark that had been dulled. Dulled by the mundanities of life.

I no longer lived in our utility room, doing and folding washing. I was working, had a reason to get out of bed in the mornings.

As always life gets in the way and during this time at the age of 49 I hit rock bottom again.

A few things happened that I don't want to divulge but these events included the loss of my Mum. This was a very difficult and traumatic experience as there were family problems and my Mum deteriorated rapidly with dementia before she passed away. Driving a 100 mile round trip to see her almost daily as well as dealing with everything else I had going on in life took its toll and my network marketing business took a back seat

After two years of working hard at it, taking my foot off the pedal made me lose my drive and once again I felt lost. Again, lots of family things were going on too which led to me having my second breakdown. Having experienced it before I recognised the signs sooner. I still remember myself falling to my kitchen floor sobbing and that's when I knew I had to take back control of my own life

I knew I had fallen out of love with network marketing but what it had given me was the ability to recognise what I didn't want to do.

I will always be grateful for the experience as I met the most amazing, inspirational people, I learned so much about business and business development and I met a woman who has been my inspiration in business and has championed me ever since.

She saw things in me that I didn't recognise in myself, she never judged me, just was always there for support and guidance. The timing of all this just happened to be as she was launching her new business Female Success Network.

I'm talking about my good friend and mentor Abigail Horne. Alongside Sarah Stone they launched this amazing platform where women could celebrate their successes, ask advice, develop themselves both personally and within business. My third lifeline, I was just picking myself up from rock bottom as all this was taking off, I could see people joining their Mastermind group and desperately wanted to join too, but I had no business idea.

So, what changed for me, well actually it was a kitchen cupboard falling on my face and cutting my nose. I honestly don't recommend anyone doing this but for me it was a wake-up call.

I was and am a great believer in higher forces and I had been practicing for some time doing morning rituals, thinking positively, using affirmations and gratitudes and believed the universe would deliver.

You might think this is all mumbo jumbo but don't give up reading this as you need to know what happened next.

That cupboard falling on my face changed my whole direction in life. I had lost my way yet again and had this conversation with my husband. How the hell could I control a cupboard falling off the kitchen wall.

What was the point of everything I believed in and practiced when unexpected accidents happen like that, that conversation led to him telling me to go back to what makes me happy, for me that was being creative in whatever form.

After this conversation I applied to start a diploma in Interior Design, something I had nearly done 9 years previously but didn't because I fell pregnant with our fourth son. I then went to see Abigail and told her my business idea, I wanted to start an interior design business but not just the big stuff I loved putting the finishing touches to a room together.

My words to her on that day were "you know like beautiful throws and the big chunky knitted cushions", that day I joined the Female Success Network Mastermind group and The Wool Boutique (www.thewoolboutique.co.uk) was born overnight and I haven't looked back since.

That all was less than a year ago, it hasn't all been plain sailing, there have been ups and downs, pretty much a roller coaster ride, but in this time, I have learned so much about developing a business and I have met the most amazing people, some of whom will be lifelong friends. I wouldn't have changed this experience for the world, as my belief 'the universe will deliver' didn't let me down.

If you had asked me on that day where my business would take me I would not have been able to answer you. I did have a vision, but it wasn't clear enough. As I have developed in the mastermind group I have met more like-minded people. I've seen them develop their amazing business ideas and we have forged relationships and I have soaked up information like a sponge.

It's not surprising that my business ideas have evolved and The Wool Boutique continues but it has developed into a much larger plan.

As I write this chapter I am less than a week from opening the doors to the public on my new venture. A shop called The Artisan Boutique (fb.com/theartisanboutique), this encompasses all my passions for interiors, being creative, encouraging others to be creative and has scope for development as my confidence and experience develops.

So how did I get to this point, I was looking for a studio to work from and display my wool boutique products when the opportunity for the possibility of a shop came up. Initially it wasn't on the cards, I honestly thought I couldn't afford it. Then lots of events just happened things just slotted into place. It was like everything I had done and learned, everyone I had met and made connections with all just fitted, the universe was certainly delivering.

Why now? I had belief in myself, I wasn't overthinking things, I was putting everything I knew into practice. All the events of the past 3 years now made sense, everything led me to this point. Being self-employed can be lonely and isolating and you can lose your direction, but I had amazing business mentors and would recommend anyone starting a new business to get one.

They help keep you on track and help you break down the steps you need to move your business forward. When you are working within something and it is your passion you can't always see and think clearly, you are too close to 'your baby' a business mentor can help you see things from a different perspective.

Before you now, is a confident business woman.

Do I know everything? No!

Have I got lots to learn? Absolutely when you have a business you have to be open minded, you have to evolve, you have to keep revisiting your business plan, your initial idea, you have to be willing to change and move with the times to keep yourself current.

Am I concerned? No because it feels right, I know I can make it work and if my initial idea doesn't work I will reinvent myself. I have done it 3 times already.

As you are reading this, my shop has opened and I will be able to sit back and reflect how far I have come in such a short time. I am grateful for all the opportunities that I have had, all the people I have met but especially grateful for having joined Female Success Network, the Mastermind group and all the wonderful inspirational women in there.

To Abi and Sarah for having my back now and always and to my business bestie Alison, for always being there for me during the highs and the lows, for being able to drag knowledge and information out of me that even I didn't know I had inside. For not being afraid to tell me when she thought I was going in the wrong direction, even if I didn't always listen to her.

If I can give you any advice from my journey it would be to surround yourself with positive people, people who are going to lift you up rather than drag you down. People who will champion you even when you don't feel like doing it for yourself.

People who inspire you, the sort that you think that you could never be like............ well guess what you can, you only have to want it enough. Go out there and believe you can conquer the world and you will, well the business world anyway.

Seize every opportunity that comes your way, no matter how big or small, face the fear, the unknown, grab it with both hands, you never know where it might lead. And if it leads nowhere then at least you've given it a go. Don't live life with regrets, with the question 'if only'. No one fails in life, it is always a lesson learned enabling you to put a different perspective on things if you are ever faced with the same scenario.

Before I go I'd just like to say a massive thank you to Abi and Sarah for giving me the opportunity to write this chapter, it has really made me sit back, reflect and look at my life and my business journey. I'm amazed at where I am today.

Always believe you can be whoever you want to be and do whatever you want to do, you just have to put the plans in place to help you on your way. Go and take the most amazing journey and do not give up at the first hurdle .

Love from an ordinary girl from an ordinary background, taking steps to do extraordinary things xx

About Susan Hughes

Susan Hughes is a busy Mum to her four boys, and has been happily married to Richard, who is a surgeon. Originally coming from Nottingham in the UK, with her husband's career she has found herself settling in Stone, a canal town in a semi-rural area of Staffordshire.

Having given up her successful nursing career over 10 years ago to become a full-time mum, in recent years Susan has been striving to find an outlet for her creative side.

As a child and into early adulthood she enjoyed being creative with sewing, embroidery and knitting. She also has a passion for interior design as she found she has a natural flare for putting colours and eclectic pieces of furniture and furnishings together.

Currently she is studying for a Diploma in Interior Design and last year also launched her own business The Wool Boutique, this idea developed on the back of her Mum passing away, she had been taught to knit by her Mum as a small girl, and has now taken this a step further to create beautiful arm-knitted jumbo merino woollen items.

The success of The Wool Boutique led Susan to develop this idea and she has now opened her own shop The Artisan Boutique to showcase her items, expand and incorporate her passion for home furnishings and beautiful home decor.

On her journey she has met many amazingly talented crafters and artists, recognising how difficult it is to have an outlet to showcase handcrafted products, she has developed a passion to give an outlet to all these people.

Susan recognised that there is a gap in the market where these skills haven't been passed on. By hosting a multitude of workshops at her shop, working with local crafters her quest is to bring back a passion for these traditional crafts and to keep them alive for generations to come.

Combining traditional crafts with today's technology she is hoping there will be something for everybody no matter what age or experience.

Contact:

Email: infotheartisanboutique@gmail.com

Website: www.theartisanboutique.co.uk

Facebook: www.facebook.com / theartisanboutique

Instagram: www.instagram.com/theartisanboutique

Tina Pavlou

Today is the first day of the rest of my life. Blessed and excited, I have been asked to write a chapter in this book with 20 something female up and coming entrepreneurs which I now regard as a sisterhood! Through laughter, tears and hard work, we have stepped into our power, in other words OWNING IT!!!

Who am I?? My name is Tina Pavlou, I am a mother to two beautiful and outstanding daughters (my greatest achievements). I live in the beautiful county of Kent, the Garden of England, by the coast.

What do I do, and what makes me who I am? I am a clairvoyant (a seer, who sees into spirit realms) a gift I have always had; an Angelic Master teacher and a Theta Healer and instructor.

From the four-year-old girl who saw Mother Mary and seeing my future when I was just 8 years of age, are just two of the extraordinary experiences I had as I grew up. I just wanted to fit in with everybody else so I put my gift to the side and YES…I found boys!

Fast forward to my thirties and my development and my initiation began.

I was so looking forward to being in my 30's and BOOM…My marriage of 12 years broke down, my career collapsed and I had a mental and emotional breakdown which was so severe I was watched over by psychiatric nurses. I was shown the truth of people all around me, veils were dropped.

Truly this was the darkest time of my life. This was my dark night of the soul experience.

I would lay on my bed and pray, 'please angels, let me sleep until this is all over'. One day as I sat on my bed saying a prayer, the sun shone on my body, I felt intense warmth when two angel wings wrapped themselves around me, it was the most beautiful serene moment that I had ever experienced; that was the phoenix rising from the ashes moment.

I knew I just had to get better and never be in that dark energy again.

I threw myself into self-development, paid by my Angel Card readings, hence this is where I got my name The Angel Lady from. I heard a voice, the voice was my angel, it said 'they will come, they will come'.

Who am I today?

Still learning, always on self-development courses and craving new knowledge; I am here to wake up the divine feminine and masculine, to teach and help as many people as I can.

Authenticity is who I am.

I was introduced to Abigail Horne and Sarah Stone from Female Success Network by my darling friend Nicky Sproson. I gave both ladies a future life reading and I think it's safe to say I blew them away – they soon became my guiding angels and have assisted me with my growth and my dream to make this world a better place.

So far I have helped and assisted over 8000 beautiful souls/clients.
'When you trust yourself, you are trusting the universe because the universe always has your back.' Tina Pavlou 2018.

About Tina Pavlou

Tina Pavlou is a clairvoyant - a seer into the spiritual realms, who works with the seven plains of existence and the spiritual laws; a Theta Healer and teacher and Angelic Reiki Master and teacher from the south coast of England.

Tina specialises in empowering people to live their best lives by giving them the spiritual tools to do so. After experiencing the Dark Night of the soul, she made it her passion to help as many people as she could, so they would never have to experience as much suffering and pain as she has.

It is impossible to be around Tina without feeling anything other than positivity and love as she vibrates on such a divine, Goddess high frequency. Her passion is just love.

CONTACT DETAILS
EMAIL: Pavloutina@yahoo.co.uk

WEBSITE: www.tinapavlou.com

FACEBOOK: www.facebook.com/tinapavlouangellady

INSTAGRAM: tina_pavlou_angel_lady_

FEMALE SUCCESS NETWORK

Printed in Great Britain
by Amazon